Never Again?

Never Again?

The United States and the Prevention and Punishment of Genocide since the Holocaust

Peter Ronayne

ROWMAN & LITTLEFIELD PUBLISHERS, INC.
Lanham • Boulder • New York • Oxford

ROWMAN & LITTLEFIELD PUBLISHERS, INC.

Published in the United States of America
by Rowman & Littlefield Publishers, Inc.
4720 Boston Way, Lanham, Maryland 20706
www.rowmanlittlefield.com

12 Hid's Copse Road, Cumnor Hill, Oxford OX2 9JJ, England

The views expressed here are the author's and do not represent the position of the Federal Executive Institute or the United States Office of Personnel Management.

British Library Cataloguing in Publication Information Available

Library of Congress Cataloging-in-Publication Data

Ronayne, Peter, 1968–
Never again? : the United States and the prevention and punishment of genocide since the Holocaust / Peter Ronayne.
p. cm.
Includes bibliographical references and index.
ISBN 0-7425-0921-4 (alk. paper) — ISBN 0-7425-0922-2 (pbk. : alk. paper)
1. Genocide. 2. Crimes against humanity. 3. United States—Foreign relations—20th century. I. Title: United States and the prevention and punishment of genocide since the Holocaust. II. Title.

HV6322.7 .R66 2001
364.15′1′09045—dc21 2001031792

Printed in the United States of America

∞ ™ The paper used in this publication meets the minimum requirements of American National Standard for Information Sciences—Permanence of Paper for Printed Library Materials, ANSI/NISO Z39.48-1992.

For Melissa

Is there a time to run for cover
A time for kiss and tell?
Is there a time for different colors,
Different names you find it hard to spell?

—The Passengers, *Miss Sarajevo*

Contents

Foreword

The twentieth century was the century of mass murder. Millions more people died at the hands of their own governments than in the combat theatres of the three world wars that defined the century. Hitler, Stalin, and Mao: the body counts produced by each are horrific to contemplate. As if to emphasize this point, the century concluded with a decade where the signature phrase "ethnic cleansing" became part of the lexicon. The horrors of Rwanda and Yugoslavia were in keeping with the pattern of internal violence and atrocities that have characterized so much of human existence in the twentieth century.

How was it that the century began with the promise of mediation, arbitration, and the peaceful resolution of conflict but ended in such tragedy? How was it that initiatives such as the Hague Conferences of 1899 and 1907, the Geneva conventions, the founding of the League of Nations, and the establishment of the United Nations were so feckless in the face of malevolent forces worldwide? Those of us who have inherited this legacy—a legacy of progressive thinking and disastrous results—are morally obligated to pursue these questions.

The question mark in the title of this book is significant. In including it, the author sagaciously signals to us the tenuous nature of our current circumstances. Nothing is resolved. Yes, some progress has been made in solidifying the moral norm against genocide as well as the obligations to both prevent its occurrence and punish its perpetrators. But the record of the United States is mixed. As the author indicates, the United States—for numerous complex reasons—"has lost significant opportunities to act against genocide." These failures are surely a matter of concern for a country that considers itself a moral nation. This book helps us to understand how and why these failures occurred and what they might portend for the future.

Never Again? tells the story of how one nation, the United States, has done so much to set international moral norms while simultaneously acting in ways that do not always fulfill and sometimes undermine those standards. Despite its good intentions—or some might say, pretensions—the United States has not escaped the exigencies of power politics. Understanding this, the author gives us an account of U.S. foreign policy that is grounded in realism without neglecting the very real weight of principle and conscience. He asks how we might build on this understanding of ethics and politics to do better in the future.

As a good scholar and social critic, Ronayne stands only a little to the side of his subject and his society. As an engaged intellectual, he asks and answers the tough questions in ways that are policy-relevant. A subject as profound as genocide demands an investigator worthy of the task. Peter Ronayne—humanist, social scientist, and social critic—brings to this work a formidable intellect leavened with a fine moral sensibility and mature political judgment. As we move ahead into a new era, an era perhaps defined by the establishment of a permanent International Criminal Court, we are fortunate to have Ronayne's analysis of the recent past as well as his diagnosis of the current state of affairs.

Peter Ronayne has provided us with a mirror. With unflinching candor, in the harsh light of reality, he has measured our behavior against our stated goals. While he does not like all that he sees, he does not succumb to despair. Skillfully avoiding the shoals of self-righteous moralism and self-defeating cynicism, this study is itself a moral act—a genuine inquiry into who we are and who we want to be.

Joel H. Rosenthal
President, Carnegie Council on Ethics and International Affairs (NY)

Acknowledgments

I owe a debt of gratitude to many people who helped make this book possible and helped me see it to the end. At the University of Virginia, Michael Joseph Smith, David Newsom, Melvyn Leffler, Kenneth Thompson, and Gordon Stewart all influenced this project in a number of ways—all for the best.

At the Federal Executive Institute, Terry Newell, Curt Smith, Pam Gwin, Bob Gest, Holly Newman, and the rest of the faculty and staff for their help, encouragement, and support.

At Rowman & Littlefield, Jennifer Knerr was greatly patient, and Janice Braunstein and Brigitte Scott were extremely helpful.

Other friends and colleagues deserve equal thanks for their support and encouragement, formal and informal: Eric Thompson and Mary Lusk, Jon and Liz Talotta, Bruce and Cindy McClelland, Al Pierce, Joel Rosenthal, Kevin Tarmann, and Alice Ba.

Of course, none of this gets anywhere without the great family that has always supported me. I am ever grateful to my parents, Claire and Vince Ronayne. On the other side of the aisle, Gerald and Jeanne Mossinghoff, Pam and Glenn Jennings, and Greg and Sandy Mossinghoff have been constant supporters. Here at home, Melissa, Jack, and Patrick can little understand the countless morale boosts they have given me.

Acknowledgments

Introduction

The United States in an Age of Genocide

The Allied liberation of Nazi concentration camps in 1945 revealed to a stunned world the scope of Adolf Hitler's murderous regime. Knowledge of the brutally systematic destruction of Europe's Jews and other "undesirable" populations shocked the world and led to a new, formal definition for an old crime: genocide.[1] In the aftermath of World War II and the horror known as the Holocaust, members of the world community took initial steps to address the hideous crime of genocide and seek to prevent its recurrence.

Behind U.S. leadership, the United Nations drafted the Convention on the Prevention and Punishment of the Crime of Genocide.[2] The document represented a significant effort to establish a new world order based on international law and respect for individuals' rights and dignity. As the opening text of the Convention made clear, states believed "that, in order to liberate mankind from such an odious scourge, international co-operation is required." Therefore, signatories to the UNGC declared "that genocide, whether committed in time of peace or in time of war, is a crime under international law which they undertake to prevent and to punish."[3]

Despite the good intentions of the UNGC, post–World War II history has proven with disturbing clarity that the Holocaust was not the twentieth century's last genocide. Crimes against humanity and genocidal massacres convulsed Cambodia and Burundi in the 1970s. Iraq's Kurdish population has suffered from Saddam Hussein's campaign of extermination. In the 1990s, "ethnic cleansing" in the former Yugoslavia and brutal images of savage, organized mass killings in Rwanda and brutality in Sudan demonstrated tragically that we have in fact been experiencing what some have called an "age of genocide." Given this, a fundamental question emerges for anyone interested in American foreign policy, the prevention and punishment of genocide, and the role of leadership and ethics in world politics: How has the United States responded to the scourge of genocide in the Holocaust era?

Countless studies exist on the Western response to the Holocaust.[4] Other scholars have investigated the origins, nature, and threats posed by genocide itself.[5] Still other works have examined in depth individual cases of genocide, and the field of comparative genocide studies continues to enjoy significant growth.[6] However, there exists a surprisingly limited body of scholarship dealing with American foreign policy and genocide since World War II. To help fill that void, this book examines how and why the United States has responded to prominent cases of genocide since the Holocaust. This issue raises a host of provocative questions about ethics and American foreign policy, the role of domestic politics, and the evolution of an international norm of genocide prevention and punishment.

These questions have attracted only occasional attention although they strike at the heart of the role of the United States in the world, its self-image and interests, and the pursuit of a world order conducive to those American interests. This book addresses these questions by investigating the record of American foreign policy vis-à-vis three prominent genocides in the post–World War II era: Cambodia, Bosnia, and Rwanda. As background to those case studies, this project investigates the important issues surrounding the forty-year delay in the U.S. ratification of the UNGC. Each of the case studies presents a blend of context and circumstance from which to draw informative comparisons and contrasts about America's diplomatic response to perhaps the most blatant and systematic violation of human rights. Much of the work here offers fertile ground for a discussion of how national interests and relevant moral considerations and imperatives have interacted in American foreign policy both during the genocidal convulsions in Cambodia, Bosnia, and Rwanda and also in subsequent efforts to bring offenders to justice for their crimes.

This study is particularly important for the United States because of its traditional national image and identity. Hans Morgenthau explained that "in order to be worthy of our lasting sympathy, a nation must pursue its interests for the sake of a transcendent purpose that gives meaning to the day-by day operations of its foreign policy," and Americans have embraced the notion of a unique national mission.[7] The United States has consistently defined itself as different, possessing a national character of generosity, altruism, and service to mankind—a worldview that transcends mere "national interest" and creates a uniquely American foreign policy. As Henry Kissinger observes in his recent book, *Diplomacy,* the United States more than any other nation has "passionately asserted that its values were universally applicable."[8] As early as the founding of the United States, Thomas Paine declared that "we have it in our power to remake the world." Woodrow Wilson injected an element of crusade into American foreign policy through his disdain for "old world" diplomacy and his zeal for American values and their promotion abroad.

The Cold War stretched beyond geostrategy to include a conflict of political ideas and philosophies, pitting the forces of democracy and human rights led by the United States against the Soviet "evil empire." Following the twin crises of Vietnam and Watergate, President Jimmy Carter sought national renewal through his efforts to make human rights the cornerstone of American foreign policy. Carter declared in his inaugural address that "our commitment to human rights must be absolute." From that point on, the notion of the United States as a champion of human rights has permeated American foreign policy language and debate. The language of "the city on the hill"—first pronounced by John Winthrop in 1630—has resonated for generations, resurrected with particular effect by Ronald Reagan. In the aftermath of the Cold War, President George Bush declared a pivotal role for the United States in fostering a "new world order." President Clinton and Secretary of State Madeleine Albright consistently referred to the United States as "the indispensable nation" in the pursuit of a liberal-democratic international society.[9]

With that American self-image in mind, this work makes a twofold presentation. First, it demonstrates clearly that the United States has lost significant opportunities to act against genocide. The United States has not been concerned enough with the horrible crime of genocide and the goals of the UNGC to call for intervention and swift retribution to prevent genocidal acts when they have occurred. In some cases, the United States even avoided possible actions and responses that did not require the use of force. Instead, a range of nonresponses has emerged, from determined nonintervention to a willingness to ignore or look away from genocide. Through this unwillingness to intervene to stop genocide when it has occurred, the United States has abdicated leadership and in part hindered the evolution of an international norm of genocide prohibition and prevention. Time and again, the United States has missed opportunities to save thousands, even hundreds of thousands, of lives by enforcing the goals of the UNGC, which it helped to draft.

However, the story is neither that simple nor entirely negative. An evolution in policy has occurred, and the United States has made a difference. This study also reveals that the fairly weak genocide norm embodied in the UNGC has nonetheless ever so gradually influenced American diplomacy. The impact of moral concerns and a weak but unique norm has emerged primarily in the form of U.S. support for postgenocide tribunals, namely for Rwanda and the former Yugoslavia.

These postgenocide initiatives show the United States pursuing judicial intervention to promote the punishment component of the UNGC. Other indicators of a normative influence on American foreign policy and American leadership in the area of genocide punishment and prevention include the use of American forces to arrest indicted war criminals in the Balkans, the creation of an interagency genocide early warning initiative, and the appointment of an ambassador-at-large for war crimes issues. In a more perverse way, the reluctance of the United States at times to use the term "genocide" for fear of the legal and moral obligations it might entail also reveals that the convention does matter.

This book explores American foreign policy and the prevention and punishment of genocide through case studies of the ratification of the UNGC and the response of the United States to genocide in Cambodia, Rwanda, and Bosnia. Although this is not an overtly theoretical work, prominent schools of thought in foreign policy and international relations inform the questions raised about American action and inaction in these cases. Stated most plainly, this analysis eschews the extreme parsimony of a traditional unitheoretical account. Too often, observers and scholars of international relations are drawn by the seductive and beguiling call of the physical sciences for a single theory, replete with simplicity and generalizability. While one should not dismiss these goals out of hand, their applicability to the study of human interaction and political behavior has limits; if taken too far, one risks sacrificing accurate descriptions and fuller understandings of the real world of international politics and foreign policy for neat and tidy explanations. This book did not set out with a preestablished agenda of arguing for or against one or another theory of international relations. A too-willing embrace, defense, or promotion of one theory over others risks ignoring relevant history and evidence that make the reality of foreign policy additionally interesting, complex, and complicated.

This study blends realist thought with more progressive notions of evolution in international ethics to understand and explain American foreign policy vis-à-vis genocide. Generally speaking, classical realism informs the limits of normative and moral imperatives in any nation's foreign policy. At the same time, a more progressive framework, including the concept that "ideas matter," urges us to realize that over time norms can and do influence foreign policy.

The most obvious or conventional explanation for how and why the United States has acted in response to genocide emerges from the classical or traditional realist school of thought. The realist emphasis on the importance of power and self-interest helps us to understand and even predict that an American administration might demonstrate reluctance to intervene to halt genocide because of other geostrategic priorities and domestic political concerns, such as opinion polls, political capital, and elections. A potentially costly adventure abroad might jeopardize a president's continued hold on power at home; therefore, humanitarian intervention is avoided.

Self-interest, fear, and power continue to hold considerable sway in human interaction, particularly at the state level. These concerns have represented significant obstacles to the development of an international society and an American foreign policy committed to the prevention of genocide.[10] Realism often accurately reminds us of the predictable chasm between American rhetoric and policy reality. However, this view of human nature is incomplete. As one critic has noted,

> To read the classic texts of international relations theory, one would never suspect that human beings have right brains as well as left; that in addition to being selfish, they also love, hate, hope, and despair; that they sometimes act not out of interest, but out of courage, politeness, or rage; and, that in addition to seeking to do *well,* they often seek to do *right.*[11]

To be fair, it should be noted that classical or traditional realists are often mischaracterized as leaving no significant room for morality in world politics. A careful reading of works by prominent realist scholars such as Hans Morgenthau, Reinhold Niebuhr, and Kenneth W. Thompson reveal a far more nuanced approach to ethics, interests, and international affairs than is often portrayed. Indeed, the national interest offers a starting point for policy formulation, and "the content of that policy and the question of its morality depend on the values one applies to defining the interest of the national community and on the extent to which those values are translated into concrete and effective policy."[12] The case studies examined here simultaneously demonstrate that policymakers at times reflect the other side of human nature in their efforts to do right and seek justice in the world.

Distinct from and often in opposition to realism stand more progressive approaches to international relations and foreign policy—whether termed liberal, Kantian, or even Wilsonian. These approaches also influence this book, in particular the theoretical lens known as "constructivism." A relative newcomer to the international relations literature (although similar ideas emerged earlier in the work of "English school" thinkers such as Hedley Bull, Adam Watson, and Martin Wight), the constructivist school of thought stresses norms as important components of state interests and actions.[13] For example, moral concerns related to issues such as racial equality and the use of nuclear weapons have in part shaped American interests and in turn American foreign policy.[14] For theorists such as Alexander Wendt and Nicholas Onuf, norms represent critical components of both the international system and states' interests.[15] They argue that world politics is "socially constructed" because the basic structures of international politics, such as security dilemmas and reliance on self-help, "are social rather than strictly material, and these structures shape actors' identities and interests, rather than just their behavior."[16] In other words, the ways of the world in international affairs are not immutable laws brought down by Moses. Sovereign states themselves have not always existed. Decisions made in 1648 with the Treaty of Westphalia "constructed" a new international society along more or less secular, state-based lines. Even great powers such as the United

States are influenced by the evolution of international ethics—prevailing global norms (e.g., racial equality, a chemical weapons taboo, or the prohibition of genocide) partially define and redefine American interests in terms of norms and accepted standards of behavior.[17]

As Wendt further explains, "To ask 'when do ideas, as opposed to power and interest, matter?' is to ask the wrong question. Ideas always matter, since power and interest do not have effects apart from the shared knowledge that constitutes them as such."[18] Attention to the role of norms in foreign policy need not give ideas priority over power and interests. All three are important. Constructivism and related schools of thought simply suggest that we recognize that ideas are often responsible not only for strategies chosen in the pursuit of interests but also for what we view to be our interests in the first place.[19] In essence, constructivism employs a rich theoretical language to remind us that statesmen are not bound by fate to follow a predetermined diplomatic script. Instead, through foreign policy, the United States and other players on the world stage can in fact change the world and impact the values and interests enshrined in international law. From the nuclear weapons use to environmental policy, the recent history of world politics bears this out.

With that in mind, this policy-oriented study leads naturally to a discussion of the influence, if any, exerted on the United States by the ideas and norms embedded in the UNGC. Tracing the U.S. response to major genocides since World War II offers a unique opportunity to contribute empirically to this developing dialogue on ideas and interests. The cases developed here illustrate the impediments faced by a new norm to become a relevant component of both the international system and states' interests. However, examining how the UNGC has influenced the United States is not enough; we must also consider the extent to which the United States has acted to promote the UNGC.

ETHICAL LEADERSHIP MOMENTS

Therefore, this book tackles the closely related and highly charged issues of leadership, ethics, and responsibility. Henry Kissinger writes, "Almost as if according to some natural law, in every century there seems to emerge a country with the power, the will, and the intellectual and moral impetus to shape the entire international system in accordance with its own values."[20] In the twentieth and early twenty-first centuries, the United States has been and is that country. Through its decisions, priorities, and influence, the United States can shape the world, acting as what some call a "norm entrepreneur" to change the behavior of others and legitimize or delegitimize certain international norms.[21] With a distribution of power in their favor, American foreign policymakers can promote the evolution of international society and the adoption of particular values in world politics. Thus, the United States can choose to work more or less actively to "construct" a particular norm or code of international conduct. As a nation, the United States can lead change.

Alexander Wendt argues forcefully that if it is possible to change the prevailing structures or the nature of world politics, "then it would be irresponsible to pursue policies that perpetuate destructive old orders, especially if we care about the well-being of future generations."[22] This sets a high standard and serves as an important frame of reference and benchmark for American foreign policy. Instances of genocide provide what will be termed here "ethical leadership moments"—distinct, even propitious opportunities for bringing about significant progress in international ethics.[23] For the more theoretically inclined, pivotal "constructivist moments" represents a worthy synonym.

Because the United States has unrivaled power to lead change in world affairs and encounters innumerable opportunities to do so given its global role, this book carefully examines and assesses the extent to which the United States has taken a leadership role in the fight against genocide. What becomes clear is that the United States has not fully capitalized on its leadership role and its ethical leadership moments. Rather, in bouts of policy schizophrenia, the United States has both supported and undermined the admirable goals of the UNGC, and this book exposes this dualism in American foreign policy. Following this introduction, chapter 1 opens the empirical section with an exploration of the U.S. ratification of the UNGC. Adopted by the General Assembly in 1948, the convention represents in large part the "birth" of a norm. Shocked into action by the horror of the Holocaust, members of the world community responded to American leadership and created a document that defined a new international crime and declared an intention to prevent its future occurrence.

Despite reasonable expectations of quick ratification by the United States, the UNGC became bogged down in the U.S. Senate, subject to attack from several sides. For over forty years, the convention languished unratified, as proponents and opponents alike mustered their cases for and against it. Finally in 1988, the UNGC garnered adequate approval and subsequent ratification. This surprising story provides essential background and raises the first in a series of important questions about domestic politics, American foreign policy, and the UNGC.

Chapters 2, 3, and 4 present case studies of the U.S. response to specific instances of genocide. Each of these chapters follows the same organizational form: briefly documents the genocide, examines U.S. policy during the genocide, and details American efforts supporting the punishment clause of the UNGC. An important qualification belongs here: This book does not purport to provide a comprehensive political and diplomatic history of the cases in question. Each chapter instead relates the important and most relevant events and actions, thus faithfully capturing the essence of each episode.

Chapter 2 examines American foreign policy during the awful ascendancy of the Khmer Rouge in Cambodia. Following the defeat of a U.S.-backed regime in South Vietnam, Phnom Penh fell to the communist Khmer Rouge and quickly descended into a genocidal nightmare directed by Pol Pot. How did the Carter administration respond to the "world's worst violator of human rights"? To answer that question, the chapter discusses issues such as U.S. attempts to secure the geopolitical "China card," the influence of the Vietnam experience, and available courses of action. To tell a complete story, the chapter also explores U.S. efforts since 1979 to bring Khmer Rouge leaders to justice.

The final two chapters turn to American foreign policy and genocide in the post–Cold War era. The end of the Cold War meant a new context for intervention and the use of force, one freed of the restraints imposed by the superpower conflict and the threat of escalation to nuclear confrontation. Chapter 3 investigates the case of U.S. foreign policy and genocide in Bosnia during the 1991–1995 war in the former Yugoslavia. In this episode, the United States faced a second genocide in Europe in just over fifty years. However, despite new freedom from the rigidity of the Cold War and bold pronouncements of a "new world order," both a Republican and a Democratic administration declined to arrest genocide in the former Yugoslavia. The United States would finally intervene, but well after significant genocidal atrocities had already occurred. Why did Cold War triumph give way to failure to block the Serbs' genocidal policy of "ethnic cleansing"? What restraints negated the freedom of action and opportunity for decidedly moral statecraft afforded by new circumstances in post–Cold War international politics? Eventually, the United States did put the weight of its considerable leadership behind the Dayton Peace Accords and the pursuit of justice at the international criminal tribunal in The Hague for crimes committed during the conflict.

Similar issues emerge in chapter 4, which examines the question of American intervention in the 1994 Rwandan genocide. Facing the most widely publicized and perhaps clearest case of genocide since the Holocaust, the United States downplayed the crisis in Rwanda and impeded UN efforts at intervention. To explain the Clinton administration's failure to respond vigorously against genocide in a small African nation, attention turns to the Somalia debacle and to the influence of domestic political concerns. The Clinton administration's decisions during the carnage and U.S. support of the subsequent UN Criminal Tribunal investigating the mass killings in Rwanda raise pertinent questions about the United States and genocide prevention in the post–Cold War world.

The final chapter considers the implications of the findings presented here for the future of American foreign policy, the prevention and punishment of genocide, and the evolution of the genocide norm. Overall, this study fills a significant gap in scholarship. This project represents the first attempt to examine, across cases, the U.S. response to prominent instances of genocide in the post–World War II world. With a focus on the intersections of and conflicts between American values and interests in foreign policy, the analysis clarifies the apparent dual track of U.S. diplomacy: nonintervention during genocides but increasing commitment to postgenocide justice. If recent history provides any indication, the United States will again confront genocide in the twenty-first century. Examining and understanding previous American responses to these horrific and massive violations of human rights will prove invaluable in formulating policies to prevent or end future episodes of genocide and subsequent human suffering.

NOTES

1. Originally coined by Polish jurist Raphael Lemkin in his book *Axis Rule in Occupied Europe* (Washington, D.C.: Carnegie Endowment for International Peace, 1944), the term "genocide" remains subject to much debate as scholars attempt to write a "better" definition than that in the UNGC. Rehashing that debate is not the purpose of this study. As of this writing, the definition of "genocide" drafted by the United Nations in 1946 remains the internationally recognized legal version (see the appendix). Furthermore, the United States and world bodies recognize the cases under examination here as fitting that definition of genocide. For an example of a proposed revision, see Frank Chalk, "Redefining Genocide," in George Andreopoulos, ed., *Genocide: Conceptual and Historical Dimensions* (Philadelphia: University of Pennsylvania Press, 1994).

2. Referred to throughout as "the Genocide Convention" and "the UNGC."

3. United Nations, GAOR Res. 260A (III), December 9, 1948.

4. See Richard Breitman, *Official Secrets: What the Nazis Planned, What the British and Americans Knew* (New York: Hill and Wang, 1999); David Wyman, *The Abandonment of the Jews: American and the Holocaust, 1941–1945* (New York: Pantheon Books, 1984); Henry Feingold, *The Politics of Rescue* (New Brunswick, N.J.: Rutgers University Press, 1970); Raul Hilberg, *Perpetrators, Victims, Bystanders: The Jewish Catastrophe, 1933–1945* (New York: HarperCollins, 1992).

5. Israel Charny, ed., *Toward the Understanding and Prevention of Genocide: Proceedings of the International Conference on the Holocaust and Genocide* (New York: Westview Press, 1984); Herbert Hirsch, *Genocide and the Politics of Memory: Studying Death to Preserve Life* (Chapel Hill: University of North Carolina Press, 1995); Helen Fein, *Genocide Watch* (New Haven, Conn.: Yale University Press, 1992).

6. Ben Kiernan, *The Pol Pot Regime: Race, Power, and Genocide in Cambodia under the Khmer Rouge, 1975–79* (New Haven, Conn.: Yale University Press, 1996); Gerard Prunier, *The Rwanda Crisis: History of a Genocide* (New York: Columbia University Press, 1995); Norman Cigar, *Genocide in Bosnia* (College Station: Texas A&M University Press, 1995); Richard Hovannisian, ed., *The Armenian Genocide in Perspective* (New Brunswick, N.J.: Transaction Books, 1986).

7. Hans Morgenthau, *The Purpose of American Politics* (New York: University Press of

America, 1960), 8. For a concise encapsulation of the concepts and history behind the "American mission," see Brian Klunk, *Consensus and the American Mission* (Lanham, Md.: University Press of America, 1985), 1–23.

8. Henry Kissinger, *Diplomacy* (New York: Simon & Schuster, 1994), 8.

9. For a general but brief discussion of ethics and American foreign policy, see Robert W. McElroy, *Morality and American Foreign Policy* (Princeton, N.J.: Princeton University Press, 1992). Works with a narrower human rights focus include Gaddis Smith, *Morality, Reason, and Power: American Diplomacy in the Carter Years* (New York: Hill and Wang, 1986), and David Louis Cingranelli, *Ethics, American Foreign Policy, and the Third World* (New York: St. Martin's Press, 1993). See also Tony Smith, *America's Mission: The United States and the Worldwide Struggle for Democracy in the Twentieth Century* (Princeton, N.J.: Princeton University Press, 1994). See also Anders Stephanson, *Manifest Destiny: American Expansion and the Empire of Right* (New York: Hill and Wang, 1995) for a discussion of the ideology of American exceptionalism, particularly the religious aspect, and its enduring influence.

10. Here I refer to international society as defined by Hedley Bull in *The Anarchical Society*: A Study of Order in World Politics (New York: Columbia University Press, 1977). Bull defines a society of states as "a group of states, conscious of certain common interests and common values, [that] conceive of themselves to be bound by a common set of rules in their relations with one another, and share in the working of common institutions" (13).

11. David Welch, *Justice and the Genesis of War* (Cambridge: Cambridge University Press, 1993), 3.

12. Michael Joseph Smith, *Realist Thought from Weber to Kissinger* (Baton Rouge: Louisiana State University Press, 1986), 164.

13. See Bull, *The Anarchical Society*; Herbert Butterfield and Martin Wight, eds., *Diplomatic Investigations* (London: Allen and Unwin, 1966); Adam Watson, *The Evolution of International Society* (London: Routledge, 1992).

14. Klotz, *Norms in International Relations: The Struggle against Apartheid* (Ithaca, N.Y.: Cornell University Press, 1996); for an article version, see Klotz, "Norms Reconstituting Interests: Global Racial Equality and U.S. Sanctions against South Africa," *International Organization* 49 (summer 1995): 451–78; Richard Price and Nina Tannenwald, "Norms and Deterrence: The Nuclear and Chemical Weapons Taboos," in Peter J. Katzenstein, ed., *The Culture of National Security: Norms and Identity in World Politics* (New York: Columbia University Press, 1996). On the school of thought overall, see Jeffrey T. Chekel, "The Constructivist Turn in International Relations Theory," *World Politics* 50: 324–48.

15. See especially "Anarchy Is What States Make of It," *International Organization* 46 (spring 1992): 91–425, and Nicholas Greenwood Onuf, *World of Our Making: Rules and Rule in Social Theory and International Relations* (Columbia: University of South Carolina Press, 1989). See also Friedrich Kratochwil, "On the Notion of 'Interest' in International Relations," *International Organization* 36 (winter 1982): 1–30. Wendt and Onuf label their perspective "constructivist" based on the sociological theory of Anthony Giddens, who argues that structures and agents reconstruct each other over time. See David Held and John B. Thompson, eds., *Social Theory of Modern Societies: Anthony Giddens and His Critics* (Cambridge: Cambridge University Press, 1989).

16. Alexander Wendt, "Constructing International Politics," *International Security* 20 (summer 1995): 71–81. Furthermore, Wendt stresses the importance of shared knowledge and understanding which manifest themselves in practice. He writes, "The Cold War was a

structure of shared knowledge that governed great power relations for forty years, but once they stopped acting on this basis, it was 'over' " (74).

17. Klotz, *Norms in International Society,* 460.

18. Wendt, "Constructing International Politics," 74.

19. Note as well that interest can be material (physical items needed for our well-being) or ideal (what is required for our spiritual or emotional health). Max Weber has been quoted for his discussion linking ideas and interests together: "Not ideas, but material and ideal interest, directly govern men's conduct. Yet very frequently, the 'world images' that have been created by ideas have, like switchmen, determined the tracks along which action has been pushed by the dynamic of interest." See Judith Goldstein and Robert O. Keohane, eds., *Ideas and Foreign Policy: Beliefs, Institutions, and Political Change* (Ithaca, N.Y.: Cornell University Press, 1993), 11–12; Hans J. Morgenthau, *Politics among Nations,* Brief ed. (New York: McGraw-Hill, 1993), 11.

20. Kissinger, *Diplomacy,* 17.

21. According to Ann Florini, John Mueller introduced the term "norm entrepreneur" at a conference on "The Emergence of New Norms in Personal and International Behavior," University of California, Los Angeles, May 1993. See Florini, "The Evolution of International Norms," *International Studies Quarterly* 40, no. 3 (September 1996): 375. Also Ethan A. Nadelmann, "Global Prohibition Regimes: The Evolution of Norms in International Society," *International Organization* 44 (autumn 1990), 4.

22. Wendt, "Constructing International Politics," 80.

23. Inspiration for this term comes from Michael Useem, *The Leadership Moment: Nine True Stories of Triumph and Disaster and Their Lessons for Us All* (New York: Times Business, 1998).

Chapter One

An Unconventional Debate: The United States and the Genocide Convention

We cannot do moral battle against genocide with one hand tied behind our backs.

—Senator William Proxmire, 1981

In November 1988, President Ronald Reagan signed legislation making the United States party to the United Nations Convention on the Prevention and Punishment of the Crime of Genocide (UNGC), and ninety days later the convention became legally binding on the United States. Thus, the United States joined with ninety-seven other members of the world community in pledging its commitment to prevent future genocides and to prosecute perpetrators of the hideous offense.[1]

At the signing ceremony, President Reagan said that the legislation "represents a strong and clear statement by the United States that it will punish acts of genocide with the force of law and the righteousness of justice."[2] Unfortunately, it had taken the United States nearly forty years to make so strong and clear a statement after President Harry Truman first requested Senate approval in 1949. Why the lengthy delay on an issue such as the UNGC? What led the United States, self-proclaimed champion of human rights issues, to reject the world's first treaty making genocide and the intent to commit it an international crime?

This chapter examines the stormy tale of ratification of the UNGC by the United States. It contrasts energetic American involvement in drafting the first and most prominent postwar attempt to prevent future Holocausts with equally determined action by American legislators and other domestic opponents to deny ratification by the U.S. Senate. In 1948, the United States took the lead in rallying the young United Nations behind the pledge "never again." Yet less than two years later, the United States would take the first steps down a path of nonratification that would last for decades.

Failure to ratify the UNGC put the United States in an awkward position. How could the United States profess concern for human rights and outrage over genocide if it refused to support the single treaty dealing with that specific and horrific atrocity? In fact, over the course of the ratification episode, several presidents and other policymakers alluded to the questions posed and criticisms levied at the United States for its anomalous position.

American reluctance to support the UNGC also had particular significance for the development of a genocide norm. No doubt, the convention is a flawed document. Some ambiguous language, definitional issues and omissions, and questions of enforcement plague the treaty. As a result, in a realist world of self-interested states, many view the document as more symbolic than anything else. Symbolic or not, the UNGC is nevertheless an important milestone. It does not prevent genocide, no more than domestic laws by themselves prevent homicide, but it creates a set of norms pertaining to a new crime. It defines a certain behavior, labels it as criminal, and declares members of the international community responsible to combat and punish the crime.

This is a significant development, quite apart from issues of enforcement and application. As convention champion Senator William Proxmire would term it, the convention is "a call for a higher standard of human conduct. It is not a panacea for injustice."[3] This normative component makes all the more important the role of the United States. With a prominent opportunity to make at minimum a strong, symbolic statement against genocide and bolster a nascent norm, the United States faltered badly. The ethical leadership moment instead took four decades to fully materialize.

ORIGINS AND DRAFTING

In his 1944 book *Axis Rule in Occupied Europe,* Polish lawyer Raphael Lemkin set out to provide "undeniable and objective evidence regarding the treatment of the subjugated people of Europe by the Axis powers."[4] He created the term "genocide" to describe Nazi efforts to exterminate European Jews. Lemkin coined the term by joining the Greek word for "race" or "tribe" (*genos*) with the Latin word for "killing" (*cide*). He explained that a conception such as the destruction of a nation requires its own term. Terms such as "homicide" or "massacre" simply did not suffice to describe the destruction or attempted destruction of a nation or ethnic group. According to Lemkin, the new term was

> intended rather to signify a coordinated plan of different actions aiming at the destruction of essential foundations of the life of national groups, with the aim of annihilating the groups themselves. The objectives of such a plan would be the disintegration of the

> political and social institutions, of culture, language, national feelings, religion, and the economic existence of national groups, and the destruction of the personal security, liberty, health, dignity, and even the lives of the individuals belonging to such groups. Genocide is directed against the national group as an entity, and the actions involved are directed against individuals, not in their individual aspects, but as members of the national group.[5]

Although this passage focuses specifically on national groups, later in the same work Lemkin addressed other offenses ("barbarities" and "vandalism") against religious and racial groups, indicating that he envisioned these groups as potential victims of genocide as well.[6]

Following the end of World War II, Lemkin lobbied vigorously for the creation of an international treaty on genocide. He pushed fervently for the newly created United Nations to take action on the issue. Lemkin's energetic determination led some to label him a "fanatic" and a "dreamer."[7] Nonetheless, the "fanatical" efforts of this dreamer persuaded the General Assembly in December 1946 to adopt a resolution that stated the following:

> Genocide is a denial of the right of existence of entire human groups, as homicide is the denial of the right to live of individual human beings; such denial of the right of existence shocks the conscience of mankind, results in great losses to humanity in the form of cultural and other contributions represented by these human groups, and is contrary to moral law and to the spirit and aims of the United Nations.
>
> Many instances of such crimes have occurred when racial, religious, political and other groups have been destroyed, entirely or in part.
>
> The punishment of the crime of genocide is a matter of international concern.
>
> *The General Assembly therefore,*
>
> *Affirms* that genocide is a crime under international law which the civilized world condemns, and for the commission of which principals and accomplices—whether private individuals, public officials or statesmen, and whether the crime is committed on religious, racial, political, or any other grounds—are punishable.

The resolution also directed the UN Economic and Social Council to begin a study that would lead to a draft convention on the crime of genocide to be submitted to the subsequent regular session of the General Assembly. Pursuant to the General Assembly's resolution, UN members began work on a document that would eventually become the UNGC. The UNGC was drafted to mark the difference between homicide and genocide. Following Lemkin's logic in coining the term, the drafters of the convention viewed homicide as becoming genocide when murders are committed because of the victim's identity as a member of a certain group, coupled with the intent to destroy that group.

The U.S. delegation to the United Nations played a central role in drafting the document, imbuing it with the language of Anglo-American legal theory and notions of common law.[8] Beyond influencing convention language, U.S.

representatives were quite vocal in their efforts to see an agreement adopted by the General Assembly. Ernest A. Gross, assistant secretary of state, urged other member states that "positive action be taken now" on so important an issue. The United States also stood at the forefront of two major areas of discussion and debate during the drafting process: the question of "intent" and the inclusion of political groups in the convention definition.

A significant issue considered early on by the drafters of the convention was whether genocide could be said to have occurred only when the entire group had been killed. Lemkin and others believed that an appropriately comprehensive document would clarify that the destruction of even part of a particular group would constitute genocide as well. To address this concern, a Norwegian delegate at the United Nations proposed the inclusion of the term "in whole or in part" in Article II of the convention. This clarification won approval by a vote of 41–8, with two abstentions.[9]

As Professor Lawrence LeBlanc of Marquette University asserts in his excellent study of the convention, the drafters, including U.S. representatives, "decidedly took the view that the destruction of parts of groups, not only entire groups, would constitute genocide, and that the crime of genocide itself had to be defined in terms of an intent to destroy groups as such."[10] Little did American proponents know that the important phrase "in whole or in part" would prove quite troublesome in the Senate ratification debate.

As it stands even today, the UNGC extends its coverage to "national, ethnic, racial, and religious groups." However, initial drafts of the convention (and the General Assembly resolution quoted previously) included protection for "political" groups. The decision to include or remove such groups from the list of the protected preoccupied the drafters for some time, and it became a serious issue of debate in the United States.[11]

Early on, the United States spoke forcefully in favor of including political groups in the convention. American representative Ernest Gross argued that political groups were not overly "unstable" as some states had claimed. Gross also took issue with the argument that opening the convention to political groups would limit the ability of governments to crack down legitimately on dangerous, subversive political groups. Indeed, states could certainly act decisively and effectively against violent opposition groups without resorting to genocidal means. As the delegate from Ecuador noted, there is a "great difference between measures for maintaining order in such a case and measures employed in the perpetration of genocide."[12]

Finally, Gross pointed to the initial inclusion of political groups in General Assembly Resolution 96 (I) and in the 1946 draft of the convention. He said that declaring that political groups were potential victims of genocide two years earlier and then removing them from convention language would undermine

UN credibility.[13] However, as debate continued over the draft, it became clear that including political groups in the convention would dissuade many states from ratifying it. As a result, states such as Egypt argued that political groups be excluded for the practical reason of securing the support of as many states as possible.[14]

Similarly practical or "realistic" concerns led the United States to compromise on the final draft. Gross essentially struck a deal whereby the United States would accept the removal of political groups from the convention in exchange for renewed consideration of language in Article VI calling for an international criminal court. Throughout the drafting process, U.S. delegates had argued for the creation of such an institution to carry out the punishment side of the convention, but that provision had been removed. The deal basically exchanging one provision for another won support. The political groups issue was resolved permanently for the United Nations but just temporarily for the United States.

SENATE DEBATE: 1950

Following UN finalization and approval of the UNGC, President Harry S. Truman asked in June 1949 for Senate advice and consent to ratify the treaty. Given the lead role played by the United States in drafting the convention, no one seemed to anticipate or expect any difficulty; the United States would naturally capitalize on this ethical leadership moment and promote the document as an important part of a postwar "new world order." The Senate Foreign Relations Committee responded to Truman's request by assembling a subcommittee to hold hearings. In January and February 1950, those initial hearings elicited an overwhelmingly favorable response to the convention. Government officials, including Deputy Undersecretary of State Dean Rusk and Solicitor-General Philip B. Perlman, spoke for the administration in strong support of the treaty.

At the opening public hearing, Rusk stressed two central rationales for ratification. Rusk did not argue that the UNGC would actually eliminate genocide. Instead, he focused mostly on the symbolic meaning of the convention and American support of it. First, in an appeal to American exceptionalism, Rusk emphasized that U.S. support for the treaty would "demonstrate to the rest of the world that the United States is determined to maintain its moral leadership in international affairs."[15] Second, according to Rusk, ratification would highlight the American commitment to the "development of international law on the basis of human justice."[16] Rusk stated that "it is an inescapable fact that other nations of the world expect the United States to assert moral leadership in international affairs."[17] He continued, suggesting that the UNGC should not be looked on as a commitment foreign to American experience because "it is a familiar role . . . for the United States to take the lead in raising moral standards of international society."[18]

For added salesmanship, Rusk placed the convention within the context of emerging tensions between the United States and the Soviet Union. He explained that the United States was "engaged in a very fundamental struggle in our foreign relations between the forces that are trying to build up a free world and the forces that are trying to tear it down."[19] In that dramatic light, he explained that the administration looked "upon this Genocide Convention as a major element in the attempt to mobilize the moral and spiritual resources of mankind . . . and through that, contribute greatly to the interests, the peace, and the well-being of the American people."[20]

Appearing before the committee in April 1950, Solicitor-General Philip B. Perlman expanded on Rusk's statement, arguing that "the Convention on Genocide is notice to the world that commission of that crime will result in punishment of the criminals and that the civilized nations will take action to make that punishment certain and severe. . . . Our duty to our country and to all of humanity forbids us to do anything less than has been written in the Convention on the Prevention and Punishment of the Crime of Genocide."[21]

Perlman buttressed his committee testimony with an essay in the *Nebraska Law Review* urging support for the convention. In the November 1950 article, he expressed his surprise that "a convention such as this, which seeks to give international legal expression to a universally acknowledged principle of human decency, epitomized in one of the Ten Commandments" would face any "serious disagreement" in the United States.[22]

Raphael Lemkin, then a professor at Yale University, also lent his voice in support of ratification. His personal history compelled him to push his adopted country to embrace an international treaty to criminalize such attempts at the annihilation of a people. Lemkin had fled from Poland following the Nazi invasion in 1939. All but two of his family of seventy-four perished in the Holocaust, and these life experiences clearly shaped his perspective on the importance of further developing and strengthening international law.[23]

Lemkin's zealous pursuit of Senate support irritated some legislators and led to some rather undiplomatic personal attacks, criticisms, and hints of anti-Semitism. Senator Alexander Smith (R-N.J.) expressed discomfort that the convention's most dedicated opponent was "a man who comes from a foreign country . . . who speaks broken English." The senator called Lemkin "a nice fellow" but noted that he and many other legislators had been "irritated no end by this fellow running around." Smith curiously added that although he sympathized with the Jewish people, "they ought not to be the ones who are propagandizing [the convention]."[24]

Lemkin bothered even those legislators in favor of ratification. Henry Cabot

Lodge (R-Mass.) mentioned that Lemkin had "done his own cause a great deal of harm" during the 1959 hearings.[25] Other senators strongly supportive of the convention gave Lemkin unfavorable reviews as well, saying that he was not the biggest problem in the ratification debate, but he was nonetheless the "least plus quantity."[26] As it turned out, the UNGC would face far more formidable obstacles to ratification than Lemkin's accent and energetic lobbying.

NGO ACTIVISM

At the start of what would develop into decades of sporadic debate over the UNGC, the administration received support from the vast majority of the nongovernmental organization (NGO) community. A wide variety of religious, political, and community organizations lined up to show their support for the administration's position. At the initial hearings in early 1950, some forty NGO representatives spoke in favor of ratification, and close to 100 submitted statements indicating their support.

Describing genocide as "the most appalling crime in all recorded history," the American Jewish Committee called for prompt action by the United States. Committee President Jacob Blaustein said that "the United States, by continual devotion to justice and humanity, has earned a reputation as the leader of world morality." He argued that any delay would damage American prestige while "shaking the temple of peace to its very foundations."[27] Other religious groups, such as the Greek Orthodox Church of North and South America, B'nai B'rith, and the Federal Council of Churches in Christ, voiced their support for ratification.

In the interest of women and children, minorities, and Americans in general, the National Council of Negro Women submitted its support for the convention. In a statement of inadvertent prescience, the council opened its testimony by explaining that "the situation of Negro people in this country is in no way involved" with the UNGC. Spokeswoman Eunice Carter declared that "the lynching of an individual or of several individuals has no relation to the extinction of masses of peoples because of race, religion, or political belief."[28] Instead, the council affirmed its commitment to the convention because women and children are often the first victims of genocide and because minorities would be safe nowhere should the destruction of any group go "unchecked or unpunished."[29] Finally, the council sought ratification because it believed that the United States "cannot maintain the respect and trust of nations or peoples unless it takes leadership in moral courage."[30]

Community organizations, such as the Business and Professional Women's Club, the Loyal Order of Moose, and the Salvation Army, also made known their unqualified support for the convention. The American Veteran's Committee, a leadership group of World War II veterans, saw the convention as a tool for attacking the causes of war. Committee representative Michael Straight argued that, as veterans, his fellow members had a "special interest in preventing war."[31] They believed that the UNGC would strengthen the United Nations as an effective organization for peace. Straight said that "if the United States should now reject or ignore the Genocide Convention . . . that would be a cruel blow to the United Nations. Ratification, on the other hand, will be one much-needed re-affirmation in its future at this critical time."[32]

Thus, to a diverse panoply of American NGOs, the Senate's choice in 1950 was clear. However, despite often eloquent arguments from NGOs and administration officials in defense of the treaty as in the interest of the United States and the world, ratification did not emerge as the clear choice. Instead, a determined minority of powerful senators and small group of NGOs on the other side of the aisle, fearful of civil rights reform at home and concerned about the Cold War abroad, contradicted the views of the administration and the mass of the NGO community.

THE AMERICAN BAR ASSOCIATION

At the forefront of this anticonvention movement stood one of America's most influential NGOs: the American Bar Association (ABA). From 1950 to the mid-1970s, the ABA, a widely respected and traditionally conservative organization, held firm in a strident campaign of opposition to the convention. Many Senate opponents of the convention received moral support and sympathetic arguments from the ABA, and together they managed to shelve the convention for years.

From the beginning of the debate, the ABA would star as the leading opponent of ratification. Despite a lack of internal consensus about the convention, the organization's House of Delegates first voted in September 1949 to oppose it.[33] During the January 1950 Senate hearings, Alfred J. Schweppe, chairman of the ABA's Special Committee on Peace and Law through the United Nations, commenced the fight against ratification. Schweppe sought to clarify in his opening remarks that he personally "took a back seat to no one in being opposed to genocide."[34] He went on to make clear the ABA opinion "that the Convention on Genocide now before the United States Senate be not approved as submitted." ABA opposition consistently revolved around a cluster of main issues: the "in whole or in part" language, states' rights versus federal power, the "domestic" nature of the genocide, and freedom of speech.

First, the ABA questioned the definition in Article II of the convention dealing with the "intent to destroy, in whole or in part, a national, ethnical, or religious group." The phrasing "in part" clearly troubled Schweppe and the ABA. While many feared a future use of the convention in connection with the treatment of Native Americans in the United States, greater concern centered on the treatment of blacks and other minorities.[35]

Both Schweppe and ABA President Frank Holman, a nationally prominent conservative, argued that the convention could serve as a tool to overturn segregation and as a powerful antilynching law. They interpreted Article II of the UNGC (which defines genocide) as a means of trying lynch mobs in the United States for genocide and as a way to erode Jim Crow laws. Holman and Schweppe described a scenario in which "in part" would apply to the murder of a single individual, and thus anyone guilty of one act of lynching could face charges of genocide. As Schweppe asked, "Certainly it doesn't mean if I want to drive 5 Chinamen out of town, to use that invidious illustration, that I must have the intent to destroy all the 400 million Chinese in the world or the 250,000 in the United States."[36]

Furthermore, the ABA opponents suggested that the clause in the convention dealing with causing "mental harm" to a racial or ethnic group could be applied to segregation statutes in the United States. Therefore, this international treaty could compel the South to integrate.[37] Such arguments resonated with a Senate leadership full of conservative southerners. As one observer has noted, "It was not surprising, given the ABA's own history, that its leadership advanced these type of objections. The organization allowed few African Americans to join, as all prospective applicants had to note their race on membership applications and obtain thirteen affirmative votes from the sixteen-member board of governors.[38]

Dean Rusk and Philip Perlman responded to these concerns by explaining that the convention defined genocide as occurring only when murderous acts were coupled with the intent to destroy an entire group. Lynching, therefore, would not fall under the convention's purview. They also pointed out that the convention required that murderous acts affect a significant portion of the group in question, and this specific requirement was further underlined in a formal understanding reached between the Truman administration and the Senate subcommittee.[39]

ABA Committee Vice Chairman Carl B. Rix raised a second and long-standing criticism of the convention: its threat to the balance of federal-state relations. Rix reported that the jurisdiction of Congress was already moving without constitutional basis into areas of civil rights. Thus, he warned that the convention would similarly contribute to such a leakage and a "dominant federalist state."[40] Rix put the question bluntly: "If there is to be a succession of treaties from the United Nations dealing with domestic questions, are we ready to surrender the power of the States over such matters to the Federal Government?"[41] The supposed "domestic nature" of genocide posed yet another fundamental problem for the ABA. Opponents argued that genocide represents an internal domestic issue rather than an international crime. Rix and others expressed concern over an apparent related attempt to expand the scope of international law beyond sovereign states and to both domestic issues and individuals.

Convention opponents from the ABA also attacked it on grounds that it undermined the Tenth Amendment and expanded federal power. They noted that the power to prosecute and punish crimes such as murder and other acts specifically prohibited by the UNGC normally fell to individual states. Therefore, they charged that ratification of the convention would federalize parts of the criminal code at the expense of states. Moreover, many also looked with horror on a provision to create an international tribunal to deal with those charged with genocide. Holman and others from the ABA feared that Americans dragged before a world court would be denied their constitutional rights.[42] Opponents additionally charged that given its scope, the UNGC would apply to all Americans and would limit their freedom of speech. They argued that anyone criticizing a minority group could be found guilty of causing "mental harm" and that anyone who indirectly wrote about genocide could be prosecuted for incitement.

Solicitor-General Perlman joined State Department legal adviser Adrian Fisher to explain that the term "mental harm" did not conflict at all with American law. During the convention drafting, Chinese representatives introduced the clause after relating a plan by the Japanese during World War II to harm millions of Chinese by administering overdoses of opium. "Mental harm" was limited to permanent mental injury and not simply temporary distress or discomfort caused by insults or heated language.[43]

Rusk contradicted the "domestic issue" reasoning, noting, "When large numbers of refugees are created through the crime of genocide . . . and when crimes like genocide so inflame the international situation as to bring us to the brink of war and are real threats to the peace, the impact on not only our foreign policy but on our domestic interest is very great, so long as such things as genocide occur in the world."[44] In addition, the ABA's domestic issue line of argument ignored previous U.S. adherence to several international agreements that criminalized certain activities such as slavery and piracy.[45] However, thus characterized, the convention appeared to its ABA opponents and many senators as unconstitutional and beyond the treaty-making power defined in the Constitution.[46]

Despite the determined support for ratification demonstrated by the Truman administration and by an expansive and varied network of NGOs and other community groups, a coalition of conservative southern Democrats and midwestern Republicans in the Senate Foreign Relations Committee continued to criticize the convention for potentially dangerous effects on race relations, civil rights, and American sovereignty. Committee Chairman Tom Connally (D-Tex.) was joined by Senator Walter George (D-Ga.) and Senator Alexander Wiley (R-Wis.) in expressing fears that the UNGC would endanger Jim Crow laws, limit freedom of speech, destroy states' rights, and jeopardize the sovereignty of the United States.

Chairman Connally, in fact, responded with near hostility to testimony in favor of the convention by State Department legal adviser Adrian Fisher. Fisher in large part repeated the central thrust of Rusk's arguments dealing with the moral leadership of the United States and its ability to condemn vocally other nations for violations such as genocide. Connally admonished Fisher sternly, stating, "I don't appreciate and don't regard with any weight at all fellows from the departments coming up here and lecturing to Congress about the morals or morality of the United States. We have been able to take care of our morality for 150 years."[47] Senator Wiley said he was "in favor of preventing mass murder" but added that he was "not in favor of leaving it to the interpretation of nations who have been indulging for centuries in just such a thing, and they have been occurring at every drop of the hat, so to speak, so that I want to be careful."[48]

Of course, the opinions of Wiley, Connally, and others like them were not shared by the rest of the subcommittee. Senators Lodge, Pepper, Thomas, and others expressed their support of the measure. Summing up the mountains of testimony, Senator Brien McMahon (D-Conn.) expressed to the Senate Foreign Relations Committee that he had been "impressed by the unanimity of the opinion of our people . . . and these are some of the petitions that have come, most of them from organizations . . . and I have not found an editorial or expression of opinion against ratification all over the country. Great organizations have passed resolutions and sent them in, urging ratification." However, the arguments of Senator McMahon and others in favor of the UNGC could not overcome the fears and determined opposition of those who charged the treaty with eviscerating states' rights and interfering with race relations in the United States. As Natalie Kaufman summarized, this conservative coalition "succeeded in labeling the Genocide Convention and all human rights treaties as un-American."[49]

On January 12, 1951, just over a year after the first Senate hearings on the UNGC, the treaty came into force following ratification by twenty UN member states. However, the United States was not among the twenty states approving the treaty. The arguments of the ABA—perhaps not surprisingly persuasive with the Senate, composed primarily of lawyers—combined with other factors to doom U.S. assent. Although the subcommittee had actually rejected the ABA's negative stance and proposed ratification by the full Senate Foreign Relations Committee, the broader committee failed to act. Chairman Connally read aloud the text of the ABA resolution against ratification and then refused to allow the committee to vote on sending the convention to the full Senate.[50]

Vocal ABA opposition, together with growing McCarthyism and its accompanying isolationist leanings (plus concerns over U.S. sovereignty), contributed to the committee's failure to move in favor of ratification.[51] The initiative of Ohio Senator John Bricker to curtail the ability of the executive to conclude treaties with foreign powers certainly did not help create a climate conducive to international human rights agreements.[52] By 1953, the Eisenhower administration moved to avoid any loss of presidential authority by essentially making a negative commitment to human rights treaties. Secretary of State John Foster Dulles, reacting to "a political environment typified by McCarthyism" and "the growing fear of 'socialism by treaty,' " promised the Senate on April 6, 1953, that the Eisenhower administration would not "become a party to any covenant [on human rights] for consideration by the Senate."[53] This effective opposition to the convention early on crippled the ratification effort. In a stunning turn of events, the Senate turned its back on an ethical leadership moment in foreign policy. Failing to receive timely ratification, the UNGC fell into relative obscurity as more pressing Cold War priorities assumed center stage in American foreign policy.

THE AD HOC COMMITTEE

As the Genocide Convention languished unratified, treaty supporters did not give up their efforts and instead sought to cure the Senate of its "lingering Brickeritis"[54] and win ratification. The year 1964 saw the formation of the Ad Hoc Committee on Human Rights and Genocide Treaties. The coalition included over fifty labor, civic, and religious groups, many of which had stepped forward in favor of ratification fourteen years earlier. Organizations such as the American Civil Liberties Union, the American Veterans Committee, B'nai B'rith, the YWCA, and several AFL-CIO groups joined the committee to promote the strengthening of international law and human rights through the ratification of UN treaties and conventions, including the UNGC. The committee counted among its members prominent lawyers such as Bruno Bitker, Rita Hauser, and Columbia law professor Richard Gardner. In part because of the new committee's lobbying efforts, the Senate Foreign Relations Committee in 1967 finally again scheduled subcommittee hearings on convention ratification.

Professor Gardner represented the Ad Hoc Committee, forcefully stating that ratification of the Genocide Convention was clearly in the interest of the United States. First, ratification would help convince other countries to accept and observe human rights treaties. Second, ratification would provide the United

States with "a better legal and moral position to protest infringement of those human rights."[55] Finally, Gardner suggested that U.S. acceptance of the convention would help bolster American influence in the drafting of future treaties and documents dealing with human rights. In this way, Gardner argued, the United States could better develop international norms and rules conducive to its interests.

The Ad Hoc Committee would lobby for three years before the executive branch publicly backed ratification again in 1970. On February 17 of that year, some twenty-one years after Truman's first call for Senate action, President Richard Nixon urged the Senate to grant its approval. The president noted that America's critics had used its continued nonratification of the convention to question the sincerity of U.S. opposition to genocide. President Nixon stated, "By giving its advice and consent to ratification of this Convention, the Senate of the United States will demonstrate unequivocally our country's desire to participate in the building of international order based on law and justice."[56]

The 1970 hearings allowed one of the convention's most dedicated proponents to be heard. Starting in January 1967, Senator William Proxmire (D-Wis.) spoke during every day of every Senate session to prompt action on the UNGC and other dormant human rights treaties. Proxmire would continue this principled practice for some twenty years. In recognition of his committed support of the convention, the Senate subcommittee called on the senator from Wisconsin to speak first during the new hearings.

Proxmire expressed both his pleasure at the fact that the Foreign Relations Committee had reopened the issue and his optimism at the prospects for ratification. Proxmire then launched into a head-on refutation of the ABA's opposition. He first stressed that the ABA itself was sharply divided on the issue, with its House of Delegates failing to support ratification by only four votes.[57] Proxmire explained that the close vote showed "no decisive or overwhelming constitutional objection to ratification."[58] Furthermore, he added that the ABA's own Standing Committee on World Order Under Law and its International and Comparative Law section—those groups most closely concerned with the convention—both strongly supported ratification.

Overall, the senator from Wisconsin stressed that the Senate of the United States and not the ABA "has the constitutional responsibility to give its advice and consent to treaties submitted to it by the President."[59] Therefore, Proxmire continued, although the ABA's position on the convention "may be interesting," the Senate "cannot allow the Bar Association to usurp our constitutional functions or to substitute its judgment for our judgment in the conduct of our foreign affairs."[60]

With support for ratification coming from the president, the secretary of state, and the attorney general, Senator Proxmire could little understand any further delay. He then appealed to American interest. He reiterated President Nixon's concern that "some of our detractors have sought to exploit our failure to ratify this convention to question our sincerity."[61] Both Nixon and Proxmire agreed that the United States should take "the final convincing step which would reaffirm that the United States remains as strongly opposed to the crime of genocide as ever."[62]

Throughout 1970 and 1971, Richard Gardner and Ad Hoc Committee President Arthur Goldberg joined Proxmire in fronting the renewed push for ratification. In a new round of testimony, Gardner worked methodically to undermine several of the ABA's main and long-standing objections.[63] Gardner disputed the claim that the convention dealt with an essentially "domestic" matter, thus leaving it beyond the scope of treaty-making power. He noted that in the 1890 case *Geofroy v. Riggs,* the Supreme Court clarified that treaty-making power may be exercised on any matter "which is properly the subject of negotiation with a foreign country." The court added that what is considered such a "proper subject" is a matter the Senate is obligated to decide. As far as the Ad Hoc Committee was concerned, "genocide is a matter of international concern on any objective basis."[64] This position echoed Dean Rusk's 1950 argument.

Gardner openly questioned whether the issue of states' rights and encroaching federal power ever had validity in the debate. He declared the issue obsolete by turning to a report by the ABA's own Section of Individual Rights and Responsibilities that explained that, "the barring of school segregation which was accomplished without any statute, the passage of the Civil Rights Acts of 1957 and 1964 and the Voting Rights Act of 1965, all sustained by the Supreme Court, show that ratification of the Convention will add no powers to those the Federal Government already possesses."[65]

As for the debate over the wording of "destruction of groups in whole or in part," Gardner challenged the interpretation offered by ABA representative Alfred Schweppe. As indicated earlier, Schweppe had argued that convention language allowed for homicide to become conflated with genocide. First, Gardner noted that "this convention is no more ambiguous than other international instruments to which we have already adhered." He then suggested that anyone struggling to interpret the phrasing simply examine the history of the convention and its drafting for clarification. Citing Dr. Nehemiah Robinson, an authority on the convention's origin and drafting, Gardner clarified that "the addition of the words 'in part' indicates genocide has been committed when acts of homicide are joined with a connecting purpose. That is, directed against persons with specific characteristics, with intent to destroy the group or a segment thereof."[66]

Turning to the fear that ratifying the convention would subject American servicemen to trial in hostile countries on charges of genocide, Gardner supplied the obvious and simplest answer. Regardless of the UNGC, the North Vietnamese or any other enemy could seek to try American soldiers under the 1949 Geneva Convention, to which the United States was party and which obligates nations to punish perpetrators of war crimes. Speaking about America's enemies, Gardner summed up: "The Genocide Convention adds nothing to their power."[67]

The efforts of Ad Hoc Committee did produce results. The ABA's Section on Individual Rights and Responsibilities had met in early 1970 and produced a report favoring ratification. The issue then moved to the organization's House of Delegates, where prominent ABA members urged support. The solicitor-general of the United States, Erwin N. Griswold, called for the ABA's support in order to "restore this nation to the great role of leadership in international law." Another powerful voice, that of former Attorney General Nicholas B. de Katzenbach, backed the convention and told ABA members, "The world is watching you."[68] However, by a margin of 130–126, the House of Delegates retreated to old concerns and convictions and voted once more against supporting ratification of the UNGC. The strenuous efforts of convention supporters made inroads but ultimately failed in their final purpose.

Furthermore, a new, outspoken critic of the convention had emerged: the Liberty Lobby. As ABA opposition wavered somewhat, the Liberty Lobby jumped into the breach. A right-wing, virulently anticommunist NGO, this organization voiced its concerns over the treaty, particularly in terms of anti-Sovietism and at times anti-Semitism. Other fairly extremist groups, such as the Voters Interest League and the Coalition of Patriotic Societies, shared this perspective and voiced their opposition as well.[69]

The Liberty Lobby not only reiterated long-standing concerns about the constitution and civil rights but also boldly accused the U.S. government of selling out to the Soviets over the issue of including political groups in the convention. In a testimonial statement in 1970, the general counsel of the Liberty Lobby, Warren S. Richardson, asked rhetorically why the concept of "political genocide" had been omitted from the definition. He supplied an answer by reading a passage from an article in the *Nevada Register* by that state's Bishop Dwyer, a vocal opponent of the convention. Dwyer wrote,

> But the convention most amazingly, neglects to list political genocide in its catalog of contents. . . . It raises a very serious question. Did the framers of the Convention genuinely intend to eliminate genocide, or was their intention, rather to provide a whitewash for what they knew was an inevitable consequence of the dialectic materialism of Marxism? This may be unjust. . . . But if they left the barn door wide open, one cannot help wondering why. It is hardly conceivable that they could have been unaware of the omissions.[70]

The Liberty Lobby considered this supposed shortcoming evidence enough to show that the Soviets had duped the United States and therefore demanded that the Senate "allow the convention to remain in committee forever."[71]

The Liberty Lobby's critique had significant shortcomings and demonstrated its slippery grasp of the historical record. As discussed earlier, the United States took full advantage of its role on the UN Ad Hoc Committee tasked with drafting the convention. American representatives maintained intimate U.S. involvement in the definition of this new international crime. When Soviet delegates proposed altering the phrasing dealing with intent (substituting "aimed at the physical destruction of groups" for "intent to destroy groups"), the United States strongly opposed it.

American representative Ernest A. Gross argued that such an alteration would introduce a "fundamental modification" in the definition since intent was a key component. The U.S. position was overwhelmingly supported.[72] Determined opponents such as the Liberty Lobby carefully ignored the fact that the Soviet Union and its allies actually abstained from the vote on deletion of political groups. The Liberty Lobby also failed to consider a strategy that would have much better served its anti-Soviet agenda: ratify the convention and then put public pressure on the Soviet Union to support revisions closing the so-called political genocide loophole.

The ABA's renewed rejection of the treaty proved an inauspicious omen for action in the Senate. Despite a 10–4 committee vote in favor of ratification, entrenched opposition in the Senate blocked further progress. Senator Sam Ervin of North Carolina led this opposition, threatening filibuster and relying heavily on unreasonable fears that American soldiers in Vietnam might be captured and tried on charges of genocide. Ervin testified that "American soldiers killing or seriously wounding North Vietnamese soldiers or members of the Viet Cong . . . who fall into the hands of the North Vietnamese, are triable and punishable in the courts of North Vietnam. No sophistry can erase this obvious interpretation of the Genocide Convention."[73]

Little about Senator Ervin's reading of the UNGC could be termed "obvious." Whether by willful intent or unfortunate misunderstanding, Ervin continued to misrepresent and misinterpret the convention from top to bottom. Once again raising the issue of "in whole or in part," Ervin incorrectly stated that "a public official or a private individual is to be subject to prosecution and punishment for genocide if he intentionally destroys a single member of one of the specified groups."[74] Ervin's bleak portrait of American life under the UNGC also predicted that "we can reasonably expect that demands will be made that every homicide, every assault and battery inflicting serious injury, and every kidnapping shall be tried in a Federal court, or in an International Court to be established pursuant to the convention."[75] In the course of his testimony, Ervin raised the other expected fears about states' rights, a sovereignty-stealing world court, and the sanctity of the U.S. Constitution.

Ervin's strong and misguided opposition did not go unchallenged by his Senate colleagues. New York Senator Jacob Javits called Ervin's testimony "the most extreme interpretation of every aspect of this convention."[76] Javits elaborated:

> With all respect, these statements are so extreme, as a sample, that I think we ought to have an opportunity—if this is the heinous thing we are going to do to our country—to analyze this statement, to check up on the law as carefully as Senator Ervin has done, and then, if the Senator would then be good enough, after we have both had an even chance, to respond to questions on this subject. I think the charge is so strong and so extreme it puts the questioners at great disadvantage. You make a big charge and in 2 minutes we are supposed to think up the whole body of law which represents the negation of that charge.

Javits subsequently submitted to the committee a point-by-point rebuttal of each of Senator Ervin's arguments against the UNGC. Still, the work of Javits and others failed to win ratification in 1970.

In 1976, the Sisyphus-like efforts of the Ad Hoc Committee received their biggest boost up to that point.[77] For years the preeminent foe of ratification, the ABA at last changed course and overturned its previously firm opposition. The ABA had for years been internally divided over the issue. However, the emergence of new leaders, such as David R. Brinks and William B. Spann, provided the organization with a fresh internationalist perspective, freed from the narrower interpretation of the UNGC supplied by the "old thinkers."[78]

In a February 1976 resolution, the ABA House of Delegates recommended ratification for the convention. The ABA resolution indicated that "statements made in the past and raised in the Senate and the ABA House of Delegates are no longer pertinent. The passage of time has confirmed that genocide is a matter of 'international concern.' . . . Acceding to the convention at this time is a positive step in the national interest of our country. The American Bar Association should come forward and place on record its positive support."[79] The ABA made its support subject to three understandings meant to clarify the controversial "in part" phrasing dealing with groups, the issue of "mental harm," and the right of the United States to try its own nationals.[80] Still, the conversion of the ABA did not entail swift Senate ratification.

In a letter to the Senate in 1977, President Jimmy Carter recommended approval, urging the body to give its advice and consent to the ratification of the convention. Explained the president, "Ratification would be a significant enhancement of the human rights commitments of this nation, demonstrating again to the world in concrete fashion our determination to advance and protect human rights."[81] Similarly, speaking on the Thirtieth Anniversary of the Universal Declaration of Human Rights, Carter said, "Eighty-three other nations have ratified the Genocide Convention. The United States—despite the support of every President since 1948—has not. In international meetings at the United Nations and elsewhere, we are often asked why. We do not have an acceptable answer. I urge the United States Senate to observe this anniversary in the only appropriate way: by ratifying the Genocide Convention at the earliest possible date."[82]

However, the subsequent brief hearings would replay previous efforts. Deputy Secretary of State Warren Christopher appeared before the Senate Committee on Foreign Relations to make the case for ratification. Calling the U.S. failure to ratify an "anomaly," Christopher argued that "adherence to the Convention is a statement to the world community that the United States stands ready to develop the international law of human rights, and to make such human rights a matter of international concern. Such a statement is in our national interest."[83] The deputy secretary touched on the importance of the ABA's support and hoped that the judgment of the nation's leading association of attorneys would influence Senate thinking. In conclusion, Christopher made a simple and straightforward statement that "there is no moral, political, or legal argument against U.S. adherence to the Genocide Convention that has merit or validity. There are strong moral, political, and legal reasons why we should become a party."[84]

Senator Jacob Javits interjected strong support for ratification and damning words for the Senate. The senator from New York called the failure to ratify "one of the most shocking failures of our country, of our system." He carefully distinguished between the majority of the Senate, which supported the convention and "a band of willful men here who stand in its way, whatever may be the dictates of humanity, or of reason, or of law, or of international community, or of friendship. It is just beyond belief."[85]

While opponents such as Helms and Ervin maintained their contrary views, the most interesting challenge to the administration's position came from the Liberty Lobby. The group predictably attacked the UNGC for its supposed assault on American citizens and their constitutional rights. This time, however, their revised critique argued that the convention was also fundamentally anti-Christian. E. Stanley Rittenhouse, a legislative aide of the Liberty Lobby, announced that under the treaty, "every missionary, both domestic and foreign, who attempted to convert anyone to Christianity would be guilty of attempting to destroy one's culture." The Lobby derived this interpretation from Article II, which provides protection to religious groups, as well as national, ethnical, and racial communities. According to Rittenhouse, "It would be genocide when a Christian missionary tries to civilize the savage and convert him to Christ. It is genocide when the whites object to black demonstrations in South Africa, but not genocide when Uganda's Idi Amin systematically kills off and eats the liver of his rivals."[86]

Rittenhouse also shared the Lobby's interesting perspectives on the Jewish faith and the convention. He added, "Another case in point is the Jewish community. Since many of those within the Jewish and Zionist community hate Christianity and Christians, and since many of these folks consider as 'traitors' Hebrews who recognize Christ to be the Messiah, any Christian who attempts to convert a Jew would be guilty of genocide under this treaty."[87]

Senator Proxmire added a healthy dose of reality to the proceedings with his continued practice of championing the convention. Proxmire said that a new president committed to human rights, ABA endorsement, and support from the Defense Department made the case for prompt Senate action stronger than before. He urged support for the UNGC, which he described as "a moral document." Proxmire termed it "a call for a higher standard of human conduct. It is not a panacea for injustice." To end his statement, Senator Proxmire referred to the words of the late chief justice of the Supreme Court Earl Warren, who said, "We as a nation, should have been the first to ratify the Genocide Convention." Proxmire added to Warren's statement a plea: "Let us not be the last."[88]

Internal Carter administration discussions revealed an interest in winning ratification for the convention and four human rights treaties transmitted by the president to the Senate.[89] National Security Adviser Zbigniew Brzezinski anticipated that the administration might have the best chance to win ratification since Truman, in part due "to the American Jewish community which continues to support the Genocide Convention as the symbol of international condemnation of the Holocaust." Brzezinski also noted that "a new conservative appeal has emerged because of recent experience with Cambodia," where Khmer Rouge atrocities were claiming the lives of millions.[90]

However, those same internal discussions quickly placed other foreign policy priorities ahead of the convention. In particular, administration officials agreed that the Panama Canal and the second round of Strategic Arms Limitation Talks (SALT II) took precedence. In a memorandum to President Carter on legislative priorities, Vice President Walter Mondale indicated the importance of timing, cautioning, "On the one hand, ratification is important to our credibility internationally on human rights. On the other hand, requesting Congressional action on the Genocide Convention could have serious potential adverse impacts on SALT."[91]

Brzezinski concurred with this approach, telling the president, "We must now decide when to push for ratification. In my view the critical issue is timing. SALT ratification is the number one priority, and no initiative should be undertaken which might affect that process."[92] Arms control came first and continued to do so throughout the administration. Having already expended precious political capital on the Panama Canal treaty, the Carter team knew it could little afford secondary skirmishes with conservative lawmakers. To push the Genocide Convention through would require much more than presidential statements and a single round of hearings. The geostrategic imperatives behind a potentially milestone arms control agreement relegated the UNGC to the second tier at best.[93] Any extra energy and effort and goodwill on Capitol Hill was reserved to win Senate support for SALT II, not for a human rights and international law treaty.

RONALD REAGAN: "LIKE NIXON TO CHINA . . ."

Convention supporters looked on the arrival in Washington of the Reagan administration with little optimism. The Reagan foreign policy team did not view human rights as a priority, and few observers expected a conservative president to champion a UN human rights treaty. The new administration initially fulfilled those bleak expectations. A new round of hearings was held in 1981, but not one official from the Reagan administration appeared.

The hearings certainly had their share of the conservative, anticonvention viewpoint despite the absence of administration representatives. The self-declared "party-pooper," North Carolina's Jesse Helms told the Senate committee that they were in truth "resurrecting an issue, a treaty, a consideration that long has been discredited, and that never has accumulated enough support in the U.S. Senate for ratification since it was signed in 1948." Helms called the hearings "a waste of time" since the convention "won't be ratified this time, either." Helms emphasized his opposition to an "entirely new theory of international law" that would wrongly infringe on American sovereignty and "diminish our own Nation and the loyalty which we as citizens owe to that nation."[94]

Strom Thurmond (R-S.C.) contributed to the conservative battle cry. Thurmond repeated much from the opposition of the 1950s and chose to ignore completely the new position of the ABA. The senior senator from South Carolina opened his testimony explaining, "The Genocide Treaty, where it should restrain atrocity, is not observed; and where it would be observed, it is unnecessary. In the barbaric nations of the world, the treaty is given lip service. In our civilized free republic, the treaty would be followed to the letter and thus could harm irreparably the fabric of our constitutional system."[95]

Thurmond then worked his way through the usual host of objections. For added effect, he included some hypothetical situations, including the grizzled specter of American soldiers in Vietnam or a similar battlefield charged with genocide (Vietnam was of course over, but the analogy lived on). As a rather unique contribution, Thurmond held out the prospect of editorial writers, citizens groups, and individual American citizens who called for the bombing of Iran during the hostage crisis being called before the International Court of Justice to face charges of "direct and public incitement to commit genocide."[96]

The Liberty Lobby again joined conservative lawmakers in opposition to the UNGC. At the 1981 hearings, the Lobby bitterly attacked their former ally, the ABA. A prepared statement lambasted the ABA:

> After 26 years of failing to ramrod the GC through the Senate, the American Bar Association labored and came up with its specious "Understandings and Declaration." . . . Clearly these "understandings (not even reservations) are not meant at all to confront and answer the grave deficiencies of the GC but to plaster over it a facade of misleading and thoroughly dishonest gloss in order to deceive Americans making a superficial inspection of the GC as it now exists and to allay apprehension. The ABA's deceitful "understandings" are an insult to the intelligence of even a superficial observer and a gross betrayal of American interest.[97]

Nonetheless, the ABA's defection had pushed the Liberty Lobby toward increased isolation on UNGC ratification.

Liberty Lobby representatives Robert Bartell and Trisha Katson felt some of this isolation during the 1981 hearings. Senate Foreign Relations Committee Chairman Charles Percy (D-Ill.) questioned them pointedly about the group's publications attacking the Genocide Convention. While Bartell described the arguments and words used by his organization as "colorful," Percy criticized the Lobby for employing "untruthful language that has no foundation" to whip up opposition to the convention.[98]

Senator Dodd (D-Conn.) joined Percy in undermining the propaganda spouted by the Liberty Lobby in their "White Paper on the Genocide Convention." Dodd quoted from a paragraph titled "Political Mass Murder Accepted," which said,

> Surprisingly, the definition of the term genocide in the Genocide Convention is substantially different than both the popular understanding and dictionary definitions. In addition to certain sorts of killing, the Genocide Convention sets forth such things as mental harm, moving children from one place to another, and even birth control. All these and less are genocide.[99]

Dodd leveled sharp criticism at the Liberty Lobby for their blatant misrepresentation of the actual convention language. For example, the "moving children" text actually reads "forcibly transferring children of the group to another group." Said Dodd, "The way you read the white paper, it sounds as though if you take your children to Disneyland, you could in effect be charged with genocide."[100]

Rising yet again to represent treaty proponents, Senator Proxmire urged ratification of the UNGC. He underlined the fact that convention ratification convention would "strengthen our hand in attacking the gross violations of human rights by the Soviet Union and its allies." Proxmire said the United States "must be free to condemn China for genocide in Tibet, Vietnamese Communists for genocide against religious groups in Cambodia, and any future Russian campaign of genocide against one of their minority populations."[101] Proxmire also attacked the convention's opponents for their consistent inconsistency, pointing out,

> On the one hand they assert that the Genocide Convention is a strong document, threatening our very civil liberties, a position which simply is not substantiated by this committee's own hearing record. On the other hand, they argue that the treaty is a "paper tiger." Where is the real enforcement authority, they ask? Yet, this question comes most often from those who would oppose any international enforcement mechanism the most.[102]

To reaffirm the ABA's commitment to the ratification of the UNGC, University of Virginia law professor John Norton Moore appeared on behalf of the association and directed the committee to reconsider testimony submitted in 1970 by then Assistant Attorney General William Rehnquist:

> In 1950 some of the questions concerning Federal jurisdiction and the treaty power were considered somewhat novel. However, developments in the intervening years—the extensive use of treaty power and the growth of Federal criminal jurisdiction—have, it seems, illuminated both these areas to the point where I believe I can safely say that the questions before the Committee and the Senate are more matters of policy than questions of legal power. Other witnesses in support of this treaty have, I believe, made this clear.[103]

Moore also appealed to the anti-Sovietism and national interest concerns of many fellow conservatives who opposed the convention. Moore borrowed from a statement by Thomas Buergenthal, dean of the American University's Law School and chairman of the ABA's International Law Section Committee on International Human Rights. Buergenthal had commented,

> [The threat of the Soviet Union] is not only military or subversive, it is also ideological and it must therefore be confronted on the ideological level as well. . . . A sound human rights policy provides the U.S. with an ideology that distinguishes us most clearly from the Soviet Union and seriously undercuts the ideological appeal of Communism. However, our ideological hand is not strong in dealing with the Soviets when our criticism of their treatment of religious or ethnic groups prompts the questions of why the United States has not ratified the Genocide Convention.[104]

Despite these statements, the favorable testimony turned in once again by dedicated senators like Proxmire and Javits (then retired), and the call for ratification by the ABA and the Ad Hoc Committee, Helms's initial comment proved correct—the convention was not ratified in 1981.

Much to the chagrin of conservatives such as Helms and Thurmond and the Liberty Lobby, the tide was slowly turning. Added to the strenuous efforts of the Ad Hoc Committee came a much-needed insider angle and an infusion of right-leaning enthusiasm and commitment to ratification. A group of ABA members, including active Reagan supporter John Norton Moore, lobbyist Craig Baab, and attorney Charles Smith, grasped the opportunity to use the prominent voice of the ABA to take the push for ratification one step further, using the invaluable "principled groundwork" laid by the Ad Hoc Committee.[105]

Concerned about the ABA's history of obstructionism on the convention issue, Baab worked to mobilize the association and established a working, coordinated coalition with the Ad Hoc Committee and other concerned groups. Moore pushed the cause of the UNGC via connections with the National Security Council.[106] At the same time, Moore and Charles Smith rallied the nonprofit organization The Conflict Analysis Center to the mission. One of the center's significant contributions was the publication in 1984 of a pamphlet calling for ratification and containing information for use by advocates and legislators.

After opening with a message from President Reagan, the pamphlet proceeded to respond in concise form to the major objections to the UNGC, including the recurrent challenges posed by the Liberty Lobby and individuals such as Phyllis Schlafly of the ultraconservative Eagle Forum. The pamphlet design even suited its purpose: Its narrow width meant that it fit perfectly inside a business envelope or the inside pocket of a man's suit coat. The Conflict Analysis Center proceeded to send a copy of the pamphlet with a cover letter calling for ratification to every House and Senate member.[107]

The new convention activists also recognized the need to tap into domestic politics. The Reagan administration's interest in using the UNGC and other human rights treaties as instruments in the rhetorical battle against the Soviets was helpful, but the convention faithful understood that it might not be enough to push the Reagan team to win Senate support. Ultimately, getting the administration on board meant also tapping into domestic politics. As election time 1984 approached and Republicans sought to woo the Jewish vote, the moment seemed ripe. Although certainly not an exclusively Jewish interest, the Genocide Convention clearly had a natural appeal to a significant number of Jewish voters. Thus, promoting the UNGC offered a new means of courting Jewish political support and making electoral inroads with other ethnic communities.[108] John Norton Moore and other fairly influential Reagan Republicans stressed this rationale. Moore argued to foreign policy officials that ratification was the right thing to do, that it served American foreign policy interests, and that it was politically wise for domestic political consumption and advantage as well.

This political context, together with renewed lobbying efforts on behalf of the convention from a wide range of groups, raised the prospects for a favorable outcome to a new round of hearings. The Reagan administration did not embrace the convention solely on its own merits but did see the potential power of human rights issues as a means of bludgeoning their Cold War adversary. To wield human rights as an effective rhetorical weapon, the administration wanted to end the ceaseless Soviet criticism of the United States for nonratification of the convention.

In December 1979, Moscow Radio taunted the United States, asking, "Why . . . has the United States not ratified the 1948 Convention of the Prevention and Punishment of the Crime of Genocide? Eighty-two countries have ratified it but the United States did not. Moreover, it is not by accident . . . but rather after very long debates in the Senate. It can hardly be said that the whole world is out of step, while the United States is in step."[109] Similarly, in 1981 the Soviet news service *Tass* produced a blistering article, explaining U.S. refusal to ratify as indicative of "Washington's unwillingness to assume firm judicial commitments in the sphere of human rights."[110]

To blunt the Soviets' rhetorical attacks and regain the moral high ground, secretary of state designate Alexander M. Haig Jr. announced his support for ratification during his Senate confirmation hearings. In his testimony, Haig argued that the convention would "unquestionably be helpful in various international fora where the United States has been criticized for its failure to ratify the Genocide Convention. This is ironic because the United States was a leader in the post–World War II effort to conclude the convention as an expression of revulsion to the Holocaust and as a deterrent to the recurrence of such crimes against humanity."[111] United States ambassador to the United Nations Jeane Kirkpatrick renewed this message in the fall of 1984 when she declared, "The Soviets and others hostile to the United States have long focused on the United States' failure to ratify the Convention as part of their anti-American propaganda. It is contrary to our national interest to provide fuel to this campaign."[112]

It would still take years, but ratification gained long-awaited momentum through the combined efforts of Craig Baab and his ABA initiative, the continued lobbying of human rights groups such as the Ad Hoc Committee, and the insider work of John Norton Moore. The president used the 1984 international B'nai B'rith convention (a main player in the Ad Hoc Committee) as a backdrop for his public call for ratification. Reagan told those assembled,

> With a cautious view, in part due to the human rights abuses performed by some nations that have already ratified the documents, our administration has conducted a

> long and exhaustive study of the convention. And yesterday, as a result of that review, we announced that we will vigorously support, consistent with the United States Constitution, the ratification of the Genocide Convention. And I want you to know that we intend to use the convention in our efforts to expand human freedom and fight human rights abuses around the world. Like you, I say in a forthright voice, "Never again!"

Reagan's endorsement received front-page newspaper coverage and secured a new round of hearings.[113] His support would prove pivotal. Lawrence LeBlanc rightly concludes, "President Reagan's endorsement virtually assured ratification of the convention since it could no longer be maintained that ratification was a dream of liberal fantasizers."[114]

As hearings got under way, the domestic politics angle troubled some Democratic lawmakers who criticized the timing of the administration's 1984, preelection endorsement, which had followed a three-year "review" of the UNGC. Connecticut Senator Christopher Dodd had difficulty understanding the need for so lengthy a review process since "not a single new question has been raised about the Convention in about 10 years." Dodd noted, "This committee has met over a dozen times since 1950 to review and debate the subject. Every question, every argument, and counterargument has been raised and answered repeatedly."[115]

Therefore, Dodd wondered aloud about the election-ratification connection. He asked Assistant Secretary of State for Human Rights and Humanitarian Affairs Elliott Abrams to explain why "it took this administration up to 8, 9 weeks before an Election Day all of a sudden to decide they support it." Senator Joe Biden raised similar concerns about political motivations and pointed out that "this is the first President who 8 weeks before the end of a campaign announced his support for it [the UNGC] having been silent up to that point."[116] Abrams perceptively replied that the decades-old problem with ratification had not been the Reagan administration's but "has in fact been the Senate."[117]

Still, Democrats continued to support the convention, despite the curious context for presidential endorsement. Meanwhile, several influential Republicans continued to oppose it, resisting the efforts of their "Great Communicator" president. Even though retired, former Senator Sam Ervin resubmitted the text of a speech he had delivered on the subject in 1970, a speech that he said "explain[ed] what a fool proposition the Genocide Treaty is."

Despite Reagan's support, there remained work to do. Senate hearings in 1984 produced only a sense of the Senate resolution that indicated support for the principles of the convention and declared an intention to tackle ratification again in 1985.[118] This represented important progress, but it still fell short of the goal. Even the resolution could not be without controversy. A product of continued conservative opposition to the convention, the resolution (known as the Lugar-Helms-Hatch Sovereignty Package for its Senate sponsors) outlined the conditions of U.S. ratification. The package included two reservations and five understandings clarifying the primacy of the U.S. Constitution over the convention, addressing issues involving the International Court of Justice, and specifying U.S. interpretation of the definition of the crime of genocide (in particular that the "mental harm" clause refers to permanent impairment of mental faculties).[119]

At the 1985 hearings, opponents continued to challenge the convention, trotting out the same objections and accusations as before. Phyllis Schlafly, president of the conservative Eagle Forum, told the senators, "Anyone who takes time to read the Genocide Convention can easily see that it is a double-edged piece of propaganda and a constitutional embarrassment. . . . Anyone reading it article by article can see from its text that it is at best an embarrassment and at worst a trap to ensnare American citizens and our allies."[120] A representative for the Conservative Caucus warned the Foreign Relations Committee about the power and sweep of the convention. He asked, "Will the day come when conservative Senators are hauled before the World Court for failing to support increased welfare benefits for minority group workers? Or will liberal Senators who support abortion be tried and prosecuted for their votes in facilitating the murder of millions of unborn children, substantial portions of whom are non-Caucasian?"[121]

The venerable Liberty Lobby, described by its legislative director Trisha Katson as "the most patriotic lovers of America and our constitution I have ever met," made its continued opposition known. With a view toward foreign plotting and scheming, Katson repeated the argument that the UNGC would "undermine our Anglo-American system of law with an international system of law which has a completely different philosophy than the ideals that guided our Founding Fathers and our constitutional republic."[122] Katson elaborated on this position and then closed her statement with a final warning about the international cabal behind the convention:

> The Genocide Convention has noble, humanitarian-sounding purposes, but it conceals the aims of those supporting it to use the issue of genocide to convince Americans to submit themselves to the jurisdiction of a World Court. . . . We believe that the internationalist forces working together fully intend to set up this machinery to institute real international law to enable the World Court to enforce its rulings, and it might be invoked against the very senators who pass it, because there are millions of Americans who could list a myriad of offenses committed by many legislators that have caused them great mental harm. You are excluded from that, Senator Helms.[123]

Despite the feverish cries of such opponents, momentum at last fell on the side of the UNGC. From the right, John Norton Moore testified again on behalf of ratification, placing the treaty in a Cold War, antitotalitarian context. Moore told the senators that "ratification is important because it will remove a propaganda theme used by totalitarian regimes against the United States." Furthermore, Moore said that U.S. support for the convention "will enable the United States to more clearly focus international attention on contemporary totalitarian genocides such as, in my judgment, that of the Khmer Rouge attack on the Cham in Cambodia, or, I believe, the Sandinista attack on the Mesquito Indians in Nicaragua."[124] Ratification by the United States would therefore translate immediately into a valuable ideological weapon for the West. Argued Moore, "It is not the democracies that by any stretch of the imagination need fear genocide. If we have false claims brought against us, let's respond on the merits as to why they are false. The totalitarian governments do fear charges of genocide, and I think without a reservation, this would be a more important instrument in the hands of the democracies."[125]

To buttress this plea from a Reagan insider came a powerful moral call to action from Holocaust survivor and chronicler Elie Wiesel. Wiesel introduced himself by contrasting his background with that of Moore and other supporters. Wiesel told the committee, "I speak to you not as a professor of law—I am not a professor of law—nor as a professor of political science—I am not a professor of political science. I am a professor in the humanities, and I would like to speak to you, Mr. Chairman and my friends, in the name of humanity. And it is in the name of humanity that I humbly urge you to approve this treaty."[126] Wiesel echoed the concerns expressed by Moore and others such as Jeane Kirkpatrick that nations around the world wondered why the United States had failed to ratify the convention despite its ideals and democratic mission. When his students asked him "why," Wiesel said, "I, their teacher, find it difficult to come up with a logical answer."[127]

To remedy that situation, Wiesel turned to the legislators before him for help:

> I urge you to give me that answer, the right answer, and reaffirm our common belief that we have been and remain a nation governed by moral principles. When those principles are jeopardized, we had the courage to defend them. Now I am asking you, isn't genocide the greatest peril to civilization's ideals and visions of peace and compassion?[128]

Senate Majority Leader Bob Dole then publicly backed the convention at the groundbreaking ceremony for the United States Holocaust Museum in October 1985 and indicated his intention to bring it to the Senate floor.[129] Dole stressed the need for Senate approval of the treaty: "As a nation which enshrines human dignity and freedom . . . we must correct our anomalous position on this basic rights issue."[130] With the support of a respected conservative president and continued work by the Ad Hoc Committee, the ABA, and other groups, the time had come for the Senate to end the debate. The convention finally made it out for a full Senate vote in early 1986. This time, it appeared that proponents did at last hold the upper hand.

The champion of the UNGC, Senator Proxmire, told his colleagues to note that "it is hard to find a major, respected organization that does not support it [the convention]."[131] From there, the senator from Wisconsin turned his ire to the remaining opponents and warned fellow senators of potential electoral consequences of support from such groups:

> And who opposed the Genocide Treaty? The John Birch Society, Phyllis Schlafly's Eagle Forum, the Liberty Lobby, and a few other far-out, extreme fringe groups. The groups that oppose the Genocide Treaty constitute a politician's dream of what each of us dearly wish we could identify with our opponent. Is there anything more embarrassing in elective politics than to be publicly and vocally supported by the John Birch Society? Does anyone really want the general public to known that a serious candidate for the U.S. Senate has the enthusiastic support of the Liberty Lobby?

Kansas Republican Nancy Kassebaum reminded the Senate that the convention could not prevent genocide, but she had nonetheless "come to agree with the view expressed by many, particularly the committee chairman, Senator Lugar, that Senate ratification of the treaty is important as a symbol." Dennis DeConcini (D-Ariz.) emphasized the importance for his vote of President Reagan's support of the convention. He explained then that "as a strong champion of human rights around the world and a firm believer in the prerogative of the Office of the President to direct this Nation's policy role in international affairs, I have been convinced by President Reagan of the need for this convention. It will strengthen his hand in dealing with the Soviet Union."[132]

Convention opponent Jesse Helms picked up on the symbol theme as well. Helms turned attention to the reservations to the treaty that he considered essential because they "defanged" the treaty of its dangerous defects, but Senator Helms would still not support the UNGC. Instead, he announced that "this Genocide Convention upon which we are about to vote is purely symbolic. . . . My vote against the treaty is likewise symbolic. Even in its present form, harmless as it now is, this treaty has the remote potential of an entangling alliance. So I shall vote against it for that reason—and also as a postscript of gratitude to a great American, Sam Ervin, who long ago took the time to make me aware of the great constitutional implications of this treaty in its original form."[133] Symbol or not, the UNGC surmounted Helms's opposition and won Senate approval by a vote of 83–11.

Given the history of the Senate and the UNGC, the story could not actually end there. Since the convention is not a self-executing treaty, the Senate then had to draft specific legislation making the United States party to the agreement.

To do this, the Senate Committee on the Judiciary drafted the Genocide Convention Implementation Act of 1988, also known as the Proxmire Act in honor of the convention's staunch Senate ally. This stage provided remaining opponents one last chance to derail ratification in some way. For example, ranking committee Republican Strom Thurmond believed the treaty would not work and did not merit ratification. Yet, in the implementation stage, Thurmond took a keen interest in the punishment assessed for conviction of genocide. He urged the death penalty. In fact, "by insisting that provision for the death penalty be made in the Proxmire Act, Thurmond was raising an issue that was guaranteed to provoke controversy and perhaps delay adoption of the implementing legislation. Those who opposed the death penalty in principle would surely oppose its being established as a penalty even for genocide."[134]

Such last-ditch obstructionism by Thurmond and others failed in the end. Finally, on October 14, 1988, the Senate approved the implementing act, and less than a month later President Reagan signed it. Even the president's signing of the convention did not pass without political undertones and mild tension. With just two days left before the presidential election, Reagan was in Chicago campaigning for Vice President George Bush. Human rights scholar William Korey, then working for B'nai B'rith, relates that a signing ceremony was quickly assembled in a hangar at O'Hare airport. For Korey, it requires no stretch to imagine political calculations contributing to the decision to have President Reagan sign the UNGC in an area with a significant Jewish population and other large ethnic communities.[135] Regardless of the prominent or minimal role of electoral process at the time, the convention at long last had the formal support of the United States.

CONCLUSION

Senate approval of the UNGC in 1988 ended a surprisingly long and arduous struggle over ratification. From the start, the persistence of nonratification provided a cautionary lesson on the risk of taking for granted U.S. support for any international agreement, no matter how noble or well intentioned the cause. Contrary to reasonable expectations, the Senate denied President Truman the approval for the treaty first sought in 1949. Thus began a sporadic and, at times, heated debate that would span almost forty years and eight administrations.

Throughout the ratification debate, Congress trumped presidential initiative and asserted its central constitutional role in defining and promoting American diplomatic interests. As a result, the Senate also held hostage an ethical leadership moment, in effect crippling for decades the U.S. commitment (even if just symbolic) to deter genocide and official American support for the norms embodied in the convention. Within the congressional arena, NGOs stood prominently in the effort to capitalize on a norm-building leadership moment and to define the interests of the United States as they applied to the prevention and punishment of genocide. Both as advocates and opponents, NGOs demonstrated a unique relevance to a foreign policy issue of at least symbolic importance. Persistent in their efforts, diverse in their opinions, and influential in terms of a final result, NGOs, such as the ABA and the Ad Hoc Committee, demonstrated early on in the debate that they, too, could play substantive roles in congressional policy deliberations and agenda setting.

NGOs helped keep the issue of ratification of the Genocide Convention alive over the course of several decades. In the end, the work of the Ad Hoc Committee, the quiet efforts of men such as Craig Baab at the "new" ABA, and insider support by John Norton Moore and others joined with the work of sympathetic legislators to propel the convention to ratification. All parties were necessary, none sufficient. Their work calls to mind Margaret Mead's suggestion that we "never doubt that a small group of thoughtful committed people can change the world. Indeed it is the only thing that ever has." This episode of NGO activity and American foreign policy hinted at the current proliferation of an ever-growing universe of NGOs lobbying to promote their specific agendas and hoping to sway decisively or at least nudge in a certain direction the course of American foreign policy. In the case of the UNGC, NGOs emerged as the primary moral entrepreneurs, pushing a reluctant Senate to support a new international norm.

From a broader perspective, this curious history reveals an intriguing combination of influences. The systemic shock of both the war and the Holocaust produced an "ethical leadership moment." Thus, prompted at the end of World War II to remake the world, the United States responded to its own sense of moral identity and responsibility by helping to create a new and significant category of international crime and establish a new norm. American representatives at the United Nations in 1949 and convention supporters in the subsequent decades—men such as Proxmire and Javits—adopted an internationalist perspective that called for an activist United States to promote a liberal-democratic world order. In essence, they wanted to make conscious policy decisions to challenge anarchy and sovereignty run amok in the international system.

However, that norm-building, leadership impulse ran into a brick wall of realism. Legislators and NGOs with more traditional perspectives, with limited views of appropriate avenues for American action in the world, criticized and challenged the UNGC. These critics promoted their own normative concern for the sanctity of America's sovereignty and the integrity of its constitutional system. Despite the shocking revelations of the Holocaust, sovereignty remained a jealously guarded possession. For influential conservative opponents of the convention, unilateral "America first" imperatives superseded the need to build international society. They also derided the ability of any international instrument to deal effectively with murderous or genocidal regimes, especially those of a communist nature. Those conservatives, from Senators Connally and Wiley to Ervin and Helms, thwarted ratification and stunted U.S. work as a norm entrepreneur. For decades, in fact, the UNGC and other human rights treaties suffered as "domestic politics ensured that the United States had neither the will nor the capability to create a strong human rights regime."[136]

Eventually, a combination of realism and normative progressivism won the day and secured ratification. Proponents of the convention maintained their faith and support and for decades worked to lay the groundwork for ratification. Interest in the UNGC endured because the ideas it embodied mattered. As described in this chapter, the arrival in Washington of the Reagan administration led to unexpectedly favorable conditions. Reagan's conservative credentials could see the treaty through. Like Nixon going to China, Reagan could support ratification, and opponents could not reasonably paint him as a wishy-washy liberal internationalist embracing some quixotic cosmopolitan goal. As a result, instrumentally enlightened realism saw value in the UNGC as rhetorical leverage in the Cold War. For the political side of the realist mind, ratification also held the promise of domestic political gain in the form of votes from a concerned Jewish constituency. Realism harnessed to an essentially ethical cause brought about the desired result. As Illinois Senator Charles Percy noted at the time, "You know, it takes a conservative Republican to get done all these progressive things we Democrats have espoused but have been unable to carry out."

The United States deserves praise for its heavy involvement in the birth of the convention. The application of hegemonic influence and persuasion in the late 1940s helped shape a treaty acceptable to most UN member states and with a wealth of potential to deter genocide and punish perpetrators. However, for the next four decades, the United States fell well short of its own high standards, rhetoric, and norm-building potential.

Although unfortunate, the caution and reluctance that characterized the U.S. attitude and action toward the UNGC set an appropriate precedent for future encounters between the United States and genocide in the postwar era.

NOTES

1. The full text of the UNGC appears in the appendix.
2. *New York Times,* November 5, 1988, A28.
3. *Hearings on the Genocide Convention before the Senate Committee on Foreign Relations,* 95th Cong., 1st sess., 1977, 4.
4. Raphael Lemkin, *Axis Rule in Occupied Europe* (Washington, D.C.: Carnegie Endowment for International Peace, 1944), ix.

5. Lemkin, 79.

6. Lemkin, 91. See also Lawrence LeBlanc, *The United States and the Genocide Convention* (Durham, N.C.: Duke University Press, 1991), 19.

7. *Current Biography* (New York: H. W. Wilson Company, 1950), 337.

8. William Korey, "America's Shame: The Unratified Genocide Treaty," in Jack Nusan Porter, ed., *Genocide and Human Rights: A Global Anthology* (Washington, D.C.: University Press of America, 1982), 283.

9. 3 UN GAOR C.6 (73rd mtg.), 1948, 97; LeBlanc, 37.

10. LeBlanc, 38.

11. The drafters of the convention simply listed the group to be protected without defining them in any detail to avoid the likely impossible task of agreeing on universally acceptable definitions. LeBlanc (60) notes that precise definition of groups was essentially left to each state and their implementing legislation.

12. 3 UN GAOR C.6 (74th mtg.), 1948, 100.

13. The Sixth Committee of the General Assembly vote to include political groups resulted in half the UN members supporting the U.S. positions: twenty-nine in favor, thirteen against, and nine abstentions.

14. LeBlanc, 66.

15. *Hearings on the Genocide Convention before a Subcommittee of the Senate Committee on Foreign Relations,* 81st Cong., 2nd sess., 1950, 20.

16. *Hearings* . . . , 1950, 20.

17. *Hearings* . . . , 1950, 19.

18. *Hearings* . . . , 1950, 20.

19. *Hearings* . . . , 1950, 21.

20. *Hearings* . . . , 1950, 21.

21. *Executive Sessions of the Senate Foreign Relations Committee* (Historical Series), 81st Cong., 2nd sess., 1950, 52–53.

22. Philip B. Perlman, "The Genocide Convention," *Nebraska Law Review* 30, no. 1 (1950): 4.

23. *Current Biography,* 1950, 336–337; LeBlanc, 20.

24. Quoted in *Executive Sessions of the Senate Foreign Relations Committee* (Historical Series), 94th Cong., 2nd sess., 1976, 645–646.

25. See note 24.

26. See note 24. See also LeBlanc, 20.

27. *Hearings* . . . , 1950, 89.

28. *Hearings* . . . , 1950, 132.

29. *Hearings* . . . , 1950, 132.

30. *Hearings* . . . , 1950, 132.

31. *Hearings* . . . , 1950, 129.

32. *Hearings* . . . , 1950, 129.

33. For details on the issues considered, see Orie L. Phillips, "Genocide Convention: Its Effects on Our Legal System," *American Bar Association Journal* 35 (1949): 623. The ABA's section on International and Comparative Law voted in favor of ratification, although with reservations. In addition, the International Law Committee of the Association of the Bar of the City of New York approved the UNGC (see *Hearings* . . . , 1950, 77).

34. *Hearings* . . . , 1950, 156.

35. For elaboration on this issue, see Natalie Hevener Kaufman, *Human Rights Treaties and the Senate* (Chapel Hill: University of North Carolina Press, 1990). See also John Rourke, *Congress and the Presidency in U.S. Foreign Policymaking* (Boulder, Colo.: Westview Press, 1983), 242.

36. *Hearings* . . . , 1950, 205.

37. *Hearings* . . . , 1950, 18–19, 199, 201–5, 304–6; Senate Genocide Convention Executive Sessions, II, 1949–50, 367–69, 371–73, 391–92; Frank Holman, *State Department Half Truths and False Assurances regarding the U.N. Charter, Genocide Convention, and Proposed Covenant on Human Rights* (Seattle: Argus Press, 1952), 33–38.

38. Rowland Brucken, "Fuel for the Growing Fire: The Genocide Convention and the Bricker Amendment" (paper presented at the annual meeting of the Society for Historians of American Foreign Relations, Georgetown University, Washington, D.C., June 20, 1997), 4.

39. *Hearings* . . . , 1950, 4, 12, 48, 71–72, 131, 251, 263. The International and Comparative Law Section of the ABA supported the convention but also sought additional wording that would define genocide specifically as acts that "directly affect thousands of persons." See *Hearings* . . . , 1950, 232.

40. *Hearings* . . . , 1950, 208.

41. *Hearings* . . . , 1950, 208.

42. Frank Holman, *Dangers of Treaty Law* (Seattle: Argus Press, 1952), 18. See also Hearings . . . , 1950, 160–62, 168–69, 171–75, and Phillips, 623–25.

43. Brucken, 6; Summary Record of the 81st Meeting of the Sixth Committee, October 13, 1948, A/C.6/SR.81.

44. *Hearings* . . . , 1950, 15.

45. See Jay Rosenthal, "Legal and Political Considerations of the United States' Ratification of the Genocide Convention," *Antioch Law Journal* 3 (1985): 126. Examples include the 1804 Convention for the Protection of Submarine Cable and the Treaty of 1862, Suppression of African Slave Trade.

46. Holman, *Dangers of Treaty Law,* 43–46; Kenneth S. Carlston, "The Genocide Convention: A Problem for the American Lawyer," *American Bar Association Journal* 36 (March 1950): 206–9.

47. *Hearings* . . . , 1950, 391.

48. *Hearings* . . . , 1950, 385.

49. Kaufman, 62.

50. *Hearings* . . . , 1950, 377–80, 384–86, 391–95, 651–53; "Genocide Action Put Off," *New York Times,* September 2, 1950, A7; Brucken, 9.

51. Vita Bite, *The Genocide Convention* (Washington, D.C.: U.S. Library of Congress, Congressional Research Service, 1980).

52. Kaufman, chap. 4.

53. Quoted in William Korey, "Human Rights Treaties: Why Is the U.S. Stalling?," *Foreign Affairs* 45, no. 3 (April 1967): 418; Tony Evans, "Hegemony, Domestic Politics and the Project of Universal Human Rights," *Diplomacy & Statecraft* 6, no. 3 (November 1995): 638; Dwight D. Eisenhower, *The White House Years: Mandate for Change—1953–1956* (London: Heinemann, 1963), 675.

54. See Korey, "America's Shame," 291.

55. Quoted in William Korey, "The United States and the Genocide Convention: Leading Advocate and Leading Obstacle," *Ethics and International Affairs* 11 (1997): 279.

56. *Hearings on the Genocide Convention before a Subcommittee of the Senate Foreign Relations Committee,* 91st Cong., 1st sess., 1970, 12.

57. *Hearings* . . . , 1970, 20.

58. *Hearings* . . . , 1970, 20

59. *Hearings* . . . , 1970, 21.

60. *Hearings* . . . , 1970, 21.

61. *Hearings* . . . , 1970, 21.

62. *Hearings* . . . , 1970, 21.

63. Gardner and Goldberg collaborated to publish a refutation of key ABA concerns in "Time to Act on the Genocide Convention," *American Bar Association Journal* 58 (February 1972): 141–45.

64. *Hearings* . . . , 1970, 12.

65. *Hearings* . . . , 1970, 108.

66. *Hearings* . . . , 1970, 110. Gardner added that such wording also protects against the argument that because a group was not completely destroyed (like the Jews in Germany) that genocide had not occurred. For details on this and other issues surrounding the drafting of the UNGC, see Nehemiah Robinson, *The Genocide Convention: A Commentary* (New York: Institute of Jewish Affairs, 1967).

67. *Hearings* . . . , 1970, 111.

68. Korey, "The United States and the Genocide Convention," 283. See also correspondence between Senator Church, Mr. Eberhard Deutsch, and Nicholas B. de Katzenbach in *Hearings* . . . , 1970, 15–28 (insertions).

69. *Hearings on the Genocide Convention before a Subcommittee of the Senate Committee on Foreign Relations,* 92nd Cong., 1st sess., 1971, 182–87. See also *Hearings before the Senate Committee on Foreign Relations,* 95th Cong., 1st sess., 1977, 82–85.

70. *Hearings* . . . , 1970, 99.

71. *Hearings* . . . , 1970, 99. Lawrence LeBlanc calls this argument "profound anti-Sovietism masked in legal and pseudolegal language." He offers an excellent chapter on "Protected Groups and Political Groups" in his book *The United States and the Genocide Convention.* For more on the anti-Soviet edge to UNGC opposition, see Jay Rosenthal, "Legal and Political Considerations of the United States' Ratification of the Genocide Convention," *Antioch Law Journal* 3 (1985): 122–24.

72. 3 UN GAOR C.6 (73rd mtg.), 1948, 96, 97.

73. *Hearings* . . . , 1970, 205.

74. *Hearings* . . . , 1970, 195.

75. *Hearings* . . . , 1970, 200.

76. *Hearings* . . . , 1970, 218.

77. Jerome J. Shestack, "Sisyphus Endures: The International Human Rights NGO," *New York Law School Review* 24 (1978): 89–123.

78. Author interview with Professor John Norton Moore, University of Virginia, August 25, 1998.

79. Statement submitted to the Subcommittee on Future Foreign Policy Research and Development of the Committee on International Relations, House of Representatives, 94th Cong., 2nd sess., August 30, 1976.

80. *Hearings* . . . , 1977, 48, 51–52.

81. Letter (May 23, 1977) reprinted in *Hearings* . . . , 1977, 54.

82. Text of Remarks of the President at Meeting Commemorating the 30th Anniversary of the Universal Declaration of Human Rights, Office of the White House Press Secretary, December 5, 1978.

83. *Hearings* . . . , 1977, 11.

84. *Hearings* . . . , 1970, 12.

85. *Hearings* . . . , 1970, 15.

86. *Hearings* . . . , 1970, 79.

87. *Hearings* . . . , 1970, 79.

88. *Hearings* . . . , 1970, 3–4.

89. The four treaties were the International Covenant on Civil and Political Rights; the International Covenant on Economic, Social, and Cultural Rights; the International Covenant on the Elimination of All Forms of Racial Discrimination; and the American Convention on Human Rights.

90. Memo from Zbigniew Brzezinski to President Jimmy Carter, December 18, 1978, Jimmy Carter Library, National Security Advisor Subject File, Human Rights Folder, December 1978–March 1979.

91. Quoted in memo from Madeleine Albright to Zbigniew Brzezinski, December 14, 1978, Jimmy Carter Library, National Security Advisor Subject File, Human Rights Folder, December 1978–March 1979.

92. Memo, Brzezinski to Carter, December 18, 1978.

93. Korey, "The United States and the Genocide Convention," 286.

94. *Hearings on the Genocide Convention before the Senate Committee on Foreign Relations*, 97th Cong., 1st sess., 1981, 96.

95. *Hearings* . . . , 1981, 8.

96. *Hearings* . . . , 1981, 11.

97. *Hearings* . . . , 1981, 4.

98. *Hearings* . . . , 1981, 106–7.

99. *Hearings* . . . , 1981, 109.

100. *Hearings* . . . , 1981,.

101. *Hearings* . . . , 1981, 16.

102. *Hearings* . . . , 1981, 17.

103. Quoted in *Hearings* . . . , 1981, 118.

104. *Hearings* . . . , 1981, 119.

105. Author interview with Craig Baab, September 4, 1998, Washington, D.C.

106. Moore later served as head of the National Advisory Commission on Oceans and Atmosphere and then as the first chairman of the board of the United States Institute of Peace.

107. Author interview with Charles Smith, September 4, 1998, Washington, D.C.

108. Author interview with Craig Baab, September 11, 1998, Washington, D.C.

109. "International Observer Roundtable," *Radio Moscow,* December 9, 1979, cited in William Korey, "Sin of Omission," *Foreign Policy* 39 (summer 1980): 173.

110. 6D042232 Moscow TASS in English, 2015 GMT 4 December 1981.

111. "Proposed Ratification of the Genocide Treaty: Pro and Con," *Congressional Digest,* December 1984, 293.

112. *Genocide Convention Report of the Senate Foreign Relations Committee,* 99th Cong., 1st sess., Exec. Rep. 99–2, July 18, 1985, 2.

113. *New York Times,* September 6, 1984, A1; "Ratify the Genocide Treaty" (Editorial), *Washington Post,* September 7, 1984, A16.

114. LeBlanc, 134.

115. *Hearings on the Genocide Convention before the Senate Foreign Relations Committee,* 98th Cong., 2nd sess., 1984, 72.

116. *Hearings* . . . , 1984, 70.

117. *Hearings* . . . , 1984, 70.

118. See LeBlanc, 6.

119. Resolution of Ratification (Lugar-Helms-Hatch Sovereignty Package), S. Exec. Rep. 2, 99th Congress, 1st session, 1985, 26–27.

120. *Hearings on the Crime of Genocide before the Senate Foreign Relations Committee,* 99th Cong., 1st sess., 1985, 101–4.

121. *Hearings* . . . , 1985, 107.

122. *Hearings* . . . , 1985, 115.

123. *Hearings* . . . , 1985, 118.

124. *Hearings* . . . , 1985, 81.

125. *Hearings* . . . , 1985, 83.

126. *Hearings* . . . , 1985, 86.

127. *Hearings* . . . , 1985, 88.

128. *Hearings* . . . , 1985, 89.

129. Senator Dole had a personal "connection" that raised his level of concern and interest in the convention. An Armenian physician, Dr. Kalikian, had helped Dole with his wartime injuries.

130. *New York Times,* February 29, 1986, A1.

131. *Congressional Record,* Senate, legislative day of Monday, February 17, 1986; 99th Cong., 2nd sess., 132, Web version (Congressional Universe), 17.

132. *Congressional Record,* 24.

133. *Congressional Record,* 32.

134. LeBlanc, 149.

135. Author phone interview with William Korey, August 26, 1998.

136. Evans, 639.

Chapter Two

The United States and the Cambodian Tragedy

Tarnished and traumatized during much of the second part of the twentieth century, contemporary Cambodia little resembles its glorious past, and few people can even imagine a Cambodia beyond civil war and the notorious "killing fields" of the Pol Pot era. However, during the high point of its civilization from the ninth to the fifteenth century a.d., the Khmer kings presided over a sizable Cambodian empire. During the Angkor era, they ruled not just the area known today as Cambodia but also sizable parts of Vietnam, Laos, Thailand, and the Malay peninsula, making them the greatest power in the region for some six centuries. Under the leadership of Suryavarman II, Angkor continued to expand its influence, developed an intensive system of agricultural irrigation, and erected Angkor Wat, the stunning Hindu funeral temple and a widely regarded architectural masterpiece of Southeast Asia. Like empires before and after it, the Cambodian hegemony would not last and suffered precipitous decline following the sacking of Angkor Wat by a Siamese army in 1353. Thus began a steady downward spiral for Cambodia that would reach an unimaginable nadir in the 1970s.

This chapter traces the story of American foreign policy and genocide in Cambodia. As the Khmer Rouge liquidated their own people and committed genocide against others, the administration of President Jimmy Carter struggled to balance its devotion to the cause of human rights with broader geostrategic imperatives. Although the genocidal regime of Pol Pot held power only from 1975 to 1979, related issues continued for decades to pose challenges both for Cambodia's domestic politics and also for the United States and the international community. Over the course of this difficult period, the United States faced several opportunities to contribute to the institutionalization and strengthening of a norm of genocide prevention and punishment. The realities and vagaries of international relations have contributed to a mixed record of American ability and willingness to capitalize on these leadership moments as they have emerged. As a result, the policies portrayed here capture the contradictory and conflicted nature of U.S. actions and norm evolution. During the early period of the Cambodia tragedy, the United States (then not a signatory to the United Nations Convention on the Prevention and Punishment of the Crime of Genocide [Genocide Convention]) failed to support and even undermined the norms of the convention, as seemingly unchallenged Cold War imperatives drove American interests and perceptions of political developments in Indochina 1970s and 1980s.

Over time, however, the United States has moved somewhat in the opposite direction toward stronger but still limited commitment to norm promotion. "Cold War" is now a twenty-four-episode CNN special documentary series, no longer the template for American foreign policy. As a result, the United States has grown more responsive and receptive to efforts to seek justice for the genocide in Cambodia, mainly by hoping to bring to trial some of the leaders most responsible for the Pol Pot regime's horrendous acts against the Cambodian population. Specifically, discussions in the spring of 1998 about capturing and trying Pol Pot and American-mediated efforts at establishing a tribunal in 2001 suggested a strengthening of the antigenocide norm as the international political context allowed for such evolution and growth.

The tale of America and genocide in Cambodia begins with a brief examination of the controversial role played by the United States in contributing unintentionally to the rise of the radical, Maoist, and savage Khmer Rouge movement in Cambodia. During the Vietnam conflict, the wartime policies of the Nixon administration unwittingly helped to destabilize Cambodia and leave it vulnerable to the machinations of Pol Pot's communist insurgency. Unlike the other cases examined in this study, the United States figured somewhat prominently in initial events that led to a cascade of genocidal brutality in a country already ravaged by war in Indochina.

Attention then turns to analyze two important foreign policy issues to emerge concerning the Pol Pot regime: the vote on Cambodia's General Assembly seat at the United Nations and American assistance to hundreds of thousands of Cambodian refugees fleeing both the Khmer Rouge and then a Vietnamese invasion. In both cases, the Carter administration came face to face with ethical leadership moments—distinct opportunities to put into practice its stirring vocal commitment to human rights. However, as the overall theme of this book suggests, the context of international politics at the time mediated and moderated a fully "rights based" response by the United States. It was only later, decades after the atrocities, that the United States stepped forward—but still not unambiguously—in its role as "norm entrepreneur." By the late 1990s, the overdue process of holding Khmer Rouge leaders accountable for genocide and crimes against humanity in Cambodia revealed evolution in international ethics and American leadership worth mentioning.

BACKGROUND

Having endured rule under joint Siamese-Vietnamese suzerainty, French colonial administration, and Japanese occupation during World War II, Cambodia faced new hardships and violent tensions brought by the war in Vietnam. As the 1960s and early 1970s wore on, Cambodia sought to preserve a position of neutrality while the rest of Indochina was at war. Cambodia's Prince Norodom Sihanouk maneuvered diplomatically to maintain his nation's independence, but he faced forces and circumstances he could not completely control. From the mid-1960s on, North Vietnamese (NVA) and Vietcong (VC) forces regularly used Cambodian territory bordering South Vietnam to hide, supply, and train their troops. A political opportunist, Sihanouk believed that the Vietnamese communists were close to winning the war, and he allowed them to land supplies at the port of Sihanoukville (later known as Kompong Som).

As NVA and VC guerrilla activity in the area grew, the administration of Richard M. Nixon reversed the restraint demonstrated by its predecessor and authorized the first B-52 raids on the Cambodian sanctuaries, hoping to destroy the supposed Central Office for South Vietnam (COSVN) located there. Beginning in March 1969 and continuing in varying intensity until 1973, over 3,600 B-52 sorties pounded Cambodian territory with bombs. The initial raids, code-named "Menu" (with specific target areas referred to as "Breakfast," "Lunch," "Dinner," "Supper," "Snack," and "Dessert"), were kept secret from Congress and the press, and military records were falsified to suggest that the missions occurred over South Vietnam.[1]

In March 1970, Sihanouk was overthrown, and former General Lon Nol, then prime minister, assumed full control. With a Nixon administration "insistent on building up Lon Nol," the new Khmer Republic received material assistance from the United States for its armed forces to support their campaign against radical, agrarian, Maoist communist rebels, known as "the Khmer Rouge," and NVA and VC troops. The United States airlifted military supplies to Phnom Penh, including thousands of captured Vietnamese rifles and ammunition.[2] In addition, ethnic Khmer battalions, known as "Khmer Krom" (meaning southern Khmers from the Mekong Delta region), trained in Vietnam by U.S. special forces, went into Cambodia to bolster the Lon Nol regime.

Nixon administration military actions in neutral Cambodia reached a pinnacle in April 1970 with an invasion by over 30,000 American troops and almost 50,000 South Vietnamese forces in search of communist rebels and the NVA command post. This "incursion," as Nixon called it, lasted until June and sparked virulent protest in the United States, including the tragic demonstrations at Jackson State and Kent State Universities. COSVN remained elusive, and the United States found itself still bolstering a corrupt anticommunist Cambodian government with rapidly diminishing popular support. As foreign powers leveled and encroached on their nation, more and more Cambodians demonstrated sympathy and support for the Khmer Rouge and its anti-Western declarations.

On April 17, 1975, following five years of intense civil war, the communist rebellion known as the Khmer Rouge took control of the Cambodian capital city of Phnom Penh and proclaimed victory over Lon Nol's Khmer Republic. Many Cambodians welcomed the end of the civil war and hoped for a new era of peace in their ravaged nation. Close to the Hotel Le Phnom, armored personnel carriers sat parked under flowering trees with yellow blossoms stuck in their headlight slots. Even government soldiers grinned as they stacked their weapons and tied white flags to their trucks.[3] Beyond the capital as well, news of the fall of the Khmer Republic caused celebration. Villagers played drums and flutes, and crowds danced and sang into the night. The celebration would not last long. Under the leadership of Pol Pot, the Khmer Rouge used starvation, war, and genocide to transform the nation (renamed "Democratic Kampuchea") according to their communist-utopian vision of a classless society. Pol Pot's radical barbarism would last until 1979, when an invasion by Vietnam toppled the despotic regime.

As soon as they declared victory, the Khmer Rouge forced the evacuation of all Cambodian cities, from the smaller provincial capitals to Phnom Penh, with its population of nearly two million. For a new Cambodia to emerge, the Khmer Rouge committed itself to the extermination of the old in a single, drastic stroke. As Khmer Rouge leader Son Sen once remarked to Prince Sihanouk, "We will be the first nation to create a completely Communist society without wasting our time on intermediate steps."[4] Cambodia's new leaders explained that emptying the nation's urban areas was a means of preventing famine and protecting civilians from American bombing attacks. In reality, cities were transformed into ghost towns as residents were ordered to the countryside to follow the agricultural life. But this was no Jeffersonian vision of an agrarian republic. By pushing all Cambodians into rural peasant life, the Khmer Rouge sought to erase what they viewed as divisive class distinctions that existed between farmer and physician, civil servant and teacher.[5]

While Cambodians faced forcible evacuation to the countryside, the regime expelled all foreigners from the country. The handful of foreign journalists who dared and managed to stay behind witnessed a truly dreadful political program put into horrible practice. John Barron and Anthony Paul described the barbaric forced marches from the city, with evacuees receiving only a few hours to gather whatever belongings they could before joining the exodus along congested streets. Lacking food and adequate water during the stifling heat of Cambodia's dry season, many collapsed and died from exhaustion if not shot beforehand as resisters.[6]

The sick and dying in hospitals received no mercy or special treatment. Adjacent to one Phnom Penh hospital "lay the remains of nonambulatory patients who had been dumped on the ground and had no friends to take them away before death did so."[7] French priest François Ponchaud called the swarm of sick and wounded men, women, and children a "hallucinatory spectacle." Ponchaud described the horror of seeing a crippled patient "who had neither hands nor feet, writhing along the ground like a severed worm."[8] Black-clad Khmer Rouge soldiers, many of them teenagers, patrolled the city to see that no one avoided the mandated program of rustication. Jon Swain of London's *Sunday Times* reported, "The Khmer Rouge army is emptying the city and its hospitals—tipping out patients like garbage into the streets. Bandaged men and women hobble by the embassy. Wives push soldier husbands on hospital beds on wheels, some with serum drips still attached. In five years of war this is the greatest caravan of human misery I have seen."[9] After merely a week of life under Democratic Kampuchea, Phnom Penh had been "transformed into a vast, still wasteland occupied primarily by corpses, stray dogs . . . and patrols standing guard to ensure that human life did not return."[10]

Life in the newly constituted countryside resembled nothing Cambodians or the outside world could have imagined. The construction of a rural-based society meant the abolition of banks and money—the National Bank was blown up, sending millions of pieces of paper money into the surrounding streets.[11] Goods were exchanged through an intercommune system of bartering. Religion was strictly forbidden.[12] The Khmer Rouge did everything possible to isolate Cambodians from one another and the outside world. They abolished postal and telephone services, controlled all mass media, dismantled the education system, and confiscated and burned books. Even medical services were reduced to the level of traditional herbs and other folk cures—imported medicines were banned and hospitals shut down.[13]

In their zeal to create a society without cities, property, money, and traditional loyalties, the Khmer Rouge engaged in widespread and systematic murder. They unflinchingly killed not just government soldiers but also civil servants and those suspected of being members of the "intelligentsia"—teachers, doctors, professors, and students. For many Cambodians, the simple act of wearing glasses—a symbol of intelligence and literacy—meant a death sentence.[14] The new regime actively sought to exterminate any Cambodians who for one reason or another represented a threat, real or imagined. Those unhappy with the new regime faced execution, along with their families, by disembowelment, by beating to death with farm implements, and even by having nails hammered into the backs of their heads—all means of eliminating opponents while deviously economizing the limited supply of bullets.[15]

A 1978 UN report charged that immediately following the 1975 takeover by the Khmer Rouge, "a large number of former military officers, senior officials, policemen, intelligence agents, country officials and military police were executed . . . and that in a very large number of cases the wives and children of such categories of persons were also executed." The report also cited the summary killings of so-called intellectuals and of many "ordinary persons whose attitudes had not been deemed satisfactory by the new authorities, or who had committed minor infractions (such as being late for work or losing their tools)."[16] The Soviet newspaper *Izvestia* described in harsh language the communist regime in Cambodia, describing Kampuchea as a "vast concentration camp" and a "gigantic prison" where "rivers of blood flow and a ruthless and systematic policy of genocide is being carried out with respect to the country's own people." Overall, a total of at least 1.5 million of Cambodia's nearly eight million people died under the Khmer Rouge.[17]

GENOCIDE

The brutality of the Khmer Rouge regime and the toll it claimed on its own people stands as one of the twentieth century's most hideous crimes. To be sure, the laundry list of atrocities alone qualifies the Pol Pot regime as one of the most grotesquely violent in human history. However, the Khmer Rouge deserve added condemnation because their radical political project included a concerted program of genocide. As Ben Kiernan, Yale University professor and founding director of the Cambodian Genocide Justice Project from 1994 to 1999, has exhaustively documented, Pol Pot directed genocidal campaigns against several distinct groups in Cambodia, strictly defined: Buddhist monks; the Cham, Buddhist, and Vietnamese minorities; and the Eastern Khmer population.[18]

Religion in general, and Buddhism in particular, were declared "incompatible with the revolution."[19] The Buddhist belief that one's station in life had been determined by conduct in a previous incarnation posed a direct challenge to Khmer Rouge efforts to redefine completely the social order.[20] To remedy this situation, the Khmer Rouge eradicated Buddhism from the country in no more than a year. Out of a total of 2,680 Buddhist monks from eight Cambodian monasteries, only seventy were known to have survived into 1979.[21] A Khmer Rouge document detailed the effort to destroy Buddhism in the new Cambodia, noting that "monks have disappeared from 90 to 95 per cent. . . . Monasteries . . . are largely abandoned. The foundation pillars of Buddhism . . . have disintegrated. In the future they will dissolve further. The political base, the economic base, the cultural base must be uprooted."[22]

Like the attacks on Buddhists, the Pol Pot regime's ruthless efforts to exterminate ethnic minority populations also fall under the jurisdiction of the UNGC. Cambodia's Vietnamese population was completely wiped out. Even before assuming control of the government, the Khmer Rouge had driven out of the country some 200,000 members of the community. Once in power, the Khmer Rouge forcibly relocated another 100,000 Vietnamese. The 10,000 or so who managed to remain suffered a worse fate—they were slaughtered in a ruthlessly organized campaign of genocidal massacres. After 1979, says Kiernan, it was impossible to find an ethnic Vietnamese who had survived the Pol Pot years.[23]

The Khmer Rouge turned their murderous attention to Cambodia's ethnic Chinese population as well. In 1975, a population of about 430,000 Chinese existed in Cambodia. Four years later, just half survived. The new regime banned the Chinese language and all other distinguishing characteristics of Chinese culture. Most Chinese resided in Cambodia's cities, and the Khmer Rouge viewed them as a particular threat to their plans for radical agricultural revolution. Most Chinese suffered systematic abuse and murder based on both geographic and social origin and on their culture and ethnic origin.

The Cham people also suffered under the genocidal policies of Pol Pot. A Muslim community that had settled in Cambodia after being ousted from Vietnam in the fifteenth century, the Cham maintained distinctive customs and religion. They posed a conspicuous challenge to the uniform Cambodian society sought by the Khmer Rouge. Initial steps by the government forced Cham women to cut their hair (worn long by tradition) to match the Khmer style. The traditional Cham sarong was not allowed, and religious activity was prohibited. When some Cham took up arms against their oppressors, the regime sought violent revenge. As journalist Elizabeth Becker relates, "The religious leadership was hunted down and killed. Mosques were destroyed or desecrated, used as granaries, pigsties or prisons."[24] Villages were destroyed, residents were massacred, the Cham language was banned. The Khmer Rouge forced thousands of Muslims to eat pork and killed many who refused. In the end, nearly 100,000 Cham were killed.[25] As a final insult, Cham who died were buried "upside down"—not facing Mecca. Other ethnic groups in Cambodia, including the Thai and Lao populations, also suffered significant death tolls.

Acts of genocide by the Khmer Rouge against minority ethnic groups in Cambodia have been well documented and clearly fall under the definition and jurisdiction of the UNGC. A more difficult question arises in terms of genocide by the Khmer Rouge against part of the majority national group. Do the murderous policies of Pol Pot against his own countrymen qualify as genocide? The drafters of the UNGC wrote the document in the context of post-Holocaust concerns—namely, the fear that one national group or its leaders might once again seek to eliminate in whole or in part *another* national group, generally a minority. However, they likely gave less thought to the scenario of "autogenocide," when a national group or significant parts of it are destroyed by its own leaders.[26]

An examination of the Khmer Rouge's record in terms of the articles of the UNGC reveals definite parallels between the regime's actions against its own people and genocide. The convention outlines specific actions that constitute genocide when "committed with intent to destroy, in whole or in part, a national ethnical, racial, or religious group as such." Article IIa focuses simply on "killing members of the group." As described previously, the Khmer Rouge consistently and remorselessly killed Cambodians for any variety of reasons. Troops killed citizens to maintain order during forced marches. Members of the bourgeoisie were regularly exterminated. Thousands of people faced execution for supposedly poor work performance in the fields or for complaining about the hard labor. Members of the Khmer Rouge itself were not immune to their own murderous regime. In 1977 and 1978, massacres against dissenters within the political elite took place in order to purge the movement of "traitors."[27] More specifically, Cambodians inhabiting the eastern zone of the country bordering Vietnam faced particularly determined efforts at their extermination. The Khmer Rouge leadership considered Eastern Khmers susceptible to Vietnamese influence. During deportation to "the killing fields," they were forced to wear blue scarves as identification and subsequently eliminated en masse.[28]

Article IIc of the UNGC defines the crime to include "destruction resulting from conditions of life." The brutal policies of the Khmer Rouge created conditions of starvation, disease, and exhaustion that killed far more people than perished from execution. As outlined previously, the Khmer Rouge forced the evacuation of Phnom Penh and other Cambodian cities under the pretext of keeping the population safe from American bombing raids. However, the merciless evacuation of all Cambodians from urban areas—no exceptions for the sick and wounded—was for ideological reasons: "To make a proletarianized nation of peasants, the Khmer Rouge instituted a policy designed to destroy the bourgeoisie and capitalist classes that had resided in the city."[29]

To further develop this new nation of peasants, the Pol Pot regime imposed collective and communal agriculture to maximize the nation's productive capacity. The Khmer Rouge approach to cultivation amounted to slave labor with all workers enduring seemingly endless days of farmwork and facing the threat of execution for any performance deemed inadequate. The brutally strict work regimen and lack of adequate food and rest led to exhaustion, especially among former city dwellers generally unaccustomed to the physical demands of rice production. Unfortunately for the Cambodian people, the new command system of agricultural production failed abysmally. Agricultural productivity declined precipitously, making already meager rations even more limited.[30]

The Khmer Rouge demonstrated little if any concern with providing adequate food to its overworked and exhausted population. Instead, the regime continued to export rice in order to import oil and military supplies despite the fact that Cambodians were succumbing to malnutrition and exhaustion.[31] Determined to remain independent from the rest of the world, Democratic Kampuchea for years refused to accept international food assistance. As former executive director of Amnesty International David R. Hawk summarizes, "The Khmer Rouge leadership is thus responsible and accountable for malnutrition and starvation that might otherwise have been avoided."[32]

A somewhat thornier issue dealing with the question of autogenocide involves the question of "intent." The intent of the Pol Pot regime to destroy specific ethnic minority groups in Cambodia is clear. The case is less clear concerning the extermination of significant portions of the majority national group in Cambodia. The UNGC in no way obviates responsibility for such a genocide simply because the genocidal acts were committed by part of a majority group against the rest of the same majority. As some argue, "The Kampucheans cannot escape responsibility for genocide simply because it was practiced on members of their *own* nationality since this massacre did not take place as part of a civil war, but as a calculated, systematic elimination of entire segments of the national population."[33] In fact, the language of the convention makes clear that any intent need only be to eliminate part of a group. David Hawk plainly states, "It was certainly the intent of the Khmer Rouge policy-makers to dissolve and if necessary eliminate the part or parts of the Cambodian nation that were perceived to stand in the way of the revolutionary transformation of society."[34] However, while many believe this to constitute genocide of a political group or a class, and although egregious, those killings do not yet fall under the UNGC. Still, genocide did occur against other groups. Overall, in the name of transformation, the Khmer Rouge regime quite intentionally led to the death of some 1.5 million fellow Cambodians.

THE U.S. ROLE IN THE RISE OF THE KHMER ROUGE

What sets the Cambodia case apart from the others examined in this work is the controversial role of the United States in contributing to the rise to power of the genocidal Khmer Rouge. Critics have argued powerfully that American actions during the Vietnam War, namely, the incursions and massive bombings of Cambodia, helped—unknowingly and certainly unintentionally—to "create" or reinvigorate a floundering, divided communist insurgency in that country.

The argument stressing U.S. complicity in the tragic events in Cambodia gained significant attention with the 1979 publication of *Sideshow: Kissinger, Nixon, and the Destruction of Cambodia* by British journalist William Shawcross. Shawcross details how the administration escalated military activity in neutral Cambodia to destroy North Vietnamese and Vietcong enclaves. He sharply criticizes Nixon and Kissinger for undertaking this campaign of secret invasion and massive aerial bombardment with little if any concern for the consequences in Cambodia.

It remains beyond dispute that the Cambodian countryside suffered devastating attacks from American B-52s. Thousands of sorties flown from 1968 until 1973 pounded Cambodian peasants, who struggled to understand the destructive force falling from the sky. The 1970 Cooper-Church Amendment, introduced by Senator Sherman Cooper and Senator Frank Church, specifically limited the use of American air power to stop men and supplies en route to Vietnam, but the Nixon administration read the legislation with a specific purpose in mind. Nixon told his advisers that although Cooper-Church reserved the use of air power for "interdiction," he wanted "this purpose interpreted very broadly."[35] Deputy Secretary of Defense David Packard, who was ordered to determine how much air power could be mustered, understood clearly that the president sought nearly unlimited bombing in Cambodia.[36]

The Joint Chiefs of Staff instructed General Creighton Adams, commander of U.S. forces in Vietnam, to "conduct the most aggressive U.S. and R.V.N.A.F. air campaign in Cambodia which is feasible."[37] American bombers subsequently destroyed village after village in Cambodia in support of the administration's policy of "Vietnamization" of the war.[38] As more bombs fell, the North Vietnamese forces pushed deeper across the border into Cambodia. The Americans responded by widening their target areas and subsequently killing more noncombatants.

The relentless bombardment of a neutral country troubled some Americans at the time. Air Force Captain Donald Dawson, on learning that a B-52 run had terrorized a wedding ceremony, refused to continue his flying duties and faced court-martial proceedings. In the American embassy, political officer William Harben expressed his outrage at the news that a peasant funeral procession walked right into a bombardment. Harben was appalled at the "reports of wholesale carnage."[39] These and other individuals had grave misgivings about the cost in human terms of American actions in and over Cambodia.

For Shawcross, the more important consequence of American military action in Cambodia was the revitalization of a declining political group—the Khmer Rouge. He sides with Cambodia's Prince Sihanouk, who argued that "Nixon and Kissinger killed lots of Americans, and many other people, they spent enormous sums of money—$4 billion—and the results were the opposite of what they wanted. They demoralized America, they lost all of Indochina to the communists, and they created the Khmer Rouge."[40] Shawcross largely agrees with this assessment, explaining that the Khmer Rouge "were born out of the inferno that American policy did much to create." He concludes that "in Cambodia, the imperatives of a small and vulnerable people were consciously sacrificed to the interests of strategic design. . . . Cambodia was not a mistake; it was a crime."[41]

In more recent research, Cambodia expert Ben Kiernan echoes much of the "Sideshow" thesis, spotlighting the unintended consequences that accompany almost any military intervention. Kiernan writes, "Although it was indigenous, Pol Pot's revolution would not have won power without U.S. economic and military destabilization of Cambodia, which began in 1966 after the American escalation in next-door Vietnam and peaked in 1969–1973 with the carpet bombing of Cambodia's countryside by American B-52s. This was probably the most important single factor in Pol Pot's rise."[42]

The Khmer Rouge leadership took opportunistic advantage of the U.S. destruction of the countryside and the incursion by outside forces, using it as a propaganda weapon against the Lon Nol regime and in favor of the communist rebellion. For the Khmer Rouge, the bombing became a handy "excuse for its brutal, radical policies and its purge of moderate communists and Sihanoukists."[43] The communist movement, torn by factionalism and internal alliances, recruited new members and solidified around Pol Pot's Red Khmer vision "because the CPK [Communist Party of Kampuchea] leadership took advantage of events that were outside its control, such as the American bombing, by appealing to Cambodian nationalism, and at the most basic level, people's desire to survive."[44]

Kiernan's review of military intelligence documents and his extensive interview data build a compelling case for the U.S. role in contributing to the resurgence of the CPK. Assessing a B-52 attack that razed the Cambodian villages of Plei Lom and Plei Blah, the U.S. Army reported that "the Communists intend to use this incident for propaganda purposes."[45]A 1973 report by the Central Intelligence Agency (CIA) pointed to the utility of B-52 raids in Khmer Rouge recruiting: "They are using damage caused by B-52 strikes as the main theme of their propaganda. . . . This approach has resulted in the successful recruitment of a number of young men."[46] The words of former CPK leader Chhit Do highlight the considerable propaganda value of the massive aerial bombardments:

> Every time after there had been bombing, they would take the people to see the craters, to see how big and deep the craters were, to see how the earth had been gouged out

> and scorched. . . . The ordinary people . . . sometimes literally shit in their pants when the big bombs and shells came. . . . Terrified and half-crazy, the people were ready to believe what they were told. . . . That was what made it so easy for the Khmer Rouge to win the people over. . . . It was because of their dissatisfaction with the bombing that they kept on cooperating with the Khmer Rouge, joining up with the Khmer Rouge, sending their children off to go with them.[47]

Not all analysts assign so much blame to the United States for helping create the Khmer Rouge. Craig Etcheson, formerly of the Cambodian Genocide Project at Yale University, notes that the Shawcross argument gives scant attention to the preexisting levels of peasant unrest, cleavages among political elites, and the problematic leadership of Sihanouk.[48] Etcheson argues that "it is untenable to assert that the KCP could not have won but for U.S. intervention. On the one hand, it does seem to be the case that between the realignment of alliance structures and the accelerated radicalization of the peasantry because of U.S. carpet bombing, U.S. actions did contribute to the ability of the KCP to recruit new members. . . . What *is* open to question is just how the balance of forces within the KCP itself might have evolved in the absence of certain U.S. actions."[49] Thus, despite his reasonable qualifications, Etcheson still sees a relevant American role.

Not surprisingly, Henry Kissinger disputes the charges levied by Kiernan, Shawcross, and others. Addressing the issue in 1991, the former secretary of state explained, "My quick response is that journalists keep saying 'bombing Cambodia.' We were bombing four Vietnamese divisions that were killing 500 Americans a week."[50] In his second volume of memoirs, Kissinger argues that the Khmer Rouge developed into a fanatical and vicious political force because of its own ideology, completely apart from U.S. bombing.

However, Etcheson notes that Kissinger's account "begs the central question: *Whose* ideology? Kissinger treats the Khmer Rouge as a monolithic organization with a unified, fixed political line, and he inexplicably maintains that U.S. actions could have had no impact on its internal policy debate. This line of reasoning fails to consider the relationship we now know to have existed between U.S. military intervention and the internal power struggle in the KCP."[51]

Some level of disagreement will always exist over the role played by U.S. policy in the growth of the Khmer Rouge. Still, it appears more than likely that American actions to end the war in Vietnam by expanding the conflict into neighboring Cambodia did contribute to a devastating future for that nation. In its zealous pursuit of communist sanctuaries, the United States violated Cambodian neutrality with an invasion and dropped over 539,000 tons of explosives on Cambodia from 1969 to 1973, three times the amount dropped on Japan during the course of World War II.[52] An estimated 150,000 Cambodians perished under U.S. bombardments. What remains unquantifiable, but nonetheless quite relevant, is the unwitting assistance the United States provided the Khmer Rouge in its struggle for power.

U.S. POLICY DURING THE FORD ADMINISTRATION

During the presidency of Gerald Ford, events in Cambodia—but not necessarily the genocide—did gain attention. As Phnom Penh fell in 1975, Americans evacuated the U.S. embassy after the new regime demanded that all foreigners depart. With few outsiders inside, indications of the growing human rights disaster trickled out from Cambodia as the Khmer Rouge worked to isolate their nation from the rest of the world. Little fully reliable information about the "new Cambodia" emerged in the early days of Pol Pot's tenure. Whatever hint of the brewing genocide that did manage to reach the Western media faced stiff competition from other stories coming out of Indochina. Reports of massive violations of human rights received considerably less attention as other events in Indochina gained prominence.

In the midst of efforts to take over islands claimed by Vietnam, forces from the Revolutionary Army of Kampuchea seized the American merchant ship *Mayaguez,* precipitating a minor crisis and putting American-Cambodian relations briefly at center stage. The Ford administration responded by shelling the Cambodian coast. Eventually, through the intervention of the Chinese, the crew and ship gained release, and Cambodia no longer attracted the attention of most Americans. Genocide in Cambodia quickly began to follow its horrifically violent course. However, news of the crimes against humanity lagged far behind and was soon overwhelmed by other stories, such as the fall of the Saigon regime and the frenzied escape of Americans and South Vietnamese and the American presidential election. Many Americans hoped to put the whole Indochina experience behind them.

As genocide began behind a veil of secrecy in Cambodia, the response from the United States to reports of massive human rights abuses was slow and infrequent if at times stern. Administration officials did announce that they anticipated a "bloodbath" in Cambodia following the Khmer Rouge takeover. The most prominent administration comment on the situation in Cambodia came from Secretary of State Henry Kissinger. Speaking to the House of Representatives Committee on International Relations the day after the fall of Phnom Penh, Kissinger indicated that the administration would "expect the Communists to eliminate all possible opponents."[53] Appearing on NBC's *Today* show in May, he said that "very tragic and inhuman and barbarous things" were happening in Cambodia.[54] Seven days later, Kissinger commented during a news conference that Cambodia's capital city was suffering "an atrocity of major proportions."[55]

A *Newsweek* story from the second week in May, "Bloodbath in Cambodia," said that U.S. officials knew that thousands of Cambodians had already faced execution and that the situation "could ultimately lead to the slaughter of tens of thousands of Cambodians loyal to the Lon Nol regime."[56] President Ford even commented publicly, emphasizing the "factual evidence of the bloodbath that is in the process of taking place."[57]

Beyond those descriptive statements, the U.S. government, under the administration of Gerald Ford, rarely commented on Cambodia, save for in the broader context of the growing Indochina refugee problem. To a considerable extent, administration statements often met with some skepticism, depending on the listener. Absolute evidence of atrocities was still lacking. In addition, several press accounts minimized the comments because they came from a strongly anticommunist administration that had supported the less-than-democratic Lon Nol regime and that was still dealing with issues following war with Vietnamese communists. For example, a writer for the *Far Eastern Economic Review* explained that

> Reports that the Khmer Rouge carried out wholesale executions of former Lon Nol government civilian and military officials immediately after their April 17 victory continue to trickle out of Cambodia through refugees and US Intelligence sources in Washington and the Thai capital. These reports can not be confirmed and should be regarded with suspicion as they come from sources which can hardly be considered detached and disinterested.[58]

As for policy initiatives in response to the communist takeovers in Cambodia and Vietnam, the United States maintained economic embargoes against both countries, but in general the Ford administration simply did not have a particular interest in or commitment to human rights issues. This response mirrored in large part congressional action. On only a handful of occasions did members of Congress raise the issue of human rights in Cambodia. One mention came from Senator Claiborne Pell, a strong supporter of the UNGC. The senator said,

> I have been shocked to read the recent press accounts of mass killings, forced evacuations from urban areas, and generally brutal treatment of the Cambodian population by the new regime . . . approximately one fifth of the Cambodian population has been annihilated—a record of barbarous butchery which is surpassed in recent history only by the Nazi atrocities against the Jews during World War II . . . I am amazed that so little has been done to investigate and condemn what is happening in Cambodia.[59]

With a 1976 victory over Ford, Jimmy Carter won the dubious privilege of dealing with genocidal developments in Cambodia.

THE CARTER VISION

Jimmy Carter began his successful drive for the presidency when many in the United States sought new patterns for international and domestic politics. American involvement in Vietnam and the scandal of Watergate scarred the nation and exacted a harsh toll on its morale and self-image. Carter was determined to make a break with the tragic past by bringing the conduct of foreign affairs into line with America's traditional political values and ideals, thus revitalizing American foreign policy and its overseas image.

Prior to the 1976 campaign, Carter presented little evidence of his foreign policy thinking. In fact, he had to become familiar with specific issues and articulate a foreign policy framework to be taken seriously as a candidate. Candidate Carter made clear that America's principal challenge consisted of sweeping the old order out of office and with it the moral bankruptcy and sins of the past.[60] He hammered away at the Nixon-Ford-Kissinger policies of "power politics," arguing that the United States had taken on Old World habits that Americans traditionally deplored. America had adopted a distasteful Machiavellian streak.

Carter believed that the anticommunist containment imperative of the Cold War forced the United States to betray its principles by supporting various tyrannical, authoritarian regimes—there would be no more Vietnams or Cambodias on his watch. To remedy such errors meant a sharp turn away from "containment at all costs." Carter stated plainly that "our government should justify the character of the American people, and our foreign policy should not short circuit that for temporary advantage."[61] Carter did not view his approach and critique of American foreign policy as a set of ambiguous and impractically grandiloquent statements of intention. He believed that his administration could successfully replace containment with greater attention to other moral imperatives: "To me, the demonstration of American idealism was a practical and realistic approach to foreign policy, and moral principles were the best foundation for the exertion of American power and influence."[62]

Therefore, human rights became a focus and catalyst of Carter's foreign policy and simultaneously a means of promoting the rebirth of faith in American values. The president summed up his approach: "I want our country to set a standard of morality. I feel very deeply that when people are deprived of basic human rights that the president of the United States ought to have a right to express displeasure and do something about it. I want our country to be the focal point for deep concern about human beings all over the world."[63]

Shortly after his inauguration in March 1977, Carter delivered a speech at the commencement exercises of the University of Notre Dame. In that speech, he stressed the need to connect American foreign policy closely with the nation's "essential character." Carter stressed, "I believe we can have a foreign policy that is democratic, that is based on fundamental values, and that uses power and influence which we have for humane purposes." Humane purposes and not single-minded obsession with the Cold War would drive a new American foreign policy, one that accepted that the United States could "no longer separate the traditional issues of war and peace from the new global questions of justice, equity, and human rights." The president urged Americans to embrace this "new world" and assume a role of revitalized, optimistic, and value-oriented world leadership.

To implement his vision of morality and American foreign policy, Carter appointed civil rights advocate Patricia Derian to assistant secretary of state for human rights. In addition, Deputy Secretary of State Warren Christopher was charged with the difficult task of making human rights goals and initiatives compatible with the overall thrust of American foreign policy. The resulting "Christopher Group" exempted the majority of military aid and food assistance programs from use as penalties for human rights violations. This initiative built on earlier congressional action.

As the human rights agenda gained momentum in the mid-1970s, Congress enacted legislation requiring the government to consider human rights conditions before providing aid and allowing the withholding of American economic and military aid to nations labeled as human rights violators.[64] Revised versions of the Foreign Assistance Act of 1974 and the International Development and Food Assistance Act of 1975 passed during the Ford interlude permitted the president to ban aid to a government "which engages in a consistent pattern of gross violations of internationally recognized human rights."[65] A later revision to the International Development and Food Assistance Act also allowed American representatives at development banks to oppose loans for nations violating human rights. Such initiatives were not available to American policymakers because the Khmer Rouge had neither asked for nor been offered either military or economic aid from the United States and did not seek loans from international development banks.[66]

CONGRESS AND CAMBODIA

Although interest in Cambodia remained fairly stagnant among most in the West, the number and accuracy of reports on Democratic Kampuchea began to grow as Carter took office. Photos of "forced Cambodian labor" appeared in the *Washington Post* on April 8, 1977, reportedly depicting "the first visual confirmation of stories by Cambodian refugees of the harsh conditions under which the Khmer Rouge are holding the country." Several books appeared as well chronicling atrocities in Cambodia, including François Ponchaud's *Cambodge*

Annee Zero and *Murder of a Gentle Land* by John Barron and Anthony Paul. The Barron and Paul account reached a wide audience through a condensed version published in the popular *Reader's Digest* magazine. The authors calculated that over one million Cambodians had died in what they termed a "new holocaust."[67]

Just months earlier, another publication had described a very different situation. *Cambodia: Starvation and Revolution* by George Hildebrand and Gareth Porter argued that the supposedly merciless evacuation of Phnom Penh and other cities was "an urgent necessity" to meet the population's needs. The authors detailed the food shortages in Democratic Kampuchea and charged the United States with criticizing the Khmer Rouge's evacuation strategy in order to distract attention away from "the actual crime committed by the United States in spreading the war to Cambodian in the first place."[68] Many viewed Hildebrand and Porter as overly sympathetic to the regime and willing to overlook clear abuses. Meanwhile, John Barron had established credentials as an anticommunist, believed by some to be connected with the CIA. Harvard Law School's Jamie Metzl explains, "The propagandist language of Barron and Paul's book and even its red cover, its absurd suggestion that [Democratic Kampuchea President] Khieu Samphan's sexuality offered an explanation for the violence in Democratic Kampuchea . . . made it seem less than authoritative to those familiar with the complexities of the Cambodia situation."[69]

A written piece that attracted considerable attention at the time was a review by French leftist Jean Lacouture of Father Ponchaud's book printed in the *New York Review of Books.* Lacouture had earlier supported the Khmer Rouge and their struggle against Lon Nol's corrupt Khmer Republic. Now, significantly, Lacouture expressed horror at the Pol Pot regime. He wrote that "after Auschwitz and the gulag we might have thought this century had produced the ultimate in horror, but we are now seeing the suicide of a people in the name of revolution, worse in the name of Socialism."[70] Dramatically reassessing his onetime advocacy for the Khmer Rouge, Lacouture declared that Ponchaud's book "can only be read with shame by those of us who supported the Khmer Rouge cause."[71]

Some news sources openly addressed the issue of conflicting reports. In the *Washington Post,* Southeast Asia correspondent Lewis Simons wrote an article, "The Unknown Dimensions of the Cambodian Tragedy," in which he discussed contradictory reports and supposedly faked photos. Summing up the debate, Simon wrote,

> Are the Communist leaders of Cambodia waging genocide there? How many Cambodians have been killed since the end of the war. . . . Tens of thousands? Hundreds of thousands? A million? All these figures are used. But no one knows. . . . This is not to

> suggest that whatever is written or said about Cambodia, however horrendous, is not true. What it does mean is that reports about Cambodia should be treated with skepticism.[72]

For its December 2, 1977, cover story, *Asiaweek* chose "Cambodia: How True?" Including in its coverage both refugee accounts and also Democratic Kampuchea government statements, the article did not come down firmly on one side or another. The very same dispute, debate, and questions would emerge during the first congressional hearing into the situation in Cambodia.

Against the backdrop of these reports and with a White House powerfully declaring its commitment to human rights as a cornerstone of American foreign policy, Congress also took the first steps to address the crisis in Democratic Kampuchea, as Cambodian refugees escaped into Thailand in 1977 and told their stories about the "killing fields."

At the prompting of New York Democratic Congressman Stephen Solarz, in May 1977 the House International Relations Committee assembled its Subcommittee on International Organizations to investigate the happenings in Cambodia. In late 1976, Solarz had visited Bangkok, where he heard horror stories about conditions in Cambodia and the evacuation of Phnom Penh. The reports echoed with stories about the Holocaust. Solarz was particularly sensitive to such parallels since his New York district included more survivors of the Holocaust than any other area in the United States.[73]

In a statement that set the tone for the hearing, Subcommittee Chairman Donald Fraser (D-Minn.) stated plainly that the United States "holds no diplomatic or commercial ties with the Cambodian government. Consequently we have very little leverage, but we still need to remain informed of developments." Solarz spoke passionately about the horrible developments in Cambodia: "I might have hoped that after Hitler . . . the world would have learned its lesson on genocide, and that holocausts would have been something of the past. Obviously it hasn't. In its own way the indifference of the world to events in Cambodia is almost as appalling as what has happened there itself."[74] Solarz charged that an "implicit racism" best explained the lack of concern or response from the West. He explained that Cambodians "are not white or Jews or westerners who are being murdered, but orientals. Perhaps to us, oriental life is not worth as much as Western life."[75] Siding with Solarz, John Barron talked of widespread killing and argued that "the people of Cambodia are being denied virtually all human rights."[76]

Not all those involved in the congressional hearing shared Solarz's grim view of developments in Cambodia. Forming a clear notion of what, if anything, the United States could or should do to respond to developments in Cambodia became difficult after somewhat conflicting testimony offered by a range of experts. Dr. David Chandler, a research fellow at Harvard University's East Asia Research Center and former Foreign Service officer in Cambodia, presented a relatively positive side of the Khmer Rouge, stressing that the communist rebels had overthrown a repressive regime. Gareth Porter, an Indochina expert from the Institute of Policy Studies in Washington (and coauthor of the controversial *Cambodia: Starvation and Revolution*), joined Chandler to produce testimony that contrasted significantly with the picture painted by Solarz.

Although not apologists for the new Kampuchean regime, Chandler and Porter suggested that reports of mass killings and brutal atrocities were exaggerated. In their opinion, refugees accounts of the crisis probably inflated death counts from the "thousands" to "tens or hundreds of thousands."[77] Porter attacked tales of a "deathmarch" from urban areas as "a myth fostered by the authors of a *Reader's Digest* book that was given massive advance publicity through *Time* magazine and again when the book was published in *Reader's Digest*."[78] Their testimony hit an even more controversial note when they blamed the United States in part for the Cambodian disaster.

Porter chastised those who blindly criticized the Kampuchean regime, explaining that "it is the worst kind of hypocrisy to express moral outrage at the revolutionary government of Democratic Kampuchea for its weaknesses rather than at the cause of overwhelmingly greater suffering: the U.S. policy in Cambodia from 1970 to 1975."[79] Chandler seconded this statement arguing that "American actions are to blame" for the rash of deaths in Cambodia. Chandler underscored his point noting that "from 1969 to 1973 . . . we dropped more than 500,000 tons of bombs on the Cambodian countryside. . . . We bombed Cambodia without knowing why, without taking note of the people we destroyed. We might have thought things through. Instead we killed thousands of people who had done nothing to us."[80] Representative Solarz disagreed and, using thinly veiled language, compared Porter with Nazi apologists. Solzarz countered, "It is beyond belief that anyone could seriously argue that this hasn't been going on."[81]

The testimony of skeptics such as Chandler and Porter hinted at the Shawcross thesis to come. It also pointed to the lack of clarity, the confusion, and the conflicting information surrounding the events in Cambodia shortly after the Khmer Rouge takeover. For even concerned American officials, gaining a clear and complete picture of the situation in Democratic Kampuchea was a significant challenge as information slowly leaked out and was then subject to conflicting analysis. As a result, formulating any appropriate policy in response was a unique challenge.

The continued dispute over what exactly was happening in Cambodia even influenced responses by nongovernmental organizations (NGOs). Prominent human rights organizations, such as Amnesty International (AI), remained fairly inactive themselves. The 1976 Amnesty report on human rights around the world had included just one page on Cambodia. Amnesty International, like national governments, was sensitive to conflicting reports coming from Cambodia and sought to avoid producing an inaccurate report. The 1976 edition mentioned claims of large-scale executions by the Pol Pot regime but added that "few refugees seem to have actually witnessed executions."[82] Therefore, AI chose not to air publicly concerns about massive human rights violations in Cambodia. Likewise, in his review of the period, Jamie Metzl has noted how the International Commission of Jurists "took no action regarding Cambodia during this period for similar reasons."[83]

CARTER ADMINISTRATION RESPONSE

However great and well placed its intentions, the Carter administration faced a difficult predicament. Democratic Kampuchea's self-imposed exile from the rest of the world made it tough to assess the situation accurately and respond appropriately to it. During a second round of hearings on Cambodia during the summer of 1977, Assistant Secretary of State for East Asia and Pacific Affairs Richard Holbrooke appeared before the House International Relations Committee and portrayed the limited options available to the administration.

Holbrooke did not soften the desperate news coming from Cambodia. He explained that "based on all the evidence available to us, we have concluded that Cambodian authorities have flagrantly and systematically violated the most basic human rights. They have ordered or permitted extensive killings, forcibly relocated the urban population, brutally treated supporters of the previous government, and suppressed personal and political freedoms."[84] Holbrooke stressed that the lack of U.S. action did not mean a lack of interest; the administration simply had few options. The assistant secretary explained that "since 1975 Cambodia has been almost completely sealed from the outside world." Holbrooke concluded that "we cannot let it be said that by our silence we acquiesce in the tragic events in Cambodia. I wish to say in the strongest possible terms that we deplore what has taken place there. I cannot tell you, however, that anything we can realistically do will improve the lot of the Khmer people in the foreseeable future."[85] Following the hearings, Representative Solarz introduced and saw passed a House resolution that expressed "deep concern over the continuing disregard for basic human rights" in Democratic Kampuchea. The resolution urged the president to work with other nations "in an effort to bring the flagrant violations of internationally recognized human rights now taking place in Cambodia to an end."[86]

Other administration officials spoke out against the horrible drama in Cambodia while also highlighting the limited policy options available to the United States. In a January 1978 speech, Warren Christopher described Khmer Rouge actions as "flagrant and massive," but he added that the United States effectively had no relations with Democratic Kampuchea. Christopher noted, "We condemn what has taken place there and will take every suitable opportunity to speak out, lest by our silence we seem to acquiesce in the unspeakable human rights abuses that are occurring there."[87]

Secretary of State Cyrus Vance addressed the issue head on following a June 1978 speech in Cincinnati when an audience member asked, "What can we do as individuals or as a nation to stop the holocaust in Cambodia?" Vance echoed the position staked out previously by his colleagues, responding that

> The situation there is, indeed, a tragic one. We have no contact at all with the Cambodians. We have tried to establish some contact so as to find out at least what is going on there. We have been unable to do this.
>
> What knowledge we have, we have to gain from others. I think that what one can do is to focus world attention on this situation and hope that the effect of world opinion may change the situation there. But in terms of what we actually can do other than working with others in the world bodies, such as the United Nations and other international fora, there is really nothing practically that I can suggest that we can do.[88]

Likewise, during the 1977 hearings, Congressman Solarz questioned Charles Twining of the U.S. embassy in Bangkok about actions to ameliorate the human suffering in Cambodia. Twining answered, "I would feel that there is a moral imperative to speak out. . . . I am not sure that it would have any influence on the Cambodian Government, unfortunately. These people are really a xenophobic lot. . . . Therefore, I think we can speak out, but I am not sure that the Cambodian leadership would care a hoot about what we or anyone else would have to say."[89]

The Pol Pot regime had already made clear its own lack of desire to hear what others had to say. During a special mission to Indochina to locate missing American servicemen and open diplomatic relations with Vietnam, an assistant to U.S. envoy Leonard Woodcock tried to contact the Kampuchean ambassador in Vientiane, Laos. The Kampuchean embassy turned the American away brusquely. Soon after, Cambodian radio announced that no representative of Kampuchea would ever meet with American officials. The radio blared forth that "the class anger of the Cambodian people against the U.S. imperialists and their running dogs is still boiling. As the Cambodian people love their independence, sovereignty, and liberty, they cannot accept the request of the U.S. imperialists to send a U.S. delegation for a visit to Democratic Kampuchea and cannot hold any meeting at any place."[90]

As news spread of brutal Khmer Rouge activity and early refugee accounts were corroborated as substantive, members of Congress and private citizens grew increasingly concerned about the reported abuses. In late March 1977, Congressman Norman Dicks of Washington wrote the president to address a "grave concern." Dicks expressed his extreme concern about human rights violations in Cambodia. The congressman wrote that "if reports I have seen are correct (and I have no reason to doubt their authenticity), atrocities are being committed now in Cambodia which rival those perpetrated in Nazi Germany during World War II." In light of the violations, Dicks urged President Carter "to take immediate diplomatic action aimed at putting an end to this revolting situation. International pressure could, and by right should, be brought to bear on the Khmer Rouge government to halt these atrocities."[91]

Oregon Representative Les AuCoin wrote the president to share his concern and the dismay of one of his constituents, a professor at Eastern Oregon State College, who believed the United States should more forcefully address the issue of genocide in Cambodia. Congressman AuCoin also made clear his own worry "about the bloodbath that has taken place" in Cambodia.[92] In December 1977, as ever more information surfaced detailing the massive violations of human rights in Cambodia, Representative Romano Mazzoli took the opportunity to press the White House. Writing critically of the communist regimes in both Cambodia and Vietnam, Mazzoli revealed his hope that "the United States will denounce—at every opportunity—the severe violations of human rights, including the senseless taking of innocent lives, occurring this day in the communist-dominated nations of Southeast Asia."[93]

Private citizens both famous and not raised their concerns about the situation in Cambodia. Illinois Representative Morgan Murphy received correspondence from a Peace Corps volunteer that was eventually forwarded to the State Department. The letter urged that U.S. intelligence work to devise "alternatives for ending the genocide in Cambodia or for bringing peace and stability to Southeast Asia."[94] Jane Fonda and Tom Hayden also sent letters to the president expressing their concern about human rights in Kampuchea.

In the Senate, a group of lawmakers on November 4, 1977, submitted a resolution to the Committee on Foreign Affairs. Sponsored among others by Senators Robert Dole, Jesse Helms, and Barry Goldwater, the resolution explained its own origin from "the moral intent of United States foreign policy" that in part seeks "to advance international human rights observance." In response to the "numerous credible accounts by refugees from Cambodia telling of countless executions and barbaric brutalities," the United States Senate strongly denounced the atrocities and killings perpetuated by the government of Democratic Kampuchea and called on the president not only to "register the deep concern of the American people about the violation of human rights in that country" but also "to cooperate with other nations, through appropriate international forums such as the United Nations, in an effort to bring the flagrant violations of human rights in Cambodia to an end."[95]

Consistent with Richard Holbrooke's initial testimony on the administration's Cambodia policy, officials responded to letters of concern about Kampuchea by stressing the drastically limited options available. Assistant Secretary of State for Congressional Relations Douglas J. Bennet Jr. answered Representative Mazzoli's letter by explaining "that the U.S. Government deplores what has taken place in Cambodia." Bennet stressed as well that the United States and Cambodia had no formal relations and that legislation already prohibited most aid. Bennet detailed humanitarian measures pursued by the Carter administration to ease suffering, including shipments of malaria medicine and resettlement assistance for refugees. However, he summarized plainly that "in the present circumstances, the United States has no leverage to affect the human rights situation in Cambodia."[96]

In response to the concerns raised by Congressman Dicks, President Carter answered with a short note thanking him for his concern. Carter highlighted his broad concern for human rights worldwide. For Cambodia specifically, however, the president noted that "at the same time, I recognize that the advancement of human rights is a complicated matter than depends upon the particular political context," a context made quite difficult given the lack of diplomatic relations between the United States and Democratic Kampuchea.[97]

Cognizant of diplomatic realities, the Carter administration nonetheless acted within the constraining sphere of U.S.-Cambodian relations. One of the administration's first steps was to request an investigation of human rights abuses in Democratic Kampuchea by the UN Human Rights Commission (UNHRC). In March 1978, the United States, Great Britain, Canada, Norway, and Australia joined Amnesty International and the International Commission of Jurists to prompt a UN initiative.

Shortly thereafter, on April 21, 1978, the president released his first formal statement addressing developments in Cambodia. In a press release roundly condemning the Khmer Rouge, Carter declared Democratic Kampuchea "the worst violator of human rights in the world today."[98] Despite the fact that the United States was still not party to the Genocide Convention (or perhaps because of it), Carter used forms of the term "genocide" twice in the statement. First, he referred to the government of Cambodia and "the genocidal policies it has implemented over the past three years." Later in the statement, Carter indicated support for a motion passed by the Canadian House of Commons that expressed horror at "the acts of genocide carried out in Cambodia." The president added that "it is an obligation of every member of the international community to protest the policies of this . . . nation which cruelly and systematically violate the right of its people to enjoy life and basic human dignities."[99] Beyond a request for broad support of an inquiry by the UNHRC and the strongly worded condemnation, the press statement included little else. Carter's pronouncement made no mention of specific actions to be taken against Democratic Kampuchea at the time or in the future.

In the course of discussions about Cambodia during a Senate Foreign Relations Committee hearing in August 1978, Senator George McGovern (D-S.D.), a longtime outspoken opponent of American involvement in Vietnam, astonished many when he proposed that the United States consider military intervention to end decisively the terror of the Khmer Rouge. McGovern explained that the use of military force should be limited to emergency cases, but in his opinion Democratic Kampuchea represented "the most extreme case I've heard of. . . . Based on the percentage of the population that appears to have died, this makes Hitler's operation look tame."[100] Although this option had little if any chance of even earning serious consideration, McGovern's argument highlighted the sense of frustration felt among those concerned about the abuses in Cambodia and aware of the limited tools available to the United States. In response to McGovern's dramatic call to action, the State Department explained that "we will do everything in our power to end the monstrous human rights situation" in Cambodia. The State Department added that the Security Council would shortly consider the UN report on the situation.

The UN report confirmed what human rights activists and thousands of refugees had suggested for some time. However, the UNHRC failed to act swiftly and decisively against the Cambodian regime, instead allowing it time to defend itself against the charges. To the surprise of no one, the Khmer Rouge denied all preliminary accusations and explained them away as nothing more than American propaganda.[101] Finally, in March 1979, a subcommission assigned to the case of Democratic Kampuchea entered its findings to the full UNHRC in Geneva. The report found that the actions of the Khmer Rouge in Cambodia "constituted nothing less than genocide," a situation "without precedent in our century except for the horror of Nazism."[102] Unfortunately, the confident and certain charges levied in the report arrived too late. Just two months earlier, in January 1979, the Vietnamese army invaded Cambodia and overthrew the Pol Pot regime.

Following the congressional hearings during the summer of 1977, the terrible situation in Cambodia continued to attract the attention of American legislators. In July 1978, a group of congressmen sponsored a letter written by New York Representative James Hanley calling on the administration to use talks with China as a means of improving conditions in Cambodia. Hanley wrote,

> Given the Cambodian government's xenophobia . . . normal avenues for temporizing the government's harshness with one exception do not exist. The exception is China,

> which maintains close ties . . . with the Cambodian government. You recently recognized this by instructing Dr. Brzezinski to repeat your April 21st statement . . . to Chinese officials during his recent trip to that country. That initial step must be carried further. We respectfully suggest that the issue of Cambodia must be included in any talks toward normalizing relations with China.[103]

Hanley stressed that the United States was approaching China in a "spirit of cooperation," which he felt the Chinese should reciprocate. He continued, "Cambodia provides the most visible area for such a demonstration, and the clearest avenue where our government can most fruitfully act to reduce the horrendous misery of the Cambodian people. We therefore hope that you will make it clear to the Chinese government that the Cambodian situation must be considered as part and parcel of any efforts for mutual cooperation between our two nations."[104]

However, the imperative of improving relations with China—strongly supported by National Security Adviser Brzezinski as a means of gaining the upper hand on the Soviets—diminished the importance of human rights in Cambodia for the Carter administration. Compared to Sino-American relations, Cambodia—even genocide there—seemed more like a distraction than anything else. The State Department responded to Congressman Hanley's concern explaining that "we believe our responsibility remains to speak out on Cambodia . . . but that it would be a serious mistake to inject Cambodian human rights violations into future US-PRC bilateral negotiations on normalization."[105] The geostrategic imperative of reestablishing relations with the People's Republic of China relegated the issue of genocide in Cambodian to secondary, even tertiary, status at best, well below the always tense issue of Taiwan.

National Security Adviser Brzezinski believed that the renewal of Sino-American relations would put the United States in better position to deal with the Soviet Union.[106] As part of that strategy, President Carter gave Brzezinski the go-ahead to travel to Beijing in May 1978. When the Carter administration decided in 1978 to pursue actively the normalization of relations with China, a new opportunity presented itself for addressing the Cambodia issue.

The China connection offered hope for pressuring the brutal regime in Phnom Penh because China was probably the one and only country capable of influencing the xenophobic Khmer Rouge leadership. Pol Pot and other Cambodian communist leaders had drawn heavily from experience of the Chinese revolution.[107] The Khmer Rouge leadership held "boundless admiration for Mao's theory of class struggle and endless revolution," and while Kampuchea divorced itself from the rest of the world, the new regime continued to accept material assistance from the Chinese, including shipments of arms and food.[108] In addition, hundreds of technical advisers from China traveled to Democratic

Kampuchea to help with matters ranging from agricultural production and military tactics to the use of railroads and factories.[109] Brzezinksi planned to focus more on the Taiwan issue during his trip to China, but many saw the meeting as a unique opportunity to raise the issue of human rights abuses in Cambodia with the Chinese leadership.

However, raising the issue and making real progress were two very different things. China traditionally resists outside pressure dealing with any human rights issues, and this reluctance extended to the Cambodia issue for a variety of reasons. As Brzezinski prepared to travel to Beijing in May 1978, Chinese leaders were rethinking the importance of their relationship with Phnom Penh, triggered by worsening relations between China and Vietnam. Territorial disputes, mistreatment of the ethnic Chinese population in Vietnam, and Hanoi's growing relationship with Moscow raised concerns in Beijing about a rift between the two nations and the growth of Soviet influence in Southeast Asia.[110]

THE KHMER ROUGE FALLS

The ouster of the Khmer Rouge by Vietnam in January 1979 and the end of the genocidal reign of Pol Pot did not elicit positive statements from Washington. Instead, reaction from Washington to the Vietnamese invasion was tempered at best, suggesting no pleasure at all in the fall of Pol Pot. At a State Department news conference, Hodding Carter III told reporters that although the United States thoroughly disapproved of the human rights abuses committed by the Khmer Rouge, nevertheless "as a matter of principle we do not feel that a unilateral intervention by a third power is justified."[111]

A week later, Secretary of State Vance reiterated his spokesman's statement, calling for the removal of foreign troops from Cambodia and urging all nations "to oppose Vietnam's actions in the name of peace."[112] The United States followed up on public pronouncements by supporting a UN Security Council resolution demanding the withdrawal of Vietnamese forces from Cambodia.

Once again, American foreign policy vis-à-vis Cambodia fell under the sizable shadow of China policy. For National Security Adviser Brzezinski, the notion of the "China card" continued to loom quite prominently in developments in Indochina. Brzezinski saw in Vietnam a Soviet proxy, and war between Vietnam and Cambodia pointed to growing tension—perhaps even the risk of direct conflict—between China and the Soviet Union. By essentially siding with the Cambodians, the United States aligned itself more closely with China and hoped to contain Soviet influence in the region. Brzezinski succeeded in persuading the more reluctant Vance and Carter that increased efforts at opening up to China would pay off.[113]

The U.S. commitment to Brzezinski's "China card" strategy faced a significant challenge in mid-February 1979, when China invaded Vietnam in response to alleged Vietnamese border aggression and their mistreatment of ethnic Chinese in Vietnam.[114] In response to China's actions, the State Department released a statement linking China's withdrawal from Vietnam with Vietnam's exit from Cambodia. Despite considerable losses at the hands of Chinese forces, the Vietnamese continued to hold firm in Cambodia. In fact, it was not at all clear to all American leaders that the collapse of the puppet regime in Cambodia best served American interests. Congressman Stephen Solarz questioned the administration's interpretation of national interests, writing that

> while the desirability of a simultaneous withdrawal of Vietnam from Cambodia and China from Vietnam is virtually self apparent, the need to prevent the restoration of the Pol Pot regime seems to have been overlooked by the Administration. What concerns us, Mr. President, is that the withdrawal of Vietnamese forces . . . would result in the re-establishment of the genocidal Pol Pot regime . . . thereby . . . guaranteeing the continued suffering of the Khmer people.[115]

Solarz suggested a step-by-step plan for Cambodia, including a cease-fire, troop withdrawals, and a UN peacekeeping force that would ensure free and fair elections.

It appears that the invasion came as no surprise at all to the United States. During Deng Xiaoping's late January visit to the United States, he told President Carter of his plans to "put a restraint on the wild ambitions of the Vietnamese and to give them an appropriate lesson."[116] The United States did respond to the February 17, 1979, Chinese attack on Vietnam by convening a special meeting of the National Security Council. At the same time, the State Department released a statement calling for both China's withdrawal from Vietnam and Vietnam's exit from Cambodia.

Despite these expressions of concern, behind the scenes the United States again pressed forward on the "China card" front, to the diminishment of policy toward Vietnam and Cambodia. When Deng informed Carter of the invasion plans in late January, the president said he could not condone such actions but quickly added that he nonetheless looked forward to developing the relationship between the two countries. As one diplomat commented, this statement made clear to China that they would not suffer for their action against Vietnam.[117] Former CIA Director Robert Gates disclosed that the United States concurrently provided periodic intelligence briefings about Soviet activity to the Chinese during their Vietnam action to help them avoid any potential retaliatory strike by the Russians.[118]

The day after the Solarz letter, the administration showed that it was not completely out of step with the representative from New York. American ambassador to the United Nations Andrew Young submitted a draft resolution to the UN Security Council requesting a cease-fire and a withdrawal of Vietnamese forces from Kampuchea. In the resolution, the United States made clear its belief that Cambodia "should be . . . truly independent and neutral with a freely chosen government which represents the will of the Kampuchean people and respects their human rights."[119]

Eventually, a compromise resolution drafted by the Association of Southeast Asian Nations (ASEAN) emerged as the favorite. It called for a cease-fire and withdrawals but without mentioning any nations by name. After a month of maneuvering and delay, mainly by the Chinese (who wanted to finish "teaching Vietnam a lesson" before agreeing to a withdrawal), the measure came to a vote in the middle of March 1979. Led by the United States, eleven other Security Council members embraced the resolution. However, to no one's surprise, the resolution met with a Soviet veto. Soviet delegate Oleg Troyanovsky argued that "the resolution shows a total disregard for the state of affairs in Kampuchea, the people of which overthrew a hateful regime."[120]

Just prior to the failure of the ASEAN resolution, President Carter delivered a foreign policy speech that included mention of the situation in Southeast Asia. Carter emphasized the limited options for American policy:

> We will not get involved in a conflict between Asian Communist states. Our national interests are not directly threatened, although we are concerned about the wider implications of what has been happening. We have been using whatever diplomatic means available to encourage restraint on all parties. . . . While our influence is limited because our involvement is limited, we remain the one great power in the world that can have direct and frank discussions with all the parties concerned.[121]

However, the imperative of the China card continued to overwhelm any real effort at such "frank discussions" with the Chinese. As historian Robert Neuringer argues, Beijing's abandonment of the Khmer Rouge was probably the only action that could have convinced Vietnam to end its occupation. Neuringer concludes bluntly (and this study supports his conclusion) that "no available evidence indicated that the United States ever put pressure on China to end its military support of what President Carter once called the 'worst violator of human rights in the world.' "[122]

In late August 1979, Vice President Walter Mondale traveled to China for talks with Deng Xiaoping. Democratic Kampuchea was on Mondale's agenda, and his staff had prepared briefing books covering the issue. The exact details of the talks are not available to the public, but the Chinese position appeared to budge ever so slightly from total support for the Pol Pot regime. Deng informed the American vice president that he could accept a Cambodian government composed of a "broad coalition of representative forces."[123] Beyond that somewhat vague statement, no real progress or pressure appears to have taken place. The administration subsequently focused efforts on assisting those who managed to escape the genocidal nightmare.

REFUGEE ASSISTANCE

Disarray in Southeast Asia, namely war-torn Vietnam and Cambodia, caused massive dislocations and an enormous refugee flow. In the United States, the media brought the story of the "boat people" into Americans' living rooms. Untold thousands of desperate people placed their faith in makeshift vessels and escaped to the high seas. At the same time, a massive human exodus took place on land as hundreds of thousands of Cambodians sought refuge in bordering Thailand, creating huge tent villages along the border of the People's Republic of China and Thailand.

The burgeoning humanitarian crisis offered the United States a new opportunity to help the Cambodian people, already suffering from famine in their homeland. The plight of Cambodia's refugees gained even wider attention following a visit to the camps in Thailand by First Lady Rosalynn Carter in November 1979. Moved by the horrible suffering she witnessed, the first lady returned to the United States and became instrumental in mobilizing a massive appeal for assistance.

The United States seized the initiative in two main ways. First, the Carter administration modified immigration restrictions to allow into the country an additional 15,000 Indochinese refugees. The administration also created an interagency task force to develop long-term solutions to refugee issues. In 1978, the United States responded to lobbying efforts from NGOs and moved to accept 25,000 more refugees from the region each year.[124] The Carter team established an American commitment to Southeast Asian refugees that endured for years. As Roger Winter, former U.S. coordinator for refugee affairs, noted in 1985, "Our nation's resettlement of over 725,000 Vietnamese, Lao, and Cambodian refugees ranks as one of the largest, most dramatic humanitarian efforts in history."[125]

As a second component of humanitarian relief, the Carter administration sought to practice their commitment to human rights by feeding Cambodians driven to desperation by chaotic political times in their homeland. However, the imperatives of realpolitik and geostrategy crept into policy, side by side with the laudable goal of helping refugees. The neediest in those camps, those most desperate for assistance, were also Khmer Rouge rebels. Not only did Khmer Rouge fighters populate many of the camps, but they also actually controlled many refugee outposts bordering Thailand. As a result, the Carter administration understood that American aid to Cambodian refugees would also mean American assistance to the Khmer Rouge.

Since the Carter national security team knew that their well-intentioned efforts at humanitarian assistance would help Cambodia's *genocidaires,* they discussed the issue and its effect on the Heng Samrin regime. Former National Security Council China expert Michel Oksenberg explains "that humanitarian assistance to the camps would help the Khmer Rouge's ability to fight the Vietnamese occupation was definitely known."[126] In the end, the Carter administration considered this double-edged assistance both a humanitarian and a geopolitical boon. Oksenberg describes it as "humanitarian relief with strategic implications that were seen as serendipitously convergent with American interests."[127] Again, the American interest involved, particularly in the view of Zbigniew Brzezinksi, was a continued "proxy war," in one interpretation, between China and its Khmer Rouge ally and the Soviet Union–Vietnam partnership. Journalist and critic John Pilger has described the resulting policy as "an extension of the Cold War, as a mechanism for U.S. revenge on Vietnam, and as part of Washington's new alliance with China, Pol Pot's principal underwriter and Vietnam's ancient foe."[128]

According to Oksenberg, he and other officials felt a certain "squeamishness" about what in essence amounted to helping Pol Pot and his rebels. Some administration officials apparently expressed more agitation than others over the policy, particularly those deeply familiar with Indochina who felt that the United States was in fact in some part responsible for the tragedies befalling the people of Vietnam and Cambodia. Still, for enough people "the strict humanitarian component of the initiative justified it while the strategic interests just happened to be congruent."[129] In the end, according to Assistant Secretary of State Richard Holbrooke, "20,000 to 40,000 Pol Pot guerrillas benefited."[130]

Administration officials raised concern publicly about the final destination of humanitarian relief. Appearing before a congressional subcommittee at the end of July 1980, American ambassador to Thailand Morton Abramowitz reported that Khmer Rouge forces were estimated from 20,000 to 40,000. According to the ambassador, the Khmer Rouge forces, "badly decimated in 1979, have recovered. They are a cohesive, disciplined fighting force with strong organization and good communications."[131] In part, Abramowitz attributed the renewal of Pol Pot's forces to Western humanitarian aid. He told the subcommittee that "a major border dilemma is assuring that relief supplies go to needy civilians in Khmer Rouge–controlled areas; not to soldiers."[132] While food aid came from the West, the Khmer Rouge were bolstered in their fight against the Heng Samrin regime by weapons from China. Geopolitics, namely in the form of the now-familiar "China card," influenced American policy once more. As one former official said, "The United States did not make a heroic effort to stop China's military supplying of the Khmer Rouge."[133]

In defense of the Carter administration and relief officials, distinguishing between Khmer Rouge and non–Khmer Rouge and denying or providing aid accordingly represented an essentially impossible logistics problem. No less a critic of U.S. policies in Southeast Asia than William Shawcross has noted that the United States and relief organizations could not deny food to Khmer Rouge rebels without simultaneously keeping it from their women and children.[134] Furthermore, the government in Thailand perceived a threat from an expansionist Vietnam and thus preferred to have a vigorous Khmer Rouge fighting and weakening the Heng Samrin regime. To this end, Thailand had little, if any, interest in restricting the flow of aid. As Robert Neuringer writes, "Many of the relief organizations wanted to cut off the feeding programs in the camps where the Khmer Rouge predominated, but the Thai government, with the acquiescence of Ambassador Abramowitz, resisted."[135]

"TO SEAT OR NOT TO SEAT": THE KHMER ROUGE AT THE UNITED NATIONS

In the fall of 1979, the Carter administration faced a symbolic but critical ethical leadership moment concerning the Khmer Rouge. As the thirty-fourth session of the UN General Assembly convened, the organization had to deal with the question of which group would represent Cambodia at the United Nations: the ousted Khmer Rouge regime of Democratic Kampuchea or the Vietnamese-imposed government of the People's Republic of Kampuchea. A third option also existed labeling the seat "vacant" until Cambodia resolved its political status.

The ASEAN nations launched the debate when they requested that the Pol Pot/Democratic Kampuchea regime be seated. Vietnam strongly protested this action, defending the legitimacy of the government of the People's Republic of Kampuchea. In response, the General Assembly turned the issue over to a special credentials committee. On September 19, 1979, that committee voted 6–3 to recommend that the General Assembly seat Pol Pot's representative. The United States, China, Belgium, Ecuador, Pakistan, and Senegal voted for Pol Pot. The Soviet Union, the Congo, and Panama voted against the Khmer Rouge.

American representative to the United Nations Robert Rosenstock said, "History contains few more abhorrent examples" of human rights abuses than the Pol Pot regime, and he stressed that U.S. support for the Khmer Rouge at the United Nations did not carry with it any implied approval or recognition of the group fighting in the jungles of Cambodia to regain power.[136] American officials explained that the committee had determined that the credentials of Democratic Kampuchea were "clearly in accordance with the General Assembly rules of procedure and . . . that in the absence of a clearly superior claim, the General Assembly should continue to seat a government whose credentials were accepted at the last session."[137] The United States consistently argued publicly that the question was in large part a technical and legal issue, quite distinct from moral sanction for one regime or another.

For their part, the Soviets did not demand that the Heng Samrin regime receive the seat but instead indicated that they would accept a proposal forwarded by the Congo that the seat in the General Assembly be left vacant. The vacant-seat option had gained at least nominal momentum when it was accepted earlier in September 1979 in Havana by the Conference of Nonaligned Nations.

When the General Assembly convened again to address the issue, the debate occasionally lost its "diplomatic" tone. Vietnam's representative lashed out at the Pol Pot regime, which had abused and murdered many Vietnamese. The representative from Vietnam called the Khmer Rouge "a phantom government, a gang of criminals who have committed the crime of genocide against their own people."

Singapore Ambassador Tommy Koh, defending the ASEAN position, conceded Democratic Kampuchea's poor record on human rights but failed to accept that as reason enough to dislodge the regime from the United Nations. The ambassador argued that rejecting the Khmer Rouge would help establish an unfortunate precedent for the notion of humanitarian intervention that would make the world "an ever more dangerous one for smaller states."[138] Singapore and other nations feared that a vote to replace Pol Pot's representatives with delegates sent to the United Nations by the Heng Samrin government would suggest tacit support for Vietnam's invasion of Cambodia and the installation of a puppet regime—the wrong message for other potentially aggressive nations considering invasion under the guise of humanitarian concerns. Singapore's representative argued that "such a doctrine . . . would harm small, weak nations whose survival could be endangered by more powerful neighbors invoking human rights violations as a pretext for intervention."[139]

Realizing they could not win outright representation for the Heng Samrin regime, Vietnam and the Soviet Union pushed the vacant-seat option. The India delegation, led by Ambassador S. N. Mishra, introduced the vacant-seat approach, explaining that it stemmed from discussions at the nonaligned nations' meeting earlier in the month. However, Yugoslavia, Senegal, Singapore, and other members of the nonaligned movement opposed the compromise. The General Assembly ruled that it would merit consideration only if the recommendation of the Credentials Committee was rejected. For its part, the United States maintained a low profile during the debate and chose not to promote the vacant-seat option. Although not perfect, this "middle ground" route offered a fairly neutral position and a way of legitimizing neither the Pol Pot regime nor the Vietnam puppet government of Heng Samrin.

However, the vacant-seat option could not vacate visions of geostrategy from the minds of key American policymakers. Brzezinksi believed that the vacant-seat formula "would imply wavering on the part of those who had gone on record against the illegal Vietnamese occupation. Both the opponents and defenders of Vietnamese . . . aggression in Kampuchea . . . have viewed the empty seat formula as a step toward the legitimization of the regime the Vietnamese imposed."[140] Brzezinski firmly held that the maintenance of good relations between the United States, China, and ASEAN should shape the American position on the Cambodia seat.

Although Secretary of State Vance ultimately sided with Brzezinksi, he struggled to square support for the Khmer Rouge at the United Nations with the broader imperatives of the administration's human rights agenda. Vance reveals in his memoirs, *Hard Choices,* that he deliberated the issue for weeks, during which time UN Ambassador Donald McHenry and Assistant Secretary of State for Human Rights Patricia Derian "argued passionately for a vote against Pol Pot." McHenry took a strong position that the United States should not follow a traditional path of geopolitics and should instead embrace the more moral side of the issue by favoring new human rights norms.[141] However, the arguments of three other advisers and the pressure of ASEAN proved definitive in Vance's final choice. Vance explained his support for the seating of the Khmer Rouge, writing,

> We faced a difficult choice. We were being asked to vote for the continued seating of one of history's most barbarous regimes. . . . Yet there were compelling reasons to consider the vote carefully. ASEAN had the full support of Japan, Australia, New Zealand, and China, which of course saw Hanoi as Moscow's surrogate in Southeast Asia. From Bangkok, our brilliant ambassador, Morton Abramowitz, who had played a vital role in refugee policy, argued the strategic consequences of not siding with ASEAN. From Peking, Leonard Woodcock, a humane and wise man, came down on the same side. Dick Holbrooke, collecting views from the entire region, concluded that the vote not to seat the DK would gain us nothing and cost us much.[142]

Vance concluded that "unpleasant as it was to contemplate voting . . . for the Khmer Rouge, we could not afford the far-reaching consequences of a vote that would isolate us from all of ASEAN, Japan, China [and] our ANZUS treaty partners."[143] He "figuratively held his nose" and instructed the U.S. mission at the United Nations to vote for the Pol Pot regime but to also make clear that the vote was based on "technical grounds" and in no way reflected "support or recognition . . . or approval of its atrocious practices."[144]

As then Assistant Secretary of State for International Organizations Charles William Maynes explains, the Carter administration found itself forced to confront "the inexorable and pitiless logic of sovereignty."[145] The key norm in the international system was—and to a large extent still is—the sanctity of borders, and the United Nations exists in large part to affirm this cornerstone of world order. However, the emergent postwar international system also placed increasing emphasis on new norms dealing with human rights, such as the prevention of the crime of genocide. According to Maynes, U.S. officials recognized the clashing norms and spoke openly about the difficult, perhaps irresolvable, "normative conflict."[146]

On September 21, 1979, with an ethical leadership moment staring it straight in the face, the United States joined the majority in voting to seat Democratic Kampuchea by a vote of 71–35, with thirty-four nations abstaining. American representative Richard Petree stressed that U.S. support for the Pol Pot delegates in no way condoned the atrocities of the Khmer Rouge regime. Petree noted that Heng Samrin's government also deserved condemnation for abysmal human rights practices and its failure to deal with the terrible famine ravaging the country. Finally, Petree added that "at this moment [the Vietnamese] invasion forces have embarked on a new offensive which can only increase the suffering of the Cambodian people."[147] The vote was considered a victory for China, both in its rift with the Soviet Union and as Pol Pot's strongest supporter. The noncommunist ASEAN states also won given their increasing alarm over the threat of Vietnamese military control spreading throughout the region.

The controversy over Cambodian credentials at the United Nations emerged in 1980 as the thirty-fifth session of the General Assembly prepared to convene. Once again, the United States found itself in a difficult position, but with a new opportunity to remove itself from even minimal association with a genocidal regime. The United States first had to deal with statements by new Khmer Rouge Premier Khieu Samphan that provided potentially embarrassing public relations for the Carter administration, particularly as the 1980 presidential election drew near. Interviewed at a hidden camp near the Thai-Cambodian border in early August, the Khmer Rouge leader openly thanked the United States for its diplomatic support at the United Nations and requested that it continue. "This is a just and clear-sighted stand," Khieu Samphan said, "And we thank the U.S. warmly."[148] Such "warm thanks" from the leader of the Khmer Rouge hit the headlines in the United States and drew renewed attention to the issue of seating the ousted and notorious regime in the General Assembly.

In response, the State Department disputed Khieu Samphan's statement that the United States actually supported the Khmer Rouge. A spokesman called the Pol Pot regime's record on human rights "wholly reprehensible" and explained that the U.S. vote to seat the Khmer Rouge at the United Nations was based on a "purely technical point" largely due to the fact that the competing Heng Samrin government was "a puppet . . . a creature of Vietnamese aggression" with no legitimate claim on Cambodia.[149] In terms of domestic politics, scars from the war with Vietnam were still fresh, and for many Hanoi posed a very real threat to Southeast Asia. Any move that even appeared to accept in any way Vietnamese aggression would face significant criticisms in much of Congress and in large segments of the population.

While Vietnamese occupiers still held power in Phnom Penh and the Khmer Rouge hid in the jungle, the other voting options received renewed scrutiny. Congressmen and American relief organizations working in Cambodia pressured the administration to support the vacant-seat formula or simply to abstain from the General Assembly vote. In a letter to President Carter, the National Council of Churches made clear its opposition to support of any kind for the Khmer Rouge:

> Clearly, the U.S. vote on the credentials question is a moral issue. Technical and geopolitical arguments can be made for one position or another, but it seems imperative that the U.S. sees this as an opportunity to acknowledge—indeed to affirm—the reality that a particularly heinous regime has fallen from power, no longer exercises effective control of the Kampuchean people or territory and is not deserving of the legitimizing prestige afforded by the retention of the UN seat.[150]

By this time, Edmund Muskie had taken over at the State Department following Cyrus Vance's resignation in the aftermath of the aborted attempted rescue of the American hostages in Iran. Muskie struggled with the issue, too, and apparently was "keen to follow the departing Secretary Vance's advice and abstain in the UN vote for Pol Pot's credentials."[151] However, facing continued pressure from China, ASEAN, and Brzezinski, Muskie agreed to a U.S. vote in favor of Democratic Kampuchea.[152]

Following the vote, U.S. ambassador to the United Nations Donald McHenry sought to moderate the perception of American support for Pol Pot, announcing that "we condemn unequivocally the savage human rights violations that have taken place under the Pol Pot regime." However, in a statement that better suited a position of abstention, the ambassador also added that "the regime that now seeks to supplant Democratic Kampuchea is also open to condemnation. It is the creation of and dependent for its survival on the military forces of Vietnam whose invasion and occupation of Kampuchea are in violation of internationally recognized principles."[153]

Three weeks after the vote, Jimmy Carter would fail to win reelection against Ronald Reagan. Thus, as its last significant policy vis-à-vis Cambodia, the Carter administration again voted in favor of the ousted Khmer Rouge regime at the United Nations.

POSTGENOCIDE JUSTICE

Justice for Cambodia and the victims of the Pol Pot regime has been elusive. In large part, postgenocide accountability in Cambodia has been sacrificed to the imperative of peace. Despite the brutality and scale of the Khmer Rouge crimes against their own country, after twenty years of instability and suffering many Cambodians want to move on with a clean break from the past. As former Congressman Stephen Solarz has noted, the dilemma for the Cambodian nation is "what is the higher priority, justice or peace and stability." However, the two options need not be mutually exclusive. In 1995, the Cambodian ambassador to the United States asserted that his nation must seek some accountability in order to reach lasting reconciliation and peace. Ambassador Huoth stated, "Every Cambodian is more or less a victim of Pol Pot."[154] In early 2001, the Cambodian legislature approved a plan for a hybrid national/international tribunal for Khmer Rouge leaders, but it took quite a long time to get there.

The United States has moved slowly to help punish Democratic Kampuchea's *genocidaires.* For quite some time, still caught up in the geopolitical gamesmanship of the time, the United States failed to pursue the Khmer Rouge leadership and in ways continued to support them indirectly during their jungle exile. The basic story of the United States and efforts at postgenocide accountability in Cambodia spans decades, and intervening issues include the establishment of the UN Transitional Authority in Cambodia (UNTAC) to promote the development of free elections and democratic institutions, several civil crises in Cambodia, and continued violence from rebel forces, including the Khmer Rouge. Although fascinating and gripping, the purpose here is not to document the history of U.S.-Cambodian relations but to focus on American efforts to address Khmer Rouge crimes.

Like most issues in Southeast Asia (beyond the POW/MIA hot button), little news from Cambodia captures American attention. The work of UNTAC and ongoing civil strife from time to time emerged on the media's radar, but for the most part Cambodia simply did not (and usually does not) garner consistent front-page coverage. Despite the dearth of media coverage, NGOs made a concerted effort to see that the United States and other world powers addressed issues surrounding the Khmer Rouge and their responsibility for Cambodia's genocidal calamity. Disturbing to many was the fact that language describing the Khmer Rouge regime as genocidal was omitted from a draft peace plan promoted by the United States and the rest of the UN Security Council. For negotiators, mentioning genocide and atrocities by the Khmer Rouge was seen as counterproductive to reaching a settlement.[155] In particular, the Campaign to Oppose the Return of the Khmer Rouge (CORKR) stood out as a group strongly committed to a democratic future in Cambodia and dedicated to "progressive change in U.S. policy towards Cambodia."

Founded in 1989, CORKR emerged as an offshoot of the Asian Resource Center, functioning independently with its own budget and staff. Much like the Ad Hoc Committee during the debate over the UNGC, CORKR represented over 100 NGOs, including the American Friends Service Committee, Oxfam America, the Union of American Hebrew Congregations, the Maryknoll Fathers, and the Federation of American Scientists. Among its agenda items were ending Thai military assistance to the Khmer Rouge, ending American aid and trade embargoes against Cambodia, expanding humanitarian assistance to Cambodia, and fighting the return to power in any form of the Khmer Rouge.

The organization achieved significant success with the drafting and passage of the Cambodian Genocide Justice Act. The group enlisted the supported of Virginia Senator Charles Robb and, following a concerted lobbying campaign, saw the initiative passed by the U.S. Congress in April 1994. Said Senator Robb, "There is no statute of limitations on genocide."[156] The act outlined the U.S. commitment, consistent with international law, "to bring to justice members of the Khmer Rouge for their crimes against humanity committed in Cambodia between April 17, 1975 and January 7, 1979." It also called on the United States to "assist appropriate organizations and individuals to collect relevant data on crimes of genocide committed in Cambodia" and "to encourage the establishment of a national or international criminal tribunal for the prosecution of those accused of genocide in Cambodia."

As a result of the Cambodian Genocide Justice Act, the State Department awarded $500,000 to the Cambodian Genocide Program (CGP) at Yale University.[157] The CGP, behind the leadership of scholar Ben Kiernan, undertook the task of documenting the killings in Cambodia during the Pol Pot years. The Cambodian Genocide Program specifically aims: "1) to collect and study all extant information about this period in Cambodian history; 2) make this information available to a court or tribunal willing to prosecute Cambodian war criminals; and 3) generate a critical, analytic understanding of genocide which can be marshaled in the prevention of political violence against populations elsewhere in the world."[158]

Following its inception, the CGP helped create an independent partner located in Cambodia, the Documentation Center of Cambodia (DC-CAM), to work on training and field research to advance the goals of the CGP. The DC-CAM has since developed into a Cambodian NGO, serving as a central point for the study of the Khmer Rouge regime and as a resource for Cambodians seeking to pursue legal redress for genocide and crimes against humanity committed by the Pol Pot regime. Through the year 2001, the CGP will provide funds for DC-CAM to continue its work. In the meantime, the center has pursued other sources of funding to continue its work, including a grant of $50,000 from the Norwegian government.

The material collected by the CGP and DC-CAM to this point represents the best collection of Khmer Rouge archives in the world. They include the "Million Documents," information containing upward of one million signatures from individuals and families surveyed in the immediate aftermath of the genocide about their losses. In 1996, researchers from DC-CAM uncovered a cache of material documenting the horrors at the infamous Khmer Rouge prison at Tuol Seng. Over 10,000 pages of material reveal the inner workings at the regime's primary torture and interrogation center. The same year, the Documentation Center obtained over 100,000 pages of records from the Santebal, the Khmer Rouge security ministry. The archive reveals Khmer Rouge planning for political violence and details the nationwide scope of the genocide and its centralized organization. Given the poor condition of the primary materials, the CGP has begun to microfilm, photocopy, and digitally store the material.[159]

In addition, to publicize their activity and make findings and data available to the public, the CGP produces CD-ROM databases and also made records available via the World Wide Web. Visitors to <http://www.yale.edu/cgp> can access almost the entire CGP database, from Khmer Rouge security files and interrogation lists from prisons to photographs of still-unidentified victims and excerpts from the diary of regime leader Ieng Sary. The innovative Web site and search engine earned the Internet Site of the Day award by *Academe Today,* the on-line version of *the Chronicle of Higher Education,* and received coverage on the Cable News Network and in the *New York Times.*[160]

The CGP assembles all the collected material to create "a comprehensive map of the terror apparatus overseen by the Khmer Rouge regime." To this end, the CGP had developed a computerized map of the prisons, torture and execution centers, and mass grave sites in Cambodia. This evidence will be integral to the success of the planned tribunal.

The CGP mandate also includes a two-part training component. First, experts travel to Cambodia to assist in the training of Documentation Center staff. Staff learn the bibliographic, database, and preservation skills necessary for the maintenance of a professional physical and electronic archive. The second component involves legal training for Cambodians. In conjunction with the Schell Center for International Human Rights at the Yale University Law School, the CGP has held legal training courses that cover basic principles for international law pertaining to genocide, crimes against humanity, and other war crimes; legal enforcement mechanisms; and due process and evidentiary requirements. One session held in Phnom Penh during the summer of 1996 focused on the practical issues involved in holding a tribunal or truth commission.[161] Training included discussions about legal accountability for the crimes of 1975–79 with members of the Cambodian National Assembly and officials from the executive branch. Among higher-level talks, CGP Director Ben Kiernan and DC-CAM Director Youk Chhang met with Vice Prime Minister Sar Kheng and His Majesty King Norodom Sihanouk to explore legal options. According to the CGP, Sihanouk made clear his preference for a UN Ad Hoc International Criminal Tribunal to be held in Phnom Penh.[162]

Of course, any trial or tribunal, whether ad hoc or under the direction of a functioning international criminal court, requires the apprehension of alleged perpetrators. Pol Pot captured attention in the Western media again in the summer of 1997. As the Khmer Rouge suffered military defeats at the hands of the government and wrangled with internal dissent, Pol Pot's former followers mutinied against him. As Pol Pot's captors held him prisoner in their jungle stronghold, the United States and other countries engaged in discussions about possible extradition and a trial on charges of genocide. On June 21, 1997, Secretary of State Madeleine Albright reportedly suggested to Canada's minister of external relations, Lloyd Axworthy, that his nation's war crimes statute could provide the legal mechanism for the extradition and prosecution of Pol Pot. However, a ministry spokesperson several days later backed away from any such commitment, suggesting that the appropriate legal structure was not in place.[163]

In addition, the Cambodian leadership at the time, a dual prime ministership between Prince Norodom Ranariddh (son of Sihanouk) and Hun Sen, had their own reasons to prefer no trial. Ranariddh led a rebel royalist faction that cooperated with the Khmer Rouge in military action against the Hanoi-installed Heng Samrin regime. For his part, Hun Sen was formerly a Khmer Rouge leader who defected and rose to head the Vietnamese client regime in Phnom Penh.[164] Both men, therefore, had reason to view a trial as potentially embarrassing and revealing of their own mixed political histories.

Some observers suggest that in such a trial the United States, too, would suffer embarrassment and face difficult questions about its previous conduct in the region. "There's certainly a major American responsibility for this whole situation," says Stephen Heder, a Cambodia scholar at London's School of Oriental and African Studies. According to Heder, "A war crimes trial could have posed a problem for the U.S. because it could have raised questions about U.S. bombing from 1969 through 1973."[165]

Such concerns dissipated somewhat when Pol Pot's captors put him on "trial" for the deaths of hundreds of thousands of his countrymen. In fact, the movement against Pol Pot had little to do with concern over his genocidal actions from 1975 to 1979 but instead centered on the murder of the former Khmer Rouge defense minister and his family in a Pol Pot–ordered purge. The resulting show trial—in large part a political move designed to remake the image of the Khmer Rouge—sentenced Pol Pot to "life imprisonment."[166] As part of that effort to reach out to Cambodians and the West, Pol Pot's captors allowed him to be interviewed on October 16, 1997, for the first time in almost twenty years.

That interview, with journalist Nate Thayer, appeared in various forms in the *Washington Post,* the *Far Eastern Economic Review,* and the *Wall Street Journal.* Pol Pot essentially denied his complicity in genocide, saying "we had no reason to kill our own people." He stressed that the Khmer Rouge had saved Cambodia from being swallowed by the Vietnamese in 1975. When pressed on the issue of the infamous Tuol Sleng prison, where an estimated 16,000 Cambodians were tortured and executed, Pol Pot called it a Vietnamese fabrication. Tuol Seng is now a museum, dedicated to documenting the horror of Pol Pot's regime, complete with a collection of the skulls of victims. Pol Pot explained this away, saying "when you look closely . . . they are smaller than the skulls of the Cambodian people."

Finally, as Thayer puts it, Pol Pot consistently turned attention away from genocide and crimes against humanity and instead "sought to elicit sympathy for his own tribulations." The leader of a genocidal regime explained to Thayer that "you look at me from the outside and you don't know what I have suffered." He continued by running down a list of his health problems, ranging from heart disease and a stroke to chronic malaria and respiratory difficulties. He said he passed his time with his wife, with his twelve-year-old daughter, and by listening to the Voice of America on the radio.

In the spring of 1998, less than a year later, the news for Pol Pot was much worse. As the Khmer Rouge's position had deteriorated even further, reports recirculated that they were working out a deal to hand him over to international authorities. As the Khmer Rouge movement continued to fracture and fall apart in the face of government offensives in the spring of 1998, the Clinton administration put into motion preliminary plans for the potential arrest of senior Khmer Rouge officials. Ambassador-at-Large for War Crimes Issues David Scheffer had long sought more concerted American effort to bring the leaders of the Pol Pot regime to justice. He had first raised the issue while working as special adviser to Madeleine Albright during her tenure as U.S. ambassador to the United Nations.

According to administration officials, President Clinton responded to developments in Cambodia by ordering the State, Defense, and Justice Departments on April 8 to prepare contingency plans for the arrest and trial of Pol Pot. Thailand apparently told the United States that it would be willing to take Pol Pot into custody provided that the United States quickly move him out of the country. American military officials considered the Northern Marianas Islands, Wake Island, and the naval base at Guantanamo Bay in Cuba as possible interim holding sites for Pol Pot.[167]

According to the *New York Times,* American military intelligence reported that Thai forces actually captured the former Khmer Rouge dictator but subsequently released him. The report suggested that the Thai leadership "may have feared that his capture would antagonize China, long an ally of the Khmer Rouge, and would complicate the foreign policy of Thailand's recently installed government, which is already struggling with an economic crisis."[168] Officials at the State Department Office for War Crimes Issues could not confirm that report.[169] Overall, the Clinton administration viewed the reported developments as perhaps the best chance to get Pol Pot up to that point. Said one American official, "If we don't get Pol Pot this time, he may die before we even have the chance to bring him to justice."[170]

As government forces closed in on him and former followers discussed handing him over to an international tribunal, Pol Pot managed to elude justice for good—he died on April 15, 1998, at age seventy-three. After suffering from malaria and the aftereffects of a stroke, the founder of the Khmer Rouge movement apparently died of a heart attack. His wife discovered that he had passed away when she went to arrange the mosquito net around his cot.[171] Although some questioned the curious timing of Pol Pot's demise, five foreign journalists were given access to the Khmer Rouge camp. They confirmed that the body was that of Pol Pot and saw no visible signs of foul play.

The death of the Khmer Rouge's "Brother Number One" did not mean the death of U.S. efforts at postgenocide accountability. Attending a Latin American summit in Santiago, Chile, President Clinton released a statement that said, "Although the opportunity to hold Pol Pot accountable for his monstrous crimes appears to have passed, senior Khmer Rouge, who exercised leadership from 1975 to 1979, are still at large and share responsibility for the monstrous human rights abuses committed during this period. We must not permit the death of the most notorious of the Khmer Rouge leaders to deter us from the equally important task of bringing these others to justice."[172] Over the course of the following week or so, the United States continued to energize its efforts to bring Khmer Rouge officials to trial.

The State Department commissioned legal experts to explore the best legal options and prepare indictments of key leaders for crimes against humanity and genocide. In addition, the United States formally requested that the Cambodian government not offer amnesty to any senior Khmer Rouge officials. According to the State Department's Office for War Crimes Issues, work continues to bring to justice figures such as Nuon Chea, Pol Pot's second in command; Ta Mok, renowned Khmer Rouge military leader; and Khieu Samphan, official president of the Pol Pot regime.[173] After months of discussion in the year 2000, Cambodian leaders and UN officials reached tentative agreement on proposed trials of Khmer Rouge leaders.

Months of discussion and deadlock were broken by the intervention of United States Senator John Kerry (D-Mass.). Kerry worked to bridge the considerable gap between Cambodia's concerns about sovereignty and UN fears about

Cambodia's politicized judiciary. The "Kerry compromise" establishes a tribunal framework that calls for both national and international judges to participate. Although more Cambodian judges will preside, decisions will require a supermajority (say, five out of seven) meaning that some UN representatives will have to concur.

The tribunal deal, originally reached in July, was approved by the Cambodian National Assembly on January 2, 2001, and by Cambodia's senate less than two weeks later. Despite approving of the deal, Cambodian Prime Minister Hun Sen argues that former Khmer Rouge Foreign Minister Ieng Sary should not be brought to trail on charges of genocide. Sary was sentenced to death in absentia in 1979 along with Pol Pot during the "show trial" and subsequently received amnesty from King Sihanouk after he defected to join the government in 1996. According to Hun Sen, Ieng Sary should not be convicted twice for the same crime. Meanwhile, discussions continue between the United Nations and Cambodia to ensure proper oversight and adequate prosecutional power for a tribunal that will, it is hoped, get under way before 2002.

CONCLUSION

The story of the United States and genocide in Cambodia is a tale replete with conflicting motives and goals, challenging contexts, and mixed results. As genocide gripped the war-ravaged nation of Cambodia in 1975, the United States faced a particularly daunting human rights and foreign policy challenge. Unlike news in today's world of instant and mass media and communications, word of the unfolding genocide in Cambodia developed slowly—but surely. The efforts of the Khmer Rouge to close their nation off from the rest of the world and to prevent horrified Cambodians from departing meant that information trickled out and its reliability was questioned. The backdrop of East-West tension further impeded a clear picture from developing quickly. Some on the left questioned the motive of Cold Warriors who charged massive human rights violations, while other observers came across as perhaps too sympathetic to the Pol Pot regime because it had overthrown a repressive right-wing government.

However, even had news about the human rights debacle come fast and furious, it seems unlikely that too much more could have been done in a preventive way. Cambodia was not receiving American aid to begin with, and the Pol Pot regime refused outside assistance. In the aftermath of a bruising experience in Indochina, military intervention by the United States simply fell well outside the realm of reality. Therefore, the United States had to resort to other avenues—public diplomacy, humanitarian assistance to refugees, and postgenocide justice initiatives—in order to take a stand on genocide in Democratic Kampuchea. Still not a signatory to the Genocide Convention, the United States was under no international legal obligation to act. Obliged or not, support of the prevention clause of the UNGC was a nonissue. However, the Carter administration had proclaimed its staunch commitment to the promotion of human rights around the world, and as news about the situation in Cambodia emerged, the crisis cried out for attention and resolution. Still, the United States stumbled, even with options well short of intervention.

In the midst of Cold War conflict, sovereignty maintained its grip as the primary norm of the international system. Therefore, a potent combination of traditional concern for national boundaries and geopolitical imperatives of the Cold War led the Carter administration to step away from an important public stance against the Pol Pot regime. The vote to seat the Pol Pot government at the United Nations stands out prominently as a lost opportunity for an important symbolic and public stand in favor of the goals of the UNGC. The Cambodian credentials issue presented the United States with a prime ethical leadership moment and a fairly "affordable" policy option with which to strengthen at least minimally the UNGC. Instead, a weak but morally significant norm took the backseat to U.S. concerns about renewed relations with China and the interests of the ASEAN nations. Although not wholly unreasonable, the power and primacy of these interests nonetheless stand as a disappointment for those urging American leadership in the struggle against perpetrators of genocide and crimes against humanity.

Lurking realpolitik also dulled the shine on the generous American program of assistance to Cambodian refugees. The United States provided invaluable help to desperate Cambodians fleeing the lethal regime in their homeland. In fact, the food aid that was provided and the relaxation of immigration restrictions were some of the only substantive actions the United States *could* take in response to the genocide. However, given the omnipresent Cold War issues and jockeying—especially in the mind of National Security Adviser Brzezinski—even this lofty and laudable project suffered from a slight taint. On the one hand, the United States perhaps deserves extra praise for providing assistance to refugees despite the fact that Khmer Rouge rebels were among their numbers. Yet, while some aid agencies and administration officials expressed consternation over supplying aid to the despicable Pol Potists, others in the Carter administration saw a distinct foreign policy benefit in helping the rebels. Under this logic, well-fed Khmer Rouge fighters would pose a much greater internal challenge to the Vietnamese-installed government in Phnom Penh at the time. One must give praise where praise is due, but it would be naive to ignore the murky constellation of motives behind so seemingly benign an operation as aid to refugees.

More norm-building efforts have taken place as the Cambodian genocide recedes further and further in history and memory. With the Cold War now in the background and the Khmer Rouge weaker and increasingly divided, more opportunities have presented themselves in the area of postgenocide justice. Unfortunately, by letting too much time pass, the international community allowed Pol Pot himself to pass away before he could stand trial for his egregious crimes. Many prominent Khmer Rouge leaders responsible for the program of genocide remain at large, and the death of Pol Pot in no way diminishes the importance of apprehending and prosecuting them, nor should it diminish plans and efforts to do so.

Projects such as the U.S.-supported Cambodia Genocide Justice Act and the resulting Cambodian Genocide Program at Yale University are important benchmarks and starting points. Both the collection of information about the genocide and the documentation of material revealing the systematic, ordered nature of the crime are essential to successful prosecution of the remaining Khmer Rouge leadership. With the tribunal agreement reached by Cambodia and the United Nations (pending details), the data and evidence collected can finally be put to use in the name of justice.

American foreign policy initiatives demonstrate that the UNGC does matter to the United States. The normative content of the UNGC resonates with the United States. Therefore, the United States pressed throughout the 1990s and into the new century for a UN tribunal to try those accused of genocide and crimes against humanity, in large part because of inadequacies in the local justice system that could jeopardize the fairness and credibility of a domestic tribunal. The efforts of American officials such as David Scheffer and John Kerry have made an important difference. One hopes that Cambodian and UN officials working on the tribunal will exercise similar leadership.

The tale of the United States, Cambodia, and the promotion of a norm of genocide prevention and prosecution of offenders offers a lesson in humility and context. History shows that despite its intentions and power, the United States could do little if anything to stop the genocidal rampage of the Khmer Rouge regime. The only potentially effective option, military intervention, had no grounding whatsoever in the domestic and international political realities of the mid-1970s.

Instead, to act as a "norm entrepreneur" and advance the cause of human rights in general and the UNGC in particular, the United States had to turn to secondary outlets—the United Nations and humanitarian assistance. Unfortunately, in the one overtly public posture the United States could assume and most clearly send a message, leadership in the realm of international ethics was sacrificed to geostrategy. Certainly, the administration had at least defensible reasons for voting to maintain the Khmer Rouge at the United Nations. Newly opened relations with China and the influence of the noncommunist ASEAN bloc of nations merited serious consideration in any regional initiative. Still,

Zbigniew Brzezinski seemed to oversell the proxy-war thesis and cared little for the repugnant public position that such Cold War jostling would require. Secretary of State Vance proved himself far more aware of the moral trade-off forced on the United States by the imperatives of realpolitik. By refusing to opt for an abstention or a vacant-seat option, the United States failed to take advantage of a leadership moment to provide powerful rhetorical support to human rights norms.

In large part, the American response to genocide in Cambodia can be explained as a straightforward, "realist" case of "interests"—unwillingness to jeopardize U.S. resources and potential Cold War advantages in the name of relatively new and weak human rights concerns and initiatives. However, over time, the moral imperatives laid out in the discourse of the Carter administration have grown stronger. The United States eventually signed the Genocide Convention. The world community continues its work to establish an International Criminal Court. Overall, the community of nations has expressed less willingness to allow states to commit atrocities against their own people and hide behind the dominant norms of sovereignty and nonintervention. Specific contextual changes matter as well, including the end of the Cold War and the increasing weakness of the Khmer Rouge in Cambodia. The crack in this door has opened a bit wider for incremental norm building supported and even led by the United States. As this chapter illustrates, international ethical evolution often takes time. The slow pace of these normative developments does not, however, diminish their importance. The postgenocide work by the United States in the pursuit of justice and accountability highlights the fact that the ideas of the UNGC matter and challenge the prevailing structure of international anarchy.

Overall, the Cambodian tragedy tested the Carter administration's attempt to retool American foreign policy and its rhetoric of human rights. The failure to take even minimal steps against the genocidal Pol Pot regime during its reign, followed decades later by initiatives aimed at bringing those responsible for the atrocities to justice, hinted at a broader policy pattern of relative inaction during the genocide and judicial action in the aftermath. The scourge of genocide reawakened almost twenty years later on two different continents, and the United States once again had serious political and moral choices to make that would influence not just American policy but also the development of important norms contained in the Genocide Convention.

NOTES

1. Arnold R. Isaacs, *Without Honor: Defeat in Vietnam and Cambodia* (Baltimore: The Johns Hopkins University Press, 1983), 195.

2. Isaacs, 203.
3. Isaacs, 203.
4. Isaacs, 285.
5. François Ponchaud, *Cambodia: Year Zero* (New York: Holt, Rinehart and Winston, 1978), 18–22.
6. John Barron and Anthony Paul, *Murder of a Gentle Land: The Untold Story of Communist Genocide in Cambodia* (New York: Reader's Digest Press, 1977), 16–36.
7. Barron and Paul, 138.
8. Quoted in Isaacs, 285.
9. See note 8.
10. Isaacs, 138.
11. Isaacs, 288.
12. Kenneth Quinn, "Explaining the Terror," in Karl D. Jackson, ed., *Cambodia, 1975–1978: Rendezvous with Death* (Princeton, N.J.: Princeton University Press, 1989), 75–77.
13. Kimmo Kiljunen, ed., *Kampuchea: Decade of the Genocide, Report of a Finnish Inquiry Commission* (London: Zed Books, 1984), 18.
14. Speaking French, the language of former colonial power France, also usually meant death. This was brought to life dramatically in *The Killing Fields* as Dith Pran struggled to avoid speaking French and revealing himself as a "threat" to the Khmer vision.
15. Leo Kuper, *Genocide: Its Political Use in the Twentieth Century* (New Haven, Conn.: Yale University Press, 1981), 157.
16. United Nations, Subcommission on Prevention of Discrimination and Protection of Minorities, E/CN.4/Sub.2/Add. 1–10, January 30, 1979.
17. Ben Kiernan, *The Pol Pot Regime: Race, Power, and Genocide in Cambodia under the Khmer Rouge, 1975–79* (New Haven, Conn.: Yale University Press, 1996), 460. See also Ben Kiernan, "The Cambodian Genocide," in George J. Andreopoulos, ed., *Genocide: Conceptual and Historical Dimensions* (Philadelphia: University of Pennsylvania Press, 1994), 191.
18. These three groups fall under the definition of genocide in Article II of the UNGC, which specifies that "genocide means acts committed with the intent to destroy, in whole or in part, a national, ethnical, racial, or religious group, as such" (UN GAOR Res. 260A [III], December 9, 1948).
19. Karl Jackson, ed., *Cambodia 1975–1978* (Princeton, N.J.: Princeton University Press, 1989), 191.
20. Jackson, 68–71.
21. Chanthou Boua, "Genocide of a Religioius Group: Pol Pot and Cambodia's Buddhist Monks," in V. Schlapentokh, C. Vanderpool, T. Bushnell, and J. Sundram, eds., *State-Organized Terror: The Case of Violent Internal Repression* (Boulder, Colo.: Westview Press, 1991), quoted in Kiernan, "The Cambodian Genocide," 197.
22. Kiernan, "The Cambodian Genocide," 198.
23. See note 22.
24. Elizabeth Becker, *When the War Was Over: The Voices of Cambodia's Revolution and Its People* (New York: Simon and Schuster, 1986), 262–63.
25. Becker, 199.
26. Jean Lacouture, "The Bloodiest Revolution," *New York Review of Books,* March 31, 1977.
27. David R. Hawk, "International Human Rights Law and Democratic Kampuchea,"

in David A. Ablin and Marlowe Hood, eds., *The Cambodian Agony* (London: M. E. Sharpe, 1987), 138.

28. Kiernan, "The Cambodian Genocide," 201.

29. Hawk, 138.

30. See note 29.

31. See note 29.

32. See note 29.

33. Letter from Professor David Weissbrodt to Senator William Proxmire, April 19, 1979, 5, quoted in Hawk, 140.

34. Hawk, 140.

35. William Shawcross, *Sideshow: Kissinger, Nixon and the Destruction of Cambodia* (New York: Simon & Schuster, 1979), 214.

36. See note 35.

37. Quoted in Shawcross.

38. Note that it is not the intention of this chapter to detail the illegal and unconstitutional employment of force by the Nixon administration in Cambodia and the attempts made to keep such actions secret, including the altering of official documents.

39. Shawcross, *Sideshow,* 272, 291.

40. See note 39.

41. Shawcross, *Sideshow,* 396.

42. Kiernan, *The Pol Pot Regime,* 16.

43. Kiernan, *The Pol Pot Regime,* 19.

44. Kate G. Frieson, "The Impact of Revolution on Cambodian Peasants, 1970–1975" (Ph.D. diss., Monash University, Australia, 1991), 188; see also Kiernan, *The Pol Pot Regime,* 19.

45. U.S. Department of Defense, *Intelligence Information Report,* No. 2 724 2116 73, 27, August 1973; also quoted in Kiernan, *The Pol Pot Regime,* 24.

46. "Efforts of Khmer Insurgents to Exploits for Propaganda Purposes, Damage Done by Airstrikes in Kandal Province," *Intelligence Information Cable,* May 2, 1973, in Kiernan, *The Pol Pot Regime*, 22.

47. Interview with Bruce Palling, quoted in Kiernan, *The Pol Pot Regime,* 23.

48. Craig Etcheson, *The Rise and Demise of Democratic Kampuchea* (Boulder, Colo.: Westview Press, 1984), 97.

49. See note 48.

50. Reply to question by Helen Thomas of UPI, Cable News Network, *Bill Moyers* program, January 19, 1991. As Kiernan points out, "500 Americans a week" translates into the much-exaggerated figure of 30,000 American casualties in 1969–1970 alone. For exploration of Kissinger's role, see Christopher Hitchens, "The Case against Henry Kissinger: Part I. The Making of a War Criminal," *Harper's Magazine,* February 2001, 33–53.

51. Etcheson, 98.

52. Anthony Lewis, "Out Damned Spot!," *New York Times,* September 24, 1979, A19.

53. *Washington Post,* April 19, 1975, A1.

54. *New York Times,* May 6, 1975, A1.

55. *New York Times,* May 13, 1975, A4.

56. *Newsweek,* May 12, 1975, 27.

57. *Newsweek,* May 19, 1975, 30.

58. *Far Eastern Economic Review,* July 18, 1975, 29.

59. *Congressional Record,* 94th Cong., 2nd sess., June 16, 1976, 18617–18.

60. Donald S. Spencer, *The Carter Implosion* (New York: Praeger, 1988), 25.

61. Brian Klunk, *Consensus and the American Mission* (Lanham, Md.: University Press of America, 1986), 129.

62. Jimmy Carter, *Keeping Faith* (New York: Bantam Books, 1982), 143.

63. Quoted in Zbigniew Brzezinski, *Power and Principle* (New York: Farrar, Strauss & Giroux, 1983), 125.

64. David Newsom, ed., *The Diplomacy of Human Rights* (Lanham, Md.: University Press of America, 1986), 223.

65. Sheldon Neuringer, *The Carter Administration, Human Rights, and the Agony of Cambodia* (Lewiston, N.Y.: East Mellen Press, 1993), 27.

66. Ibid.

67. *Reader's Digest,* February 1977, 228.

68. George C. Hildebrand and Gareth Porter, *Cambodia: Starvation and Revolution* (New York: Monthly Review Press, 1976), 15.

69. Jamie Frederic Metzl, *Western Responses to Human Rights Abuses in Cambodia, 1975–1980* (New York: St. Martin's Press, 1996), 57.

70. Lacouture, 9.

71. Lacouture, 10.

72. *Washington Post,* February 19, 1978, C3.

73. Becker, 393.

74. U.S. House of Representatives, Subcommittee on International Organizations, *Hearings on Human Rights in Cambodia,* 95th Cong., 1st sess., May 3, 1977, 32.

75. See note 75.

76. *Hearings* . . . , 1977, 12.

77. *Hearings* . . . , 1977, 12–14, 19–39.

78. *Hearings* . . . , 1977, 19.

79. *Hearings* . . . , 1977, 32.

80. *Hearings* . . . , 1977, 14.

81. *Hearings* . . . , 1977, 34–35.

82. Amnesty International, "Annual Report: 1975–76," London, 1976, 137–38.

83. Metzl, 64.

84. "Human Rights Situation in Cambodian," *Department of State Bulletin,* September 5, 1977, 323.

85. U.S. House of Representatives, Subcommittee on International Organizations, *House Hearings on Cambodia,* July 26, 1977.

86. *Congressional Record,* 95th Cong., 1st sess., September 27, 1977, 31045–46.

87. Warren Christopher, "Human Rights: Cambodia," *Department of State Bulletin,* February 1978, 32.

88. Cyrus Vance, "Question and Answer Session Following Cincinnati Address," *Department of State Bulletin,* June 1978, 19.

89. *House Hearings on Cambodia,* July 26, 1977, 15.

90. Nayan Chanda, *Brother Enemy: The War after the War* (New York: Harcourt Brace Jovanovich, 1986), 147–48.

91. Letter to President Carter from Representative Norman Dicks, 6th District, Washington, March 24, 1977 (Jimmy Carter Library, White House Central File, box CO-81).

92. Letter to President Carter from Representative Les AuCoin, 1st District, Oregon, July 8, 1977 (Jimmy Carter Library, White House Central File, subject file, box CO-81).

93. Letter to President Carter from Representative Romano Mazzoli, 3rd District, Kentucky, December 16, 1977 (Jimmy Carter Library, White House Central File, box CO-40).

94. Letter to Representative Morgan F. Murphy from Ed Strinko, September 13, 1978, cited in Carl Lieberman, "The Reaction of the Carter Administration to Human Rights Violations in Cambodia," in Herbert D. Roesenbaum and Alexej Ugrinsky, eds., *Jimmy Carter: Foreign Policy and Post-Presidential Years* (Westport, Conn.: Greenwood Press, 1994), 275.

95. Senate Resolution 323, "Relating to Human Rights in Cambodia," 95th Cong., 1st sess, November 4, 1977.

96. Letter from Douglas J. Bennet Jr. to Representative Romano L. Mazzoli, January 31, 1978 (Jimmy Carter Library, White House Central File, box CO-81, box CO-40).

97. Letter from Jimmy Carter to Congressman Norman Dicks, April 5, 1977 (Jimmy Carter Library, White House Central File, box CO-81, box CO-40).

98. *American Foreign Policy Basic Documents, 1977–1980* (Washington, D.C.: U.S. Department of State, 1983), Document 550.

99. See note 98.

100. *Congressional Quarterly Almanac* 34 (1978): 88; Neuringer, 34.

101. Kuper, 134–35.

102. Kuper, 136.

103. Letter from James M. Hanley et al. to President Jimmy Carter, July 6, 1978, (Jimmy Carter Library, White House Central File, box CO-40).

104. See note 104.

105. Letter from Douglas J. Bennet to James M. Hanley, August 17, 1978 (Jimmy Carter Library, White House Central File, box CO-40).

106. Gaddis Smith, *Morality, Reason, and Power: American Diplomacy in the Carter Years* (New York: Hill and Wang, 1986), 86–87.

107. Neuringer, 30.

108. Chanda, 17.

109. *House Hearings on Cambodia,* July 26, 1977, 15.

110. Robert G. Sutter, "China's Strategy toward Vietnam and Its Implications for the United States," in David W. P. Elliott, ed., *The Third Indochina Conflict* (Boulder, Colo.: Westview Press, 1981), 175–78.

111. *New York Times,* January 4, 1979, A4.

112. *New York Times,* January 12, 1979, A6.

113. Smith, 91–94, 97–99; Neuringer, 51.

114. Neuringer, 54.

115. Letter from Stephen Solarz to President Jimmy Carter, February 22, 1979 (Jimmy Carter Library, White House Central File, box CO-66); Neuringer, 55.

116. Robert M. Gates, *From the Shadows: The Ultimate Insider's Story of Five Presidents and How They Won the Cold War* (New York: Simon and Schuster, 1996), 121.

117. Author interview (confidential), 1998.

118. Gates, 122–23.

119. *American Foreign Policy Basic Documents, 1977–1980,* Document 596; Neuringer, 56.

120. *New York Times,* March 17, 1979, A4.

121. *New York Times,* February 21, 1979, A4.

122. Neuringer, 58.

123. *New York Times,* August 29, 1979, A3.

124. Telegram to President Carter from John Richardson Jr., president, Freedom House, April 25, 1978; Letter to Leo Cherne, chairman, International Rescue Committee, from Zbigniew Brzezinski, May 17, 1978 (Jimmy Carter Library, White House Central File). See also "The Vice President: America's Role in Southeast Asia and the Pacific," *Department of State Bulletin,* July 1978, 25.

125. "An Edited Transcript of a Conference on Ethical Issues and Moral Principles in U.S. Refugee Policy, March 24–25, 1983," U.S. Center for Refugee Affairs, Washington, D.C., 34–35. For more on this issue, see Valerie O'Connor Sutter, *The Indochinese Refugee Dilemma* (Baton Rouge: Louisiana State University Press, 1990).

126. Author interview with Michel Oksenberg, October 8, 1998.

127. See note 126.

128. John Pilger, "The Long Secret Alliance: Uncle Sam and Pol Pot," *Covert Action Quarterly,* fall 1997, 1.

129. See note 128.

130. See note 129.

131. *American Foreign Policy Basic Documents, 1977–1980,* Document 585; Neuringer, 62.

132. See note 131.

133. Author interview (confidential), 1998.

134. William Shawcross, *The Quality of Mercy: Cambodia, Holocaust, and Modern Conscience* (New York: Simon & Schuster, 1984), 340–56.

135. Neuringer, 62.

136. *Washington Post,* September 20, 1979, A25.

137. U.S. Department of State, "United States Participation in the UN (1979)," 39.

138. *New York Times,* September 22, 1979, A1, A2.

139. Neuringer, 72.

140. Letter from Zbigniew Brzezinski to Sam Brown, October 29, 1980 Jimmy Carter Library, White House Central File, Section File, box IT-10).

141. Author interview with Charles William Maynes, September 11, 1998.

142. Cyrus Vance, *Hard Choices: Critical Years in America's Foreign Policy* (New York: Simon and Schuster, 1983), 126.

143. Vance, 126–27.

144. *American Foreign Policy Basic Documents, 1977–1980,* Document 551; Smith, 99.

145. Author interview with Charles William Maynes, September 11, 1998.

146. See note 145.

147. *Washington Post,* September 22, 1979, A19.

148. *Washington Post,* August 8, 1980, A1.

149. See note 148.

150. Letter from the National Council of the Churches of Christ, Claire Randall, general secretary, to President Jimmy Carter, July 18, 1980 (Jimmy Carter Library, White House Central File, Box ND-47).

151. Neuringer, 78.

152. Chanda, 382.

153. U.S. Department of State, *United States Participation in the UN: Report by the President to Congress, 1980* (Washington, D.C., 1981), 41.

154. "Accounting for War Crimes in Cambodia," *PeaceWatch,* vol. 1, no. 6 (Washington, D.C.: United States Institute of Peace, October 1995), 2.

155. This semantic practice continued until the start of the 1989 Paris peace process, when the word "genocide" was first spoken in reference to the Pol Pot regime (*New York Times,* April 17, 1998, A15). See also John Pilger, "Pol Pot's Safe Haven," *New Statesman and Society* 26 (April 1991): 10.

156. Office of Senator Charles S. Robb, "Charles S. Robb News," July 16, 1993 (press release).

157. A special office of Cambodian Genocide Investigations was created within the State Department's Bureau of East Asia and the Pacific to administer the funds.

158. Cambodian Genocide Program, "A Report to the United States Department of State, Bureau of East Asia and the Pacific," 1994–1997, 1.

159. Cambodian Genocide Program, 18–19.

160. Cambodian Genocide Program, 8–9.

161. Cambodian Genocide Program, 11.

162. Cambodian Genocide Program, 12.

163. *Washington Post,* June 24, 1997, A11.

164. See note 163.

165. *New York Times,* April 17, 1998, A15. See also Hitchens, 33–53.

166. *Washington Post,* July 27, 1997, A24.

167. *New York Times,* April 9, 1998, A1.

168. See note 167.

169. Author interview with Shelia Berry, special assistant to Ambassador David Scheffer, Washington, D.C., September 25, 1998.

170. *New York Times,* April 9, 1998, A1.

171. *New York Times,* April 17, 1998, A1.

172. *New York Times,* April 17, 1998, A15.

173. Author interview with Shelia Berry, September 25, 1998.

Chapter Three

The United States and Genocide in Bosnia

In mid-February 1984, over 1,200 athletes from forty-nine countries and almost half a million spectators traveled to Sarajevo, Yugoslavia, for the Winter Olympics. As a cosmopolitan, ethnically diverse city of Serbs, Croats, and Muslims, Sarajevo offered the world a model of multiculturalism, tolerance, and citizenship—an ideal city to host the games and embody the Olympic movement. The 1984 Winter Olympics produced many memorable highlights. Scott Hamilton and Katarina Witt became household names for their figure skating. Britain's ice dancing team of Jayne Torville and Christopher Dean brought the crowd to their feet with their gold medal–winning performance to Ravel's *Bolero.* On the slopes, the United States had much to cheer about as brothers Phil and Steve Mahre finished first and second in the alpine slalom and newcomer Bill Johnson captured gold in the men's downhill.

Less than a decade later, facilities such as Zetra Olympic Hall and the prominent ski jumping venue, once packed with cheering fans, stood damaged and ravaged by a brutal war that pitted the region's ethnic groups against one another. Alpine skiing, bobsled, and luge sites overlooking the city bristled with Serb artillery and tanks. Once prestigious and admired, Sarajevo fell under siege as Yugoslavia disintegrated into war and Serbs bent on "ethnic cleansing" attacked the Muslim civilian population, terrorizing them with countless bombardments and the threat of starvation. In the Balkans, the hope and idealism of the Olympic movement had been replaced with a terrible war and Serbian aggression that included genocide as one of its goals. A poster circulated in the city portrayed blood dripping from the interlocking Olympic rings. Sarajevo recaptured public attention, but this time as a city of death, destruction, and war crimes.

This chapter further examines the issue of the United States and the prevention and punishment of genocide, this time in its first "new world order" context: the 1992–1995 war in Bosnia. The dominant theme of this episode is the abdication of leadership by two successive administrations. In the aftermath of the Cold War, the United States emerged as the preeminent world power, unrivaled militarily and economically. With this "lone superpower" status, the United States faced a clear opportunity to stop the second European genocide in fifty years at minimal cost. However, as this chapter demonstrates, instead of exercising political and moral leadership to influence and shape international society, both the Bush and the Clinton administrations balked. A combination of potent factors—domestic politics, historical analogies, and personal histories—prevented decisive action by the United States and thus crippled any international action to fulfill the goals of the United Nations Convention on the Prevention and Punishment of the Crime of Genocide (UNGC).

While the outside world dithered and passively watched a moment for decisive ethical leadership take shape, power hungry, ethically challenged individuals took advantage of dire conditions in the Balkans. In the name of self-aggrandizement, men such as Serbian President Slobodan Milosevic and Bosnian Serb leader Radovan Karadzic willingly launched the region into a period of brutal ethnic hostilities and genocide in pursuit of their vision of "Greater Serbia."

In terms of ethical leadership and norm building, this chapter describes a two-track evolution. On one hand, America's Bosnia policy—namely, its fairly decisive policy of nonintervention over the course of three years—took the norm of genocide prevention backward or at least stalled it. The United States deferred to its European allies, providing them the chance to demonstrate leadership they had yet to manifest. An incapable Europe and an inert United States meant that genocide in the Balkans proceeded relatively unhindered. The normative pronouncements and commitments of the UNGC to stop the crime remained *impuissant* and inactive. A chance to invigorate the pledge of "never again" with real action fell by the wayside, and the UNGC in part remained more vision than reality.

On the normative progress side, however, the evolving influence of concern about genocide prevention and punishment did make itself felt. The postgenocide developments described in this chapter demonstrate progress. These initiatives also suggest the importance of hegemonic involvement in norm promotion. Despite omnipresent realist obstacles to action as dramatic and transformative as intervention, forward normative evolution can nonetheless occur.

BACKGROUND: YUGOSLAV BREAKDOWN

Many observers of Yugoslavia's dissolution and subsequent war, including Presidents Clinton and Bush, their secretaries of state, other high-level policymakers, and media commentators, dismissed the events as the tragic result of "ancient ethnic hatreds" existing in the Balkans. Resort to such language also often emphasized the likely "quagmire" scenario awaiting outside intervention and helped excuse Western passivity. Somewhat persuasive on the surface, these arguments reflect inaccurate understandings of history and flawed interpretations of more contemporary events in the Balkans. Balkan history includes considerable tension, but in Bosnia-Herzegovina no inherent, timeless hatred and hostility existed between Serbs and Muslim Slavs.[1]

Yugoslavia sprung into existence initially as the Kingdom of Serbs, Croats, and Slovenes in 1918 (renamed "Yugoslavia" in 1929). Competing nationalist agendas troubled the country following its birth without destroying it. World War II brought Nazi occupation and partition. The so-called Independent State of Croatia, little more than a Nazi puppet government with no real legitimacy or significant popular support, collaborated with the Germans. Croatia's distasteful Ustasha regime committed massacres against the Serb population within its borders—crimes that Serb leaders would revisit repeatedly in the 1990s to argue falsely their status as the true victims of genocide. At the same time, Serb "Chetniks" (nationalists fighting for the monarchy) massacred many Muslims and Croats. No group held a monopoly as perpetrator or victim of wartime intercommunal violence.

Following the war, Yugoslavia entered a new period of stability under the domineering communist leadership of Josip Broz Tito. Tito and his partisans earned a strong and respected reputation as freedom fighters during the occupation that propelled them to power in peacetime. A devoted authoritarian, Tito also held a firm commitment to a multiethnic society and rejected the domination of one people by another. He controlled the country as a whole while simultaneously establishing a federal state composed of republics that enjoyed limited autonomy.

This combination of strict control from above and strong distaste for ethnic intolerance ushered in a lengthy period of stability and relative ethnic harmony for the Balkans. Census figures from Bosnia-Herzegovina from as late as 1991 showed that Bosnian Muslims accounted for 44 percent of the population, Serbs 31 percent, and Croats upward of 18 percent, making Bosnia the most ethnically diverse of the republics in the region. Many villages were homogeneous, but the cities revealed considerable ethnic mixing, including high rates of intermarriage.

Tito's death in 1980 set in stage a slow but certain period of fragmentation that accelerated dramatically with the death of the Soviet Union less than a decade later. The loss of firm control from above, coupled with serious economic downturn—complete with high unemployment and recession—lent additional volatility to the mix. The end of the Cold War revealed to the Yugoslav republics a whole new context for action and national aspiration. As in the Soviet Union and Czechoslovakia, the disappearance of communist repression manifested itself not only in calls for democracy but also in resurgent nationalist sentiment and solidarity. Rising economic uncertainty, particularly among the middle and lower classes, heightened a sense of dependence on one's individual republic and increased receptivity to nationalist rhetoric as all sides feared becoming victims of economic moves by others.[2]

Into this increasingly tense and volatile environment stepped political opportunists willing to exploit such conditions for their own gain. As former Assistant Secretary of State and chief Bosnia negotiator Richard Holbrooke plainly asserts, "Yugoslavia's tragedy was not foreordained. It was the product of bad, even criminal, political leaders who encouraged ethnic confrontation for personal, political, and financial gain."[3] Croatia's Franjo Tudjman deployed extreme nationalism and xenophobia, heightening fears of Serb domination. This tactic in turn resurrected Serb fears of a reborn Ustashe for the 1990s. However, no one stood more prominently among these "criminals" than Serbian President Slobodan Milosevic.

As conditions worsened in Yugoslavia, Milosevic embraced extreme nationalism and used it to consolidate his own political power. According to the last American ambassador to Yugoslavia, Warren Zimmerman, "Milosevic is a man almost totally dominated by his dark side . . . an opportunist, not an ideologue, a man driven by power rather than nationalism. He has made a Faustian pact with nationalism as a way to gain and hold power."[4] To cement his leadership, "Slobo" dusted off Serbian mythology and reinvigorated a quest for a "Greater Serbia" at the expense of other ethnic groups in the region, particularly the Bosnian Muslims. As early as 1987, Milosevic established his nationalist credentials by ousting his patron, Ivan Stambolic, for purportedly being too conciliatory toward Albanians in the Kosovo province, who happened to make up 90 percent of the population. With "Greater Serbia" in his sights, Milosevic abolished Kosovo's autonomy and brought it fully under Belgrade's control.

When Kosovars protested against this action, the Milosevic regime responded in kind by orchestrating mass demonstrations of its own. Most dramatic among these was a gathering of a million Serbs in 1989 to honor the 600th anniversary of the Battle of Kosovo at Polje. For Serb nationalists, the 1389 defeat of King Lazar at the hands of the Turks under Sultan Murad very much "defines their nationhood, their Christianity against the infidel, and their self-styled role as Europe's protectors."[5] Milosevic filled his oration with images of Serbs as a great people historically wronged and oppressed, Serbs as the unrecognized and unappreciated defenders of Europe against Ottoman barbarity, and Serbs ready to reassert themselves and rejuvenate their historical mission and destiny. Myth blended with reality as Milosevic played shamelessly to the hundreds of thousands before him, prodding them with his speech that read "as a paradigm of nationalist madness."[6]

This militant Serb vision of manifest destiny—a bizarre combination of victimhood and virulence—culminated as Milosevic exclaimed, "For six centuries now the heroism of Kosovo has inspired our creativity, fed our pride, and not allowed us to forget that we were an army, great, brave, and proud, one of the few that in defeat stayed undefeated. Six centuries later, today, we are again in battles and facing battles. They are not armed, although such battles cannot be excluded yet."

The implicit message rang clear to the other groups in the Balkans—Serb domination in a reconstituted, postcommunist Yugoslavia would reduce them to second-class status at best. Invoking a 600-year-old war in his inflammatory speech, "Milosevic opened the floodgates" and presaged the bloody conflict to come with his pregnant words.[7] Within a few short years, the disintegration of Yugoslavia would reach full speed as other republics sought escape from a Yugoslav federation dominated by irredentist, and eventually genocidal, Serbs.[8]

Milosevic and his followers and partners, men such as Bosnian Serb leader Radovan Karadzic, spread their nationalist epidemic of hatred through the media. For Milosevic, a "fortuitous" combination of economic and political unrest played into his hands, providing hyperreceptivity to the message of fear and hate he and Karadzic zealously peddled through radio, television, and print media. State-controlled television and radio provided the perfect medium for rallying anxious Serbs around Milosevic and Karadzic and against their neighbors. In the Serbian press, all Muslims became "Islamic fundamentalists, all Croats Ustase."[9] Ambassador Zimmerman observes,

> Those who argue that "ancient Balkan hostilities" account for the violence that overtook and destroyed Yugoslavia forget the power of television in the hands of officially provoked racism. While history, particularly the carnage of World War Two, provided plenty of tinder for ethnic hatred in Yugoslavia, it took the institutional nationalism of Milosevic and Tudjman to supply the torch. . . . The nationalist media sought to terrify by invoking mass murderers of a bygone time. The Croatian press described Serbs as "Cetniks"—the Serbian nationalists of World War II. For the Serbian press, Croatians were Ustase (and later Muslims became "Turks"). People who think they're under ethnic threat tend to seek refuge in their ethnic group. Thus did the media's terror campaign establish ethnic solidarity on the basis on an enemy to be both hated and feared. The virus of television spread ethnic hatred like an epidemic throughout Yugoslavia. . . . An entire generation of Serbs, Croats, and Muslims were aroused by television images to hate their neighbors.[10]

British journalist and author Noel Malcolm echoes Zimmerman's point, writing, "Having watched Radio Television Belgrade in the period 1991–1992, I can understand why simple Bosnian Serbs came to believe that they were under threat from ustasa hordes, fundamentalist jihads, or whatever. . . . It was as if all television in the USA had been taken over by the Ku Klux Klan."[11] On the Serbian side, these threats—more perceived and manufactured than real—drove and justified a brutal war and an accompanying genocide. Michael Sells, in *The Bridge Betrayed,* succinctly summarizes: "The national mythology, hatred and unfounded charges of genocide in Kosovo and imminent genocide in Bosnia had shaped into a code: the charge of genocide became a signal to begin genocide."[12]

GENOCIDE IN BOSNIA

The crime of genocide, according to the accepted UN definition, occurred in Bosnia, perpetrated by the Serbs against the Bosnian Muslims. The intent of "ethnic cleansing," to remove Muslims from the land by any means necessary, including rape, torture, deportation, and killing, was genocidal. Serb actions clearly fall under the terms of Article II of the UNGC (see appendix). The Commission of Experts established by the Security Council (Resolution 780) concluded in May 1994 that atrocities committed by the Serbs were the products of an intentional policy. The commission's report stated that Serb atrocities qualified as crimes against humanity and that it would also likely "be confirmed in court under due process of law that these events constitute genocide."[13] Indictments and convictions brought by the International Criminal Tribunal for the Former Yugoslavia against Serb leaders further amplify the fact that the distinct crime of genocide took place in Bosnia.

However, throughout much of the war, observers and principals alike debated the nature of Serb crimes in Bosnia. Many sought to avoid finger-pointing and blaming. Britain's Lord Owen, a chief Balkan negotiator for the European Community, seemed to excuse the Serbs for their genocidal actions by erroneously claiming that the Serbs themselves were victims of genocide during World War II at the hands of both Croatians and Muslims. The Serb propaganda machine worked hard to sell this fallacious history, and it certainly helped their cause when someone such as Owen repeated it. Even if true, past victimhood would hardly legitimize or make "okay" genocidal retribution in the 1990s. Still other critics suggested that the number of victims was too low for genocide to have occurred.[14] Such arguments ignored the simple fact that no magical threshold exists at which point murders or atrocities become genocide. The UNGC makes clear that genocide does not require a certain number of murders or a group's total annihilation.

Some argued that all sides were guilty of atrocities, and they considered it unfair to single out the Serbs as villains. This line of reasoning received considerable attention when supported by individuals such as Canadian General Lewis

MacKenzie, chief of staff of the UN Protection Force (UNPROFOR) providing humanitarian assistance in Sarajevo. MacKenzie reflected this view with statements such as, "Dealing with Bosnia is a little like dealing with three serial killers—one has killed fifteen, one has killed ten, one has killed five. Do we help the one that's only killed five?"[15] MacKenzie also contended, without evidence, that the Muslims often attacked their own people to win international sympathy and support.[16]

Muslims and Croats did commit unjustifiable atrocities during the war. No one should offer excuses for their abhorrent behavior. However, the claim that since all sides committed atrocities they all share equal guilt borders on absurd reductionism; it is simply wrong. An equivalent argument would lump together the United States and its allies with Hitler's Germany because soldiers on both sides committed atrocities and the Allies firebombed cities. While all human rights violations and crimes committed by any and all parties in the former Yugoslavia demand strong condemnation, the facts clearly reveal that the Serbs committed the vast majority of atrocities as part of a distinct plan of genocide.

This is not new news; prominent media sources covered it at the time. The *New York Times* reported on April 24, 1994, that "the overwhelming majority of crimes were committed by Serbs in an orchestrated campaign to eliminate Muslims from Serb held territory." The next day, a *New York Times* editorial on "ethnic cleansing" in the region concluded that "the overwhelming responsibility for this practice lies with the Serbs." The *Wall Street Journal* likewise reported that "UN investigators blame Serbs for the worst atrocities, from the creation of Nazi-like detention camps to forced deportations and systematic rape of Muslims."[17]

Information from a leaked Central Intelligence Agency (CIA) report in 1995 also refutes the notion of equivalent, shared blame across among ethnic groups in Bosnia. As revealed in the *New York Times,*

> The report makes nonsense of the view—now consistently put forward by Western European governments and intermittently by the Clinton administration—that the Bosnian conflict is a civil war for which guilt should be divided between Serbs, Croats, and Muslims rather than a case of Serbian aggression. . . . "To those who think the parties are equally guilty, this report is pretty devastating," one official said. "The scale of what the Serbs did is of a different order. But more than that, it makes clear, with concrete evidence, that there was a conscious, coherent, and systematic Serbian policy to get rid of Muslims through murder, torture, and imprisonment."[18]

Subsequent congressional and State Department reports confirmed the CIA findings, indicating that 80 to 90 percent of the war crimes were attributable to the Serbs.[19]

Genocide is no accident. Genocide does not emerge from adding up "x" number of atrocities. It requires intent, and the Serbian leadership and their forces clearly demonstrated genocidal intention. In *Genocide in Bosnia,* Norman Cigar concludes that "the genocide—or ethnic cleansing, as it has been commonly known—that befell the Muslims of Bosnia-Herzegovina was not simply the unintentional and unfortunate byproduct of combat or civil war. Rather, it was a rational policy, the direct and planned consequence of conscious policy decisions taken by the Serbian establishment in Bosnia-Herzegovina. This policy was implemented in a deliberate and systematic manner as part of a broader strategy intended to achieve a well-defined, concrete, political objective, namely, the creation of an expanded, ethnically pure Greater Serbia." Ambassador Zimmerman lays the intent at the feet of Milosevic and Karadzic, charging that "they are as guilty as if they had primed the explosive charges, pulled the triggers, or driven the bulldozers over the grave sites."[20] Furthermore, a plan known as "RAM" (source of the abbreviation is unknown) drafted by Serb military officials set out the plan for military conquest and the ethnic cleansing of land in Bosnia they considered rightfully Serb. The plan was straightforward in its aim. According to a former Serbian political leader who read the document, RAM aimed "to destroy Bosnia economically and completely exterminate the Muslim people."[21]

The duration of the war and the countless atrocities prevent a full chronicling here. However, select examples deserve mention and provide adequate evidence that Serb war crimes and atrocities fit into an organized campaign of genocide against Bosnia's Muslim population. As the 1995 CIA report details, "Serbian authorities made use of concentration camps as tools for their campaign of genocide against Bosnian Muslims. The creation of Greater Serbia required that Muslim civilians be taken from their homes, brought to concentration camps, terrorized, and killed." In a sharp burst of Serbian violence, more than three-quarters of a million Muslims were ousted from a swath of territory covering 70 percent of the country.[22] Initial reports of torture and death at Serb controlled "labor camps" surfaced as early as 1991.[23]

In a series of Pulitzer Prize–winning reports, *Newsday*'s Roy Gutman publicly exposed the Serbs' system of concentration camps set up in northern Bosnia. His initial reports from survivors came in August 1992 and suggested that over a thousand civilians had already perished and that thousands more were being detained and starved. From these reports, the world first learned of the term "ethnic cleansing," the sterile, Orwellian term used by the Serbs to describe and mask their campaign of genocide. At the Omarska camp, civilians were held in metal cages while awaiting execution in groups of ten to fifteen. The United Nations estimated that Omarska held 11,000 prisoners at its height.[24] At a separate camp set up in a customs warehouse in the city of Brcko, the Serbs executed (usually by firing squad or by slitting their throats) an estimated 1,350 Bosnians from mid-May to mid-June.[25]

The UN Commission of Experts established to investigate atrocities and other international crimes in the former Yugoslavia found that the Serb-run detention camps were part of a state policy of "ethnic purification" via terror and genocide.[26] Typically, Serbs emptied Muslim villages, rounding up the inhabitants and transporting them to the camps in buses or on train cars. They provided no food, water, or sanitation. On arrival, "a few were often killed on the spot. Men between the ages of sixteen (or younger) and sixty were separated from older men, women, and children. These men, considered of military age, were transferred to larger, more heavily guarded camps, where tortures and murder were the rule."[27] Testimony from camp survivors revealed a horror show of sadism as Serb guards decapitated prisoners with chain saws, forced others to bite off body parts of fellow prisoners, and beat others to death with clubs, rifle butts, pipes, and cables. "We won't waste our bullets on them," said a guard from Omarska to a UN representative. "They have no roof. There is sun and rain, cold nights, and beatings two times a day. We give them no food and no water. They will starve like animals."[28] According to an official at the U.S. embassy in Zagreb, "The Nazis had nothing on these guys. I've seen reports of individual acts of barbarity of a kind that hasn't come up in State Department cable traffic in 20 years."[29]

For Bosnian women, the Serbs often turned to rape as a tool of genocidal terror. Overwhelming documentary evidence exists of Serbian forces engaging in the systematic rape of thousands of women.[30] Serb troops even established temporary bordellos where they would gang rape women for days at a time, with victims ranging in age from twelve to sixty-two. Serbs reportedly told many of their victims that they acted under orders.[31] In her startling book *Rape Warfare,* Beverly Allen asserts that rape was a preconceived, premeditated tactic of genocide, such that the military even debated who would command "this new military operation aimed at noncombatant women and children."[32] The Yugoslav army's special services section, which included "experts in psychological warfare," drafted a report meant to assist with ethnic cleansing:

> Our analysis of the behavior of the Muslim communities demonstrates that the morale, will, and bellicose nature of their groups can be undermined only if we aim our action at the point where the religious and social structure is most fragile. We refer to the women, especially adolescents, and to the children. Decisive intervention on these social figures would spread confusion among the communities, thus causing first of all fear and then panic, leading to a probable [Muslim] retreat from the territories involved in war activity.[33]

Another troubling but telling document from the army to the secret police reported that "sixteen hundred and eighty Muslim women of ages ranging from twelve to sixty years are now gathered in the centers for displaced persons within our territory. A large number of these are pregnant, especially those ranging in age from fifteen to thirty years. In the estimation of Bosko Kelevic and Smiljan Geric, the psychological effect is strong, and therefore we must continue [the practice of genocidal rape]."[34]

Historian Philip Cohen writes, "State-sponsored rape was an integral part of 'ethnic cleansing' and was designed to accomplish several goals. Mass rapes destroy the victims' core social institutions, the family and community. Mass rapes instill terror so that the victims will never seek to return to their homes and villages. . . . Rape victims were forced to bear the children of their tormentors thus compounding their personal suffering. . . . Forcibly impregnated rape victims have a tragically high incidence of suicide and infanticide. Mass rape, then, was an integral part of genocide."[35] David Rieff underlines the point in *Slaughterhouse:* "The Serbs had used rape as a weapon of war all over Bosnia as a way of terrorizing the Muslim population into flight and thus fulfilling the Serb war aim of ethnic cleansing."[36]

To heighten the terror, children also suffered rape. According to former State Department human rights official Jon Western, children were systematically raped. Western recounts, "There was one account that affected me: a young girl was raped repeatedly by Serb paramilitary units. Her parents were restrained behind a fence and she was raped repeatedly and they left her in a pool of blood and over the course of a couple of days she finally died, and her parents were not able to tend to her." Western and his colleagues initially doubted the story but changed their minds after many witnesses corroborated its terrible authenticity.[37]

The more "fortunate" Bosnian Muslims faced removal from their homes and deportation. In July 1992, the Yugoslav government chartered an eighteen-car train to deport forcibly an entire Muslim village of almost 2,000 to Hungary. Similar scenes repeated themselves across the region, some involving train transport, others with deportees packed into buses. Once they depopulated the areas, the Serbs often renamed the towns and carefully and completely destroyed the monuments, religious sites, and other institutions closely identified with the Muslim community. For example, in Banja Luka, "Serbian authorities destroyed 99 percent of the Mosques, 13 of which dated to the sixteenth and seventeenth centuries."[38] From their positions outside Sarajevo, Serb artillery units targeted the National Museum and the National Library, touching off an inferno in which "over a million books, more than a hundred thousand manuscripts and rare books, and centuries of historical records of Bosnia-Herzegovina went up in flames."[39] The report by the UN Commission of Experts also found evidence that Serb forces systematically destroyed or damaged "cultural property" in the former Yugoslavia.[40]

When war broke out between Serbia and Croatia, Serb militia and Yugoslav National Army (JNA) forces soon thereafter indiscriminately bombarded civilian populations in Dubrovnik and Vukovar. These war crimes provided practice and preface for similar acts against communities in Bosnia. For nearly two years, Sarajevo suffered a tireless siege by Serb forces. Sniper bullets and mortar shells bloodied the one-time jewel of multiethnic coexistence and terrorized its civilian population a little more every day, hoping to drive them out. In total, the assault killed upward of 10,000 Sarajevans, including at least 1,500 children.[41]

In a modern city that had hosted the Olympics just a decade earlier, 60 percent of the buildings were destroyed or seriously damaged. So great was the devastation that a UN team estimated it would cost a minimum of $4 billion to return the Bosnian capital to its prewar condition. The determined Serbs relentlessly terrorized Sarajevo, disrupting power service, holding up food and water supplies, and controlling all access to the city. No one was safe, whether scurrying next door to see neighbors or standing in line at the market for bread. The barbaric siege of Sarajevo and other cities fit perfectly in the overall Serb strategy—terrorize and murder civilians at every opportunity and hope that they give up and flee, leaving behind them "ethnically pure" territory. For smaller communities, the Serbs relied on outright attack and invasion to ply their genocidal agenda. Srebrenica stands as one of the darkest representatives of this murderous plan.

SREBRENICA

An overtly genocidal assault on an entire community in Bosnia occurred when the Serbs launched a final attack on the "safe area" of Srebrenica in July 1995. Once a rich mining town—its very name means "silver"—the war in Bosnia turned it into a refugee camp, bursting with starving and homeless Bosnian Muslims. The vicious move against Srebrenica—really a culmination of several violent campaigns—"constituted the most serious single war crime in Europe since the Second World War."[42] With impunity, Serb troops led by General Radislav Krstic, under the command of General Ratko Mladic (both men would be indicted war criminals), deported almost 20,000 Muslim women and children, attacked the essentially defenseless enclave, and massacred close to 8,000 mostly unarmed men and boys.[43] With no defenders—UN forces were present but unable to provide resistance—Srebrenica first endured a massive bombardment. As the collapse of their enclave appeared imminent and inevitable, the Muslims fled Srebrenica. For men such as Mladic and his followers, simply capturing the town itself was not enough. With "ethnic cleansing" as their guiding star, the Serbs embarked on a manhunt. They tracked down and executed as many of the fleeing men as possible, remaining faithful to their genocidal mission even at the risk of allowing Croatian military advances across the country.[44] On a recording played at General Krstic's trial in The Hague, his voice is reportedly heard ordering a major to "kill each and every one of them. Do not leave a single one alive."[45]

The sum of these details—camps, rape, bombardments, cultural destruction—amounts to genocide but not a predestined genocide that sprang from deep-rooted ethnic hatred. Genocide by Serbs against Bosnian Muslims was calculated and put into motion by political forces with a monstrous nationalist agenda. Guided from above and pushed to hatred and aggression, Serb forces carried out systematic atrocities and war crimes with genocidal intent. Genocide and war in Bosnia resulted in the death of upward of 200,000 people, the rape of thousands of women, and a massive refugee population. Croatian and Bosnian Muslim forces also perpetrated some atrocities for which they rightly face criminal indictments, but these acts remained relatively sporadic and spontaneous rather than the result of a program of genocide.[46] The UN Commission of Experts concluded that there exists "no moral equivalency" between the Serbs, Bosnian Muslims, and Croats as perpetrators of war crimes.[47] Belgrade coordinated with the local so-called Bosnian Serb Army to destroy Bosnia and eliminate its non-Serb inhabitants. In less than two months' time, Serb forces occupied 60 percent of Bosnia-Herzegovina. Within one year, the Serbs "cleansed" close to two million people—half of Bosnia's population—from the region.[48]

THE BUSH ADMINISTRATION: "NO DOG IN THAT FIGHT"

President George W. Bush presided over the first of two American administrations challenged with the difficult task of dealing with the breakup and breakdown of Yugoslavia. From the start, the Bush team adopted an overtly "hands-off" policy regarding the disintegrating state of Yugoslavia. As tension, nationalism, and the potential for violence grew in the former communist state, the administration made quite clear its preference for Yugoslavia's continued political and territorial integrity. In part, the United States hoped to avoid a negative precedent for dissolution in other regions, namely in the former Soviet Union. Secretary of State James Baker traveled to Belgrade on June 21, 1991, just short of a deadline for secession set by Slovenia and Croatia. During his visit, Baker stressed the U.S. preference for a "complete" Yugoslavia and said that the United States would not grant recognition to breakaway republics.[49] Baker also criticized Serbian President Milosevic for actions pushing the region toward disaster.[50] With time, as breakup seemed increasingly inevitable, the administration signaled its willingness to accept changes in the composition of Yugoslavia if change or separation took place in a peaceful, negotiated way.

However, peaceful methods did not have the day in Yugoslavia. Fighting broke out almost immediately after Slovenia and Croatia formally declared independence in June 1991. Serb and JNA militia forces attacked the breakaways. Foreshadowing sieges to come, they indiscriminately shelled the cities of Vukovar and Dubrovnik. The United States limited its response to statements that voiced dismay at Serbian aggression and expressed disapproval at JNA and militia actions.[51] American officials discussed a show or use of force by the Sixth Fleet in the Adriatic to end the attacks against Dubrovnik and Vukovar, but strong Defense Department opposition quickly scuttled that possibility.[52] As Warren Zimmerman explained, "The use of force was simply too big a step to consider in late 1991. . . . I didn't recommend it myself; I should have."[53]

As crisis conditions developed and worsened in Yugoslavia and as an ethical leadership moment took shape, the United States willingly embraced disengagement. This grew in large part from the Bush administration's belief that events in Yugoslavia fell outside the orbit of central or vital American interests. Having recently prosecuted a war in the Persian Gulf, the United States receded into the background in deference to Europe's desire to assert itself, especially in its own backyard. After all, Yugoslavia's troubles were first and foremost a European problem.

With the Cold War over, the Europeans sensed a golden opportunity to exercise leadership on the continent and wiggle out from the ever-dominant and at times overbearing presence of their Atlantic ally. Lord David Owen explains that "there was a feeling that Europe could do it all on its own. . . . Europe wanted to stand on its own feet—Yugoslavia was the virility symbol of the Euro-federalists. This was going to be the time when Europe emerged with a single foreign policy and therefore it unwisely shut out an America only too happy to be shut out."[54]

As the crisis took shape, Europe's officials publicly stated their preference for U.S. "distance." The chairman of the European Commission, Jacques Delors, declared, "We do not interfere in American affairs. We hope they will have enough respect not to interfere in ours."[55] Luxembourg's Foreign Minister Jacques Poos boldly declared, "This is the hour of Europe, not the hour of the Americans."[56] The United States took advantage of this hour to rest following the January/February 1991 Persian Gulf War against Iraq and to placate Europe, deferring to the "wish that transatlantic coordination take place in EC-US channels instead of in NATO," where the United States held a more dominant role.[57] Indeed, "there existed an undercurrent in Washington that Yugoslavia was as good a place as any for Europe to step up to the plate and show they could act as a unified power."[58]

In the Balkans, fighting abated in Slovenia because the Slovenes offered surprisingly strong resistance. Croatia remained problematic. Violence continued, and attacks by Serb forces on civilians increased, including more bombardment of Vukovar and Dubrovnik. In response to the growing intensity of the fighting, the European Community joined the Soviet Union in supporting a UN arms embargo against all of Yugoslavia, breakaway republics included. On September 25, 1991, the Security Council voted to approve the arms embargo, which was intended to limit the fighting and smother its potential intensity. The Yugoslav government of Milosevic also endorsed the embargo. As the federation crumbled, the Serbs had secured most of the military assets of the armed forces, some of which they distributed to local militias. With essential control of the JNA and its assets, Belgrade saw the arms embargo as a way to add to its already decisive advantage over its neighbors.[59]

In the winter of 1992, attention turned to Bosnia-Herzegovina as it held a referendum on independence. The choice seemed simple if not obvious for Bosnia. President Izetbegovic and his fellow Bosnian Muslims faced the prospect of total domination by an increasingly nationalist, assertive, and exclusionary Serbia; or, they could declare independence, become their own country within the UN system, and fight it out. The February 29, 1992, vote revealed overwhelming support for independence. However, the region's Serb minority boycotted the vote and renewed their commitment to their own autonomous area. Bosnian Serb leader Radovan Karadzic told those favoring independence, "I warn you, you'll drag Bosnia down to hell. You Muslims aren't ready for war—you'll face extinction."[60]

Given the Serb reaction to declarations of independence by Slovenia and Croatia, the next development came as no surprise. By the end of March, Bosnian Serb forces, supported by the JNA, attacked Bosnian Muslim forces hastily assembled by the Bosnian government (they had maintained no armed forces). The war in Bosnia was on, with genocide soon to follow.

When war engulfed Bosnia-Herzegovina, the United States recognized the futility of pressing for the integrity of the state of Yugoslavia. Following that reasoning, the United States, on April 7, 1992, announced its recognition of the newly independent states of Croatia, Slovenia, and Bosnia-Herzegovina.[61] At this "independence" stage of Yugoslavia's disruption, the French reportedly presented the Bush administration with a preemptive measure to avoid a Balkan-wide war. According to a former State Department official, "The French came to the administration at very senior levels . . . once in the early phase of Belgrade's attack on Croatia, and at least once well before the military campaign against Bosnia, and they made a proposal to join with the United States, and other willing states, to put preventive peacekeepers on the ground across Bosnia—to support the legitimate elected government of Bosnia, to stabilize and prevent the outbreak of conflict, and to see Bosnia through that transition process to becoming a new independent state."[62] The Bush administration, having recently fought a war in the Persian Gulf, had little interest in a new military campaign and remained content in its sideline role.

Instead, the Bush administration continued to cede leadership to Europe. Statements such as "We continue to place a high value on the European Community's leading role in seeking a political settlement of the Yugoslav crisis, as mandated by the CSCE [Organization for Security and Cooperation in Europe]" detached the administration from responsibility.[63] In a firmer statement of disengagement and passivity, and one that American officials would repeat throughout the Bosnia crisis, the deputy assistant secretary of state for European and Canadian affairs, Ralph Johnson, told Congress that "the world community cannot stop Yugoslavs from killing each other so long as they are determined to do so."[64]

By May 1992, as Serb aggression continued and the extent of the burgeoning humanitarian disaster (particularly in Sarajevo) became clearer, Secretary of State Baker publicly expressed outrage and suggested comparisons between Serb and Nazi behavior. To express its displeasure with the Milosevic regime, the United States recalled Ambassador Warren Zimmerman from his post in Belgrade, a move aptly described as "cautiously diplomatic." Beyond that, the administration followed Baker, who remained firm that a general policy of staying out of Balkan issues represented the best strategy. Baker decided "to disengage from the issue" and simply follow policy made in Brussels. Baker summed up his take on the former Yugoslavia with the homey phrase "We don't have a dog in that fight."[65]

Despite his own personal revulsion at the increasing violence and civilian casualties in Sarajevo and surrounding areas, President Bush wrote the area out of American interests. In reference to Yugoslavia, the president said, "I don't think anybody suggests that if there is a hiccup here or there or a conflict here or there that the United States is going to send troops." The United States exerted some pressure at the United Nations to secure a 13–0 Security Council vote for a trade embargo against Yugoslavia, a measure sparked in part from the May 27, 1992, "breadline massacre," when Serb shells killed sixteen people standing in line for food relief. To ensure passage, the measure included language noting that the Serbs alone were not responsible for events in the Balkans.[66] As the siege of Sarajevo ran on into the summer, the Bush administration raised concern over the limited food and medicine available to the city's civilians. Once again, the United States applied some pressure at the United Nations to explore seriously the use of force to ensure delivery of humanitarian aid—not to end the war. Then the ugly face of genocide appeared clearly for all to see during the first week of August 1992.

Roy Gutman broke the story with a dispatch on a concentration camp in Omarska in the August 2 edition of *Newsday.* Television broadcasts of the camps, complete with images of emaciated prisoners huddled behind barbed wire, followed shortly thereafter. Visual parallels to Nazi concentration camps were inevitable. The day after the Gutman piece, State Department spokesman Richard Boucher told reporters that the administration knew that "abuses and torture and killings [were] taking place" in what the Serbians referred to as "detention centers."[67] When questions arose about why the Bush administration had said or done nothing about such atrocities, the official word mutated. On August 4, Assistant Secretary of State for European Affairs Thomas Niles appeared before the House Foreign Affairs Committee and stated that "we don't have, thus far, substantiated information that would confirm the existence of these camps."

Fearing a public outcry and demands that something be done, the administration tried to backtrack and decelerate the issue.[68] As Mark Danner suggested in his *New York Review of Books* article "America and the Bosnia Genocide," "The Bush people, having concluded nearly two years before that taking strong action posed unacceptable risks, now feared that popular outrage momentarily fueled by this sort of 'telegenic' but (in their view) ephemeral atrocity might drag them toward such involvement—or else, popular sentiment would penalize them politically (with the election barely three months away) for doing nothing."[69]

Lawrence Eagleburger admitted later, "We kind of waffled around a little bit. All of us were being a little bit careful . . . because of this issue of whether or not it was going to push us into something that we thought was dangerous."[70] Avoiding the issue became more difficult when Arkansas Governor Bill Clinton, in full campaign mode, lambasted Bush for failing to act against "the renegade regime of Slobodan Milosevic." Clinton called on the United States to provide the United Nations with assistance necessary to stop the slaughter, including the use of military force. White House spokesman Marlin Fitzwater fired back that the governor's statement was "the kind of reckless approach that indicates he better do more homework on foreign policy."[71] After waffling, President Bush publicly denounced the camps and called for immediate access to them by international observers. The Serbs, caught quite publicly, shut down some camps and simply moved others. For those camps opened to the outside, they trotted out the prisoners in the best health to satisfy the demands of inspectors.

AVOIDING THE "G" WORD: ACT I

As evidence amassed that genocide was taking place in Bosnia, the pressure grew on the United States to actually call it "genocide." The Bush administration felt pressure externally from the media, nongovernmental organizations (NGOs), Congress, and states at the UN General Assembly. Pressure also emerged from within the government, namely from foreign service officers (FSOs) directly involved in Bosnia reporting and policy.[72] With their detailed knowledge of events in Bosnia—and believing them to amount to genocide—some FSOs spoke out. According to Paul Williams, then a State Department lawyer with the Office of European and Canadian Affairs, these officials believed that "if the United States identifies what is occurring in Bosnia as genocide, then it ups the ante, it creates a moral obligation as well as a legal obligation to take action."[73] Several FSOs turned to the State Department's dissent channel mechanism to voice their views and concerns about genocide in Bosnia and U.S. inaction.[74] The former chief political officer at the embassy in Belgrade relates, "As I've read the definition of genocide, this was genocide. But we did not want to say that. The marching orders from President Bush were that Yugoslavia was essentially a European problem and we were to stay out of it."[75]

A high-profile sign of internal dissent came late in August 1992, when George Kenney, the acting chief of the Yugoslav desk at the State Department, resigned from his position to protest the U.S. government's failure to act against the genocide in Bosnia-Herzegovina. According to Kenney, he tried several times to introduce the word "genocide" into administration accounts and statements: "I thought it was warranted, but there was absolutely no acceptance of that."[76] Kenney blasted the administration for its do-nothing policy and called negotiations then under way in London a "charade" that would result in nothing without military muscle to back them up. The London Peace Conference, Kenney concluded, would fail without "very strong pressures, including military pressures against Serbia to stop its campaign of genocide in Bosnia." He did not expect such action, however, for two reasons: first, because the administration feared public blame if military action failed and, second, because Secretary of State Eagleburger "feels we should wait until they exhaust themselves and then move in."[77]

In response to the budding controversy, the Bush administration decided to submit evidence about war crimes and other atrocities in Bosnia to the UN War Crimes Commission. The State Department delegated this responsibility to a foreign service officer with no background in Balkan affairs and an intern recently graduated from college. As FSO Richard Johnson describes, "Hardly a commitment of personnel and expertise commensurate to the recognized gravity of the issue."[78] It would only be months later, in December, that the administration would formally, if quietly, label Serb atrocities in Bosnia as "genocide." Just before the Bush administration left office, the United States voted with 101 other nations in support of a UN General Assembly resolution that included a statement equating Serb "ethnic cleansing" practices with genocide.[79]

Debate continued in August at negotiations in London aiming at a solution to the Balkan conflict. Although the discussion reportedly opened with a "rousing condemnation of the Serbs," little of substance took place to punish them further for their atrocious behavior. The traditionally cautious and prudent Bush administration raised the tone of their rhetoric. Acting Secretary of State Lawrence Eagleburger declared, "The civilized world simply cannot afford to allow this cancer in the heart of Europe to flourish, much less spread. We must wrest control of the future from those who would drag us back into the past, and demonstrate to the world—especially to the world's one billion Muslims—that the Western democracies will oppose aggression under all circumstances, not oppose it in one region and appease it in another."[80] Similarly, Assistant Secretary for International Organization Affairs John Bolton reminded that in the post-Holocaust world, the international community vowed to "never again" allow such genocidal barbarity to occur. Bolton nonetheless proposed no preventive action but only ensuring "accountability for those responsible for criminal acts under international law."[81]

The Serbs made a flurry of promises in London—to end the siege of Sarajevo, to shut down detention camps, and to return captured territory—none of which they would honor or have to honor because no one pressured or forced them to do so once they left the bargaining table.[82] With the United States and its allies unwilling to demand and compel compliance with the various London agreements, the conference devolved into "a lost opportunity, a turning point, and a sorry chapter in the West's mishandling of the conflict."[83] As political scientist and former Defense Department analyst Wayne Bert argues, "The summer of 1992 was the time of decision on the Bosnian war. . . . During the summer the extent to which rape, concentration camps, ethnic cleansing, and destruction of cities and cultural edifices were routine Serb policy had become clear."[84] More precisely, the Serb campaign of war buttressed by atrocities and genocide had revealed itself clearly, but the United States and Europe limited themselves to toothless diplomacy and negotiation, and very quickly the Bush administration retreated back to the "pox on all their houses" approach, shunning a moment ripe for leadership. Just over two months after the concentration camp news broke, acting Secretary of State Eagleburger lectured, "I have said this 38,000 times and I have to say this to the people of this country as well. This tragedy is not something that can be settled from outside and its about damn well time that everybody understood that. Until the Bosnians, Serbs, and Croats decide to stop killing each other, there is nothing the outside world can do about it."[85]

The failure at London highlighted the Bush administration's consistent and almost principled unwillingness to commit any significant use of force to end the war or to halt "ethnic cleansing" in Bosnia. At most, the United States entertained the notion of providing air and naval escort protection for supplies sent to Sarajevo. Otherwise, the Bush team repeated its lack of interest in any unilateral use of force to end the brutality in the Balkans. James Baker always emphasized that force would always remain a last resort after all other options had been explored.

Influential and well respected, General Colin Powell helped reinforce this approach. As chairman of the Joint Chiefs of Staff, he openly questioned the wisdom of American military engagement in Bosnia. Powell championed the need for well-defined objectives, the use of overwhelming force, and a clear exit strategy. General Powell initially opposed the use of force to expel Iraq from Kuwait, and he saw Bosnia as a quagmire of ancient ethnic hatred and a mission that failed to fit any of his conditions for intervention. Bosnia tapped a wellspring of Vietnam analogies in Powell's mind, analogies that he revealed in a *New York Times* interview and in a follow-up editorial. Many senior Pentagon officials drew lessons directly from Vietnam and overlayed them reflexively on the conflict in Bosnia.[86]

Speaking from his position as secretary of state, Lawrence Eagleburger provided analogous thinking. After replacing Baker as secretary of state, he appeared on television and openly disagreed with those calling for more decisive, forceful action. Despite his strong words in London, Eagleburger now fumed, "I'm not prepared to accept arguments that there must be something between the kind of involvement of Vietnam and doing nothing, that the *New York Times* and the *Washington Post* keep blabbing about, that there must be some form in the middle. That's, again, what got us into Vietnam—do a little bit, and it doesn't work. What do you do next?"[87]

Although he exclaimed, "By God, we've kicked the Vietnam syndrome once and for all!" following the overwhelming military success in the Persian Gulf War, President Bush struggled with his own lingering Vietnam fears.[88] On August 7, 1992, pressed on the use of force to shut down the concentration camps, Bush told reporters, "I don't care what the political pressures are. Before one soldier is committed to battle, I'm going to know how that person gets out of there. And we are not going to get bogged down in some guerilla warfare. We lived through that once."[89] Warren Zimmerman emphasizes that Vietnam infected every discussion Bush had about intervention: "The 'lesson' drawn from Vietnam was that even a minimum injection of American forces could swell inexorably into a major commitment and produce a quagmire." With this quagmire-phobia came "an almost obsessive fear of American casualties."[90] David Gompert, who served from 1990 to 1993 on the National Security Council staff as special assistant to the president and senior director for European and Eurasian affairs, buttresses that analysis, writing that "intervention in Bosnia was viewed as more akin to the Vietnam experience (high casualties, lengthy stay, poor prospects) than to Desert Storm (few casualties, short stay, good prospects)."[91]

Following the election loss in November 1992 to Governor Clinton, the Bush administration returned briefly to the Bosnia tragedy, as Secretary Eagleburger floated a proposal to exempt Bosnia from the UN arms embargo. The Security Council did not receive the idea warmly. Instead, Britain and France vetoed the proposal, in large part out of concern over the impact of intensified hostilities on the safety of their military personnel on the ground in Bosnia.[92] Some critics suggest that the proposal to lift the embargo on Bosnia was at best halfhearted, a calculated public relations maneuver that the administration knew would fail. Former State Department official Stephen Walker explains that "Eagleburger took none of the usual steps to make something come of his proposal."[93] Indeed, shortly after the failed attempt to lift the embargo and arm the Bosnians, Eagleburger once again shared condemnation for all parties in Bosnia while making no reference to genocide at all. Eagleburger repeated, "It's Serbs, it's Croats, it's Bosnian Muslims, the whole panorama. If you're intent on killing each other, don't blame it on somebody else."[94]

However, no one was blaming the West for causing the violence. Many were, however, hoping that the United States and its allies might act to stop genocide. The Bush administration left office supporting humanitarian relief but still resolutely opposed to the use of American force in Bosnia. Concern about winter casualties from starvation and exposure pushed the United States to provide relief, including an airlift to Sarajevo and airdrops to outlying enclaves. This relief effort saved thousands, even tens of thousands, of lives. While an admirable effort, it nonetheless did nothing to stop or slow the genocidal war creating the perilous conditions in the first place; in fact, it helped keep potential victims alive.

CLINTON'S TURN

As a presidential candidate in the 1992 election, Bill Clinton levied some heavy criticism against the Bush administration for its Bosnia policy. He attacked the administration for timidly standing by as "ethnic cleansing" proceeded, particularly after stories broke about the concentration camps. In the Arkansas governor's opinion, this unacceptable bystanding left Bosnia's civilians to perish and diminished American values and its role as a champion of human rights in the world. Taking an unequivocal stance, Clinton stated on August 4, 1992, "I am outraged by the revelations of concentration camps in Bosnia and urge immediate action to stop this slaughter." Clinton added, "If the horror of the Holocaust taught us anything, it is the high cost of remaining silent and paralyzed in the face of genocide." Just a day later, Clinton built on his powerful call to action, declaring, "We cannot afford to ignore what appears to be a deliberate and systematic extermination of human beings based on their ethnic origin. I would begin with air power against the Serbs, to try to restore the basic conditions of humanity."[95] He also supported lifting the arms embargo to allow the Bosnians to equip and defend themselves.

Governor Clinton's pronouncements on Bosnia even bolstered those in the State Department still struggling with Bush's insistence on keeping out of Bosnia. Policy Planning's John Fox told ABC News that Clinton's statements "were raising hopes within the department that perhaps there would be sufficient pressure to bring about a change, if not before the election then after."[96] At first, it appeared that the new administration would follow through and invigorate a lifeless Bosnia policy. Newly minted Secretary of State Warren Christopher delivered a strong message when he appeared before the Senate Foreign Relations Committee on February 10, 1993. Christopher told the senators,

> The events in the former Yugoslavia raise the question whether a state may address the rights of its minorities by eradicating them to achieve ethnic purity. Bold tyrants and fearful minorities are watching to see whether ethnic cleansing is a policy the world will tolerate. If we hope to promote the spread of freedom, if we hope to encourage the emergence of peaceful ethnic democracies, our answer must be a resounding no. Beyond humanitarian concerns, we have direct strategic concerns as well. The continuing destruction of a new United Nations member challenges the principle that internationally recognized borders should not be altered by force. In addition, this conflict itself has no natural borders. It threatens to spill over into new regions, such as Kosovo and Macedonia. It could then become a greater Balkan war like those that preceded World War I. Broader hostilities could touch additional nations such as Greece and Turkey and Albania.[97]

Quickly, however, President Clinton adopted a very different and more restrained stance on the genocide in Bosnia. With amazing alacrity, the previously urgent appeal for immediate action ceded to the more immediate demands of President Clinton's domestic agenda.[98] The administration found it fairly easy to ignore the tragedy in Bosnia. As a plurality president, Clinton feared a potentially costly foreign policy issue that could weaken him politically and jeopardize his initiatives at home, such as health care reform.

Influential advisers such as Dick Morris explicitly reinforced this mind-set. In his memoirs, Morris explains that "noninvolvement in Bosnia had been a central element in my advice. You don't want to be Lyndon Johnson, I had said early on, 'sacrificing your potential for doing good on the domestic front by a destructive, never-ending foreign involvement. It's the Democrats disease to take the same compassion that motivates their domestic policies and let it lure them into heroic but ill-considered foreign war.' "[99] Tim Wirth, former Colorado senator and counselor to Clinton, remarked, "We can't let Bosnia endanger the best liberal hope for a generation."[100]

Furthermore, for a new domestically oriented president with problematic military "issues," namely alleged draft dodging and controversy over gays in the military, deploying ground troops was highly unlikely. The likelihood of any intervention dropped even further given Colin Powell's adamant opposition. Powell was highly critical of the Clinton foreign policy team and its policy discussions, which he described as "group therapy—an existential debate over what is the role of America, etc. . . . like a graduate student bull session or the think-tank seminars in which many of my new colleagues had spent the last twelve years while their party was out of power."[101] Opposed to hard thinking about American foreign policy, the general expressed his continued, firm, and influential opposition to the use of force in Bosnia by the United States.

The new administration also rejected the Vance-Owen plan for Bosnia. Vance-Owen was the diplomatic mission initiated by the United Nations and the European Community. Former U.S. Secretary of State Cyrus Vance joined with Britain's Lord David Owen to produce a settlement. They proposed reorganizing Bosnia-Herzegovina into ten cantons, three for each ethnic group and a separate jointly administered Sarajevo. Overall, 43 percent of the territory would go to the Serbs. Clinton and his foreign policy advisers believed it rewarded Serbian aggression and sanctioned ethnic cleansing. While the Clinton administration expressed its dislike for Vance-Owen, it failed to offer a viable alternative and undermined the difficult negotiations with obvious apathy.

With ground troops and cantonization essentially ruled out, the use of air power surfaced as a potentially viable and palatable option. For proponents, air strikes held the promise of punishing and even dissuading the Serbs at relatively low risk in terms of American casualties and deep entanglement. Thus, the Clinton administration sought to create movement with a proposal known as "lift-and-strike" that combined air power with a modified arms embargo. Under this plan, the United Nations would exempt Bosnia from the arms embargo. The North Atlantic Treaty Organization (NATO) would strike at Serb positions to provide cover for the Bosnians while they rearmed themselves (including heavy artillery) and received some training.

Lift-and-strike appeared to provide the administration with the best of both worlds: "the US would be taking a principled position to resist Serbian aggression and support the efforts of the Bosnian government by securing a restricted lifting of the UN arms embargo against the territories of the former Yugoslavia in favour of the Bosnian authorities, providing air deterrence to prevent Serbian forces taking advantage of a transitional period and avoiding a commitment of US forces on the ground."[102]

The plan had immediate appeal in its apparent simplicity and common sense. The idea of selectively puncturing the embargo resonated strongly with congressional Republicans, especially Bob Dole, who found it absurd to prevent the

Bosnians from defending themselves. President Clinton expressed his own personal understanding of the Bosnians' plea to lift the arms embargo, saying in private, "If there were other countries keeping us from defending ourselves, I'd be pissed as hell or goddamn resentful."[103] As for air strikes, the notion of air power enjoyed significant afterglow following its high-profile use against Iraq during the Persian Gulf War.

The administration hammered away at lift-and-strike behind the scenes in preparation for a trip to Europe by the secretary of state to discuss the plan. Meanwhile, the president had the opportunity to preside over the opening of the United States Holocaust Memorial Museum. On a dark and unseasonably cold April 22, 1993, the president joined Nobel Peace Prize laureate and Holocaust survivor Elie Wiesel to "dedicate the United States Holocaust Museum and so bind one of the darkest lessons in history to the hopeful soul of America."[104] The president invoked the pledge "never again" and spoke of ethnic cleansing, commenting, "We learn again and again that the world has yet to run its course of animosity and violence. Ethnic cleansing in the former Yugoslavia is but the most brutal and ever present manifestation."

Midway through his address, Wiesel turned to Clinton and said, "And Mr. President, I must tell you something. I have been in the former Yugoslavia last fall. I cannot sleep since what I have seen. As a Jew I am saying that. We must do something to stop the bloodshed in that country . . . something, anything, must be done."[105] For the administration, that something was lift-and-strike.

Yet the plan's simplicity was illusory. Actual implementation of an effective lift-and-strike proposal meant much greater involvement than publicly discussed, including the very type of intervention that Clinton sought to avoid. David Rieff explains,

> Many of the calls for lifting the arms embargo against the Bosnians took no account of the military realities on the ground. To the question of how the weapons were going to be gotten into Sarajevo or Tuzla, supporters of this approach at best tended to respond vaguely. When pressed they would concede that some outside force would have to bring in the arms the Bosnians needed. And yet, if one took them at their word, what they were calling for was military intervention in the strictest sense. . . . In reality, there was never any possibility of getting arms in sufficient quantities to Bosnian government forces without at least a limited intervention.[106]

Thanks to the European allies, the administration would never have to address publicly such operational details involved in making lift-and-strike a reality.

When Secretary of State Warren Christopher traveled to the Continent in May 1993 to discuss the plan with the allies, it soon became clear that Europe thought little of lift-and-strike. Paris and London gave both Christopher and the plan a fairly chilly reception. Responding to an earlier American argument that removing the burden of the embargo from Bosnia would work to level the playing field, Britain's foreign secretary had suggested that it would rather establish "a level killing field."[107] The Europeans remained reluctant to use force and put at risk their troops already deployed with the UN force in Bosnia. European officials did not enjoy being lectured or prodded in any direction by a country without people in harm's way. To compound this, Christopher reportedly did more listening than active promotion of the policy.[108] Then-Belgian foreign minister Willy Claes observed, "I had the feeling, when he [Christopher] came to Brussels, that he had felt very clearly that there was not a possibility to convince the Europeans."

Still other allies believed that, if determined, the United States could make lift-and-strike a reality despite Europe's objections. Wayne Bert captures this attitude: "Several observers were of the view that if the United States had insisted on stronger military action, then the Europeans would have had no option but to go along. They would have been shamed into it."[109] However, the administration apparently did not push the policy with much enthusiasm, opting instead for an exchange of views instead of forceful promotion. Describing this "exchange of views" between the United States and the allies, former Assistant Secretary of Defense Richard Perle stated, "It was an exchange alright: Warren Christopher went to Europe with an American policy, and he came back with a European one."[110]

In the end, it was British, French, and Spanish troops who were on the ground. If the Americans were not willing to insist—in effect, threaten to breach NATO itself—the Europeans certainly could not take the proposal seriously. While one can understand the concern in London, Paris, and Madrid for their people in Bosnia, this approach also made virtual hostages of the UN Protection Force in the region. The overriding concern for the safety of personnel on the ground invited Serbian audacity without fear of reprisal, including taking "blue helmets" hostage to avoid strikes.

Europe wanted an end to the war, not a more intense and prolonged conflict. The allies feared that arming Bosnians would extend a war that the small republic could not win. An in-flow of weapons would also and push them away from negotiating a settlement such as Vance-Owen, which, however flawed and unjust, would stop the bloodshed. David Gompert states flatly that Europe's "unspoken aim was to deprive the Bosnian Muslims of any reasonable hope of rescue so that they would accept defeat and agree to a settlement."[111] Lord Owen in particular feared the false encouragement that the lift-and-strike rhetoric alone would likely foster. Owen went so far as to warn the Bosnians, "Don't, don't, don't, live under this dream that the West is going to come in and sort this problem out. Don't dream dreams."[112]

Concerns about Russia and the survival of the Yeltsin government also softened American insistence on the use of force against the Serbs. The influential Deputy Secretary of State Strobe Talbott expressed strong concerns that too much U.S. support for the Bosnians and too much U.S. and NATO action against the Serbs would hurt Yeltsin's position and strengthen right-wing nationalist forces in Russia that already sharply attacked him for his "Atlanticism."[113] Bosnia was a particularly sensitive issue because of historical Russian-Serb affinity and the lingering ethos of Orthodox Christianity and "pan-Slavism."

To avoid putting Yeltsin in a more difficult position at home and to build a foundation for Russian-American partnership, the United States gave Moscow's reservations about any initiative "more than their due."[114] As a result of this accommodation, Russia emerged as a significant foreign policy presence in the region (a presence denied it during the Tito regime), returning to "foreign policy prominence beyond its own—or even the former Soviet Union's—borders."[115] Moscow often impeded progress and openly favored the Serbs, for example, opposing air strikes, opposing resolutions of condemnation by the Organization for Security and Cooperation in Europe (OSCE), and supporting an end to the economic sanctions.

Instead of taking the lead, the United States followed its reluctant allies and backed off on lift-and-strike, its only serious proposal on Bosnia. Christopher reassessed Bosnia and began to see the need for the United States to keep clear. The European Community's response to lift-and-strike informed him of "what a loser this policy was." The secretary of state also wanted the president to end the bold rhetoric that damaged American credibility and hurt an already tremendously difficult situation.[116] Christopher found the president more receptive to that message than expected.

An avid reader and history fan, Clinton had picked up a copy of Robert Kaplan's *Balkan Ghosts.* In the book, Kaplan highlights the "ancient hatreds and longstanding feuds" interpretation of events in Bosnia. Finding Kaplan's argument compelling, the president entertained new doubts on the potential to influence war and atrocities in the region.[117] Clinton was apparently also influenced by an opinion piece by Arthur Schlesinger Jr., published in the *Wall Street Journal* on May 3, in which the historian "warned the president that, like Lyndon Johnson and Vietnam, intervention in the Balkans could undermine his domestic policy."[118] Before long, the administration moved from describing Bosnia as a pivotal challenge to America's "ability to nurture democracy in the post-cold war world" to labeling it with phrases such as "an intractable problem from hell that no one can be expected to solve . . . less as a moral tragedy . . . and more as a tribal feud that no outsider could hope to settle."[119]

America's Bosnia policy disappeared from view. As Joshua Muravchik puts it, "Having tiptoed up to the line of military action in Bosnia and then flinched, the Clinton administration spent the next months trying to define down the importance of the crisis to America."[120] The administration now viewed Bosnia only in humanitarian terms, with no reference or connection to vital interests. Previous moral indignation pushed aside, Warren Christopher in June 1993 fully eviscerated his bold and visionary statement on Bosnia from the previous February. He now referred to Bosnia as "a humanitarian crisis a long way from home, in the middle of another continent."[121]

This "downgrading" of Bosnia contrasted markedly both with earlier Clinton administration rhetoric and also with the approach of the Bush administration. Right or wrong, the Bush administration had no intention of committing American forces in any form to Bosnia, and they adjusted their rhetoric accordingly. Bush's well-known (and often mocked) prudence led him to a consistent embrace of two rules: "Do not make the United States responsible for a problem it cannot solve and make no threat that the United States cannot execute."[122]

Although cautious in action, President Clinton had demonstrated little such rhetorical restraint, particularly in his first years in office. However genuine his concern for Bosnia's victims, the president too often made promises he could not or would not keep. Over the course of the war, debate continued throughout the country over the appropriate course of action for Bosnia, most clearly evidenced by the constant opposing commentaries and opinions in the media. However, such inconsistency from the United States government was unacceptable: "The President talked too much about what he was going to do—and then didn't do it."[123] It soon became painfully clear that the Clinton team had no policy, nor did it seem to want one beyond a general stance of noninvolvement even as genocide marched on in Europe.

Instead of lift-and-strike, the Clinton administration now suffered from what James Gow of London's King's College called "rift-and-drift."[124] American policy on Bosnia, now lacking any deep commitment to any particular cause or principle—except maybe nonintervention—stood still. Relations with Europe and Russia had taken a frosty turn. The dying continued in Bosnia; the genocide proceeded. Vocal critics such as Leslie H. Gelb called administration policy "a farce." He wrote, "Diplomacy without force is farce, but that is the present Western-UN course. It is cynical farce, for all the realists and neo-isolationists who espouse it know they are winking at Serbian genocide and merely delaying their inevitable confrontation with Serbia, at unforgivable cost in Muslim lives."[125] Lord David Owen captured the essence of Clinton's early struggle with Bosnia policy, observing that "the US could neither advocate a settlement nor abdicate from a settlement. They could not forgo the appearance of exerting power, but they were not ready or seemingly able to accept the compromises and the responsibility that go with the exercise of power."[126]

This abnegation of responsibility bothered some in the State Department so much that they chose to follow the precedent set by George Kenney a year earlier and resign in protest. Marshall Freeman Harris began the miniexodus when he left on August 4, 1993, saying his morale bottomed out at the end of July, when Secretary Christopher said that the United States was doing all it could. Jon Western, a war crimes analyst, left shortly thereafter, announcing that he was "thoroughly demoralized and depressed" and "heartsick by the failure" of the United States to make Bosnia a top priority. Eight-year foreign service veteran Stephen Walker, then at the Croatia desk, completed the triumvirate. Following his late August resignation, he criticized "U.S. support for a diplomatic process that legitimizes aggression and genocide."

Before 1993 became 1994, the State Department would lose another prominent voice: Warren Zimmerman. The former ambassador to Yugoslavia had grown increasingly frustrated with "a policy whose tentative nature was being exploited by the Serbian aggressors." In his memoirs, Zimmerman explains that his "frustrations with Bosnia and with an unrelated personnel issue pointed inexorably to leaving." He informed Secretary Christopher of his intention to retire in large part over Bosnia and arranged a farewell meeting. Zimmerman ended his State Department tenure by making one last case for the use of force against the Serbs, to which he received "no substantive comment."[127]

VIRTUAL BACKBONE

As 1993 became 1994, the war dragged on, oblivious to the roller-coaster nature of American policy. Croat forces demonstrated a newfound effectiveness against the Serbs. The siege of Sarajevo also continued, complete with shelling of the supposedly "safe" city. NATO opted not to respond to the almost daily assaults "on the grounds that these attacks remained below an undefined threshold of intensity."[128] However, a mortar shell fired on February 5, 1994, changed all that, however briefly. The shell landed in an outdoor Sarajevo marketplace, killing sixty-eight civilians and wounding hundreds of others.

The attack—accurately described as "an obscene act but no worse than other atrocities routinely committed in Bosnia"[129]—stirred the American public, who reacted powerfully to the grisly footage broadcast on television and printed in the papers and magazines. Senator Dole used the tragedy once again to press President Clinton to exempt the Bosnians from the UN arms embargo. He called the Serb attack "not surprising in light of the international community's utter lack of will and principle in responding to nearly two years of aggression against Bosnia."[130] The Clinton administration translated its newest pang of outrage into policy and pushed NATO to issue an ultimatum to the Serbs requiring that they move their heavy weapons and artillery out of range of Sarajevo (a twenty-kilometer radius) within ten days or face air strikes. The Serbs slowly complied, or at least reached what was termed "virtual compliance."[131] The United States also dispatched planes to Sarajevo to evacuate victims to an American-run hospital outside Zagreb, Croatia.

Earlier proponents of the use (or threatened use) of air power claimed vindication. The celebration did not last long. Within weeks, the Serbs simply transferred many of the artillery pieces for use against other locations, including the "safe area" of Gorazde and its 65,000 Muslim inhabitants. Serbian compliance/defiance then manifested itself in the shelling of Gorazde, the detention of UN peacekeepers, and firing on NATO aircraft enforcing a no-fly zone.[132] Instead of newfound will, administration inconsistency resurfaced. Secretary of Defense William Perry ruled out American action to save the threatened enclave.[133] Days later, National Security Adviser Anthony Lake undercut Perry's statement, announcing that "neither the president nor any of his senior advisors rules out the use of air power to help stop attacks such as those against Gorazde."[134]

On April 11, 1994, the use of air power to prevent the fall of Gorazde was ruled in, as NATO undertook its first-ever air-to-ground attack mission. The attack itself was slight. Two American jets struck a tent and several vehicles. When Serb intransigence continued, NATO withheld additional sorties and instead applied the Sarajevo ultimatum, demanding that Serbian forces withdraw from the area and pull back their heavy weapons to twenty kilometers from Gorazde. The Serbs followed a predictable script and watched the April 22, 1994, deadline come and go without reprisals. Shortly thereafter, they did redeploy their forces to avoid at the last minute any additional strikes from the air.

The record of threatened and delivered air strikes remained mixed. Joshua Muravchik argues that "despite Serbian cheating and probing, NATO seemed at last to have established that it was prepared to use some degree of force to protect at least some of the proclaimed safe areas."[135] However, the force used amounted to little more than "patty cake" bombing."[136] The strikes did represent progress, but it had come too little and too late. David Gompert argues persuasively that "the Clinton administration demonstrated instead how sharply limited any use of force would be, which is why the Serbs merely licked their wounds and went on with their basic strategy after Gorazde and other instances of selective use of Western air power."[137]

The NATO ultimatums resulted in some progress on the diplomatic side. In exchange for European support of military action (however limited), the United States agreed in June 1994 to a plan to split Bosnian territory in two, with 51 percent going to a Muslim-Croat federation and the remaining 49 percent going to Serbia. Endorsement of the plan was a significant departure for Washington, which had long supported Bosnia's territorial integrity and sought to avoid a settlement such as Vance-Owen, which appeared to reward Serb aggression and ratify the results of ethnic cleansing. The Clinton administration's failure to lead and take unilateral action forced it to accommodate European conditions for their support of NATO air strikes. As a *Washington Post* editorial accurately explained,

> Creation of the map is the result of a major change of heart within the Clinton administration, which had said it would never endorse a map, much less pressure the Bosnian factions to agree to one. However, the Americans agreed to help design such a solution in exchange for the acquiescence of Europe in general, and France in particular, to use NATO air strikes as a threat to deter Bosnian Serb attacks on the capital, Sarajevo, and the besieged Muslim enclave of Gorazde.[138]

The new plan reflected a renewed diplomatic effort among the so-called Contact Group of the United States, Russia, France, Germany, and Great Britain. The Bosnians, losing the fight and dependent on humanitarian aid from the West, accepted the plan and assumed that the Serbs would reject it. With sanctions hurting at home, Slobodan Milosevic lobbied his Bosnian Serb counterparts to accept the proposal and end the war. Milosevic failed to persuade Karadzic to accept the deal, and the United States revived its efforts to win Bosnian exemption from the arms embargo.

Toward that same end, the United States ceased enforcing the embargo on the Adriatic, and an amendment sponsored by senators Sam Nunn and George Mitchell called for a November 15 cutoff of funds for enforcement activity. Still stymied on the embargo issue at the Security Council, the United States supported a General Assembly resolution calling for an end to the embargo. The resolution passed 94–0 with sixty-one members abstaining. The Contact Group, unable to muster consensus for additional military threats, turned its attention to pressure Belgrade further to push its comrades. In exchange for a softening of the economic sanction against Serbia, Belgrade agreed to end material support for the militias. The Serb leader did not completely cut off the flow of supplies but did make noticeable reductions.[139] Despite the deal, the Bosnian Serbs were not impressed with either Milosevic or the Contact Group, and they continued their genocidal aggression. Related bargaining continued throughout much of the first half of 1995. The Contact Group proposed a complete lifting of the economic sanctions against Serbia if Milosevic recognized the borders of Bosnia-Herzegovina, if not its government. Belgrade flatly refused.

At the end of 1994, as war and genocide proceeded apace in Bosnia, a group of over seventy members of the world's political and cultural elite published a unique obituary in the *New York Times.* The death notice read,

IN MEMORIAM

Our commitments,
Principles, and moral values
Died: Bosnia, 1994
On the Occasion of the 1,000th Day
Of The Siege Of Sarajevo[140]

ATROCIOUS OVERREACH

Meanwhile, the shelling of Sarajevo once again grew more intense as summer approached in 1995. NATO flexed its muscles momentarily by bombing Serbian ammunition dumps. Rather than back down, the Bosnian Serbs responded by taking almost 400 UN peacekeepers hostage. Some were chained to trees and bridges near potential target sites to deter NATO action. Instead of a vigorous UN/NATO response, this terrorist tactic won a halt in the bombing and secret negotiations between Serb commander Ratko Mladic, UN military official General Bernard Janvier, and UN representative Yashushi Akashi. At those talks, Akashi and Janvier allegedly assured Mladic that NATO would cease air strikes in return for the hostages. This deal grew in importance by mid-July as Maldic's forces, commanded by General Radislav Krstic, moved on the "safe haven" of Srebrenica.

Two years earlier, on May 6, 1993, the UN Security Council established Sarajevo, Tuzla, Bihac, Srebrenica, Zepa, and Gorazde as supposed "safe areas" where Bosnian Muslims could find refuge. Later that month, France, England, Russia, Spain, and the United States sponsored a "Joint Action Program" that pledged protection for the six "safe havens." The Security Council only provided for 220 troops from UNPROFOR to "defend" Srebrenica; an additional fifty military observers were sent to protect civilians in the other areas.

Srebrenica had suffered for years from shelling and disrupted aid. Intermittent airdrops of supplies (including some by American Hercules transport planes) barely kept the inhabitants alive. By the summer of 1995, the population in Srebrenica had swollen to 50,000 people in a community with adequate facilities for no more than 15,000.[141] A small UN force of Dutch troops was stationed at Srebrenica but could not offer much given their limited mandate, minimal equipment, and the much larger Bosnian Serb force opposing them. Air strikes might have held off the Serb offensive, but none were forthcoming. According to the *New York Times,* "General Janvier convened his top military advisors. . . . The general asked for advice. The response was nearly unanimous: airstrikes. The United Nation's credibility was at stake. Srebrenica was a safe area. It had to be defended. . . . General Janvier was unpersuaded. He announced that he would sleep on it. He left his aides 'aghast' as a United Nations official put it."[142]

The Clinton administration remained unwilling to act unilaterally. NATO could not agree on action. Free of threats from the air, Krstic advanced his troops into Srebrenica as thousands of Muslims fled. The United States and Europe stood by as tens of thousands of Bosnian Muslims were "cleansed" from the area. Serb forces systematically butchered over 8,000 men and boys. UN peacekeepers, ever neutral, fueled buses used to deport Bosnian Muslims from the area and transport others to remote areas for execution. Serb forces even donned Dutch UN uniforms to lure people out from hiding to be killed.[143] Judge Fouad Riad, a member of the International Criminal Tribunal for Yugoslavia, described the genocidal atrocities in Srebrenica as "from hell, written on the darkest pages of human history."[144]

As the world witnessed a genocidal assault against an area designated by the international community as "safe," French President Jacques Chirac phoned President Clinton on July 13, 1995. Bob Woodward reports that Chirac stunned Clinton by suggesting that they "ought to go in with French ground forces and American helicopters to recapture the city." According to Woodward, Clinton "made it clear that he didn't consider that practical and wouldn't go along."[145] Leadership once again waned when faced with a moment for decisive, ethical action.

Genocide at Srebrenica created powerful shock waves. The media flooded viewers with news of the catastrophe. With detailed intelligence on the rapes, exterminations, and refugees fleeing the area, the administration had an even sharper picture of the dark events. At a July 18, 1995, meeting of the foreign policy principals, exasperation and disgust swelled to the surface. Vice President Al Gore, a longtime proponent of stronger action, told those assembled, "The worst solution would be to acquiesce to genocide." Gore referred to a front-page *Washington Post* photograph of a young refugee who had hanged herself. Gore challenged his colleagues and the president: "My 21-year-old daughter asked about that picture. What am I supposed to tell her? Why is this happening and we're not doing anything. My daughter is surprised the world is allowing this to happen. I am too."[146]

Given the recent record of the United States, the United Nations, and NATO, the Serbs were not surprised. More confident than ever of their ability to perpetuate genocide with relative impunity, the Bosnian Serbs moved against other enclaves, quickly taking Zepa (protected by seventy-nine Ukrainians) on July 25, 1995, and then once again menacing Gorazde.

NO MORE "PATTY-CAKE"

When the genocidal horror of Srebrenica threatened to repeat itself at Gorazde, American outrage and resolve coalesced. Predictably, the administration drew fire from concerned newspaper columnists and television commentators. However, more important, the Clinton policy came under attack by a focused campaign in Congress. With a majority in both the House and the Senate, Republican legislators coordinated their criticism into actual support for legislation. Long a critic of the arms embargo, Senator Bob Dole mustered enough support for the so-called Bosnia Self-Defense Bill. The bill threatened to force the government to unilaterally lift the arms embargo on Bosnia. Dole was also prepared if necessary to seek a two-thirds majority to override the president's veto. With a presidential election less than a year away, President Clinton finally had to face the immediate legacy of his "passive and ineffectual role in a war he had promised to do something about three years earlier."[147] The domestic agenda president now felt significant domestic pressure to tackle a difficult and risky foreign policy issue about which he had once spoken grandly but had recently all but ignored.

The prospect simultaneously loomed that the Europeans would remove their UNPROFOR troops if the United States cracked the embargo. Europe's leadership had consistently argued that flooding Bosnia with more arms would intensify the fighting and further jeopardize their personnel. Paris, London, and other troop-contributing capitals made clear their intention to remove the force if this occurred. Under those circumstances, the Clinton administration would find itself having to honor a NATO commitment to support the evacuation. That effort would involve 25,000 American military personnel in an overall force of 60,000 tasked with the embarrassing job of essentially declaring defeat, completely abandoning the Bosnians, and pulling out the humanitarian presence out of the battle zone. Not only would evacuation smack of defeatism, but it was also bold and dangerous. As Richard Holbrooke describes the plan, known as "OpPlan 40–104," "It used twenty thousand American troops, some of whom were assigned to carry out a risky nighttime U.S. heliborne extraction of U.N. troops from isolated enclaves, an operation likely to produce casualties."[148] The bizarre logic now before the administration was clear: They had to find a way to avoid a "disastrous UN withdrawal," and to avoid that actually meant greater American involvement.[149]

Determined to keep U.S. troops out of an active Bosnian war zone, the administration needed UNPROFOR and its European contingents to stay put. This required a fully intact arms embargo. The administration knew that they could not fend off the Republican Congress indefinitely. The optimum solution, then, was an end to the war. With mounting pressure at home and abroad, the administration suddenly gave Assistant Secretary of State Holbrooke "real authority to act in the name of the United States" and energized its negotiating efforts.[150]

Significant developments in the Balkans also contributed to improved conditions on the ground and at the negotiation table. On August 4, 1995, the Croatians launched a massive (and at times brutal) offensive. With its forces rebuilt, resupplied, and retrained (in part with U.S.-funded personnel from MPRI, an American private military company), Croatia's "Operation Storm" overran the Croatian Serb position at Knin and recaptured almost all Serb-held territory in the region. With a successful military campaign, the Croats dealt a serious blow to the image of invincible and unshakable Serb forces. These results deflated at least momentarily the powerful notions of a supposedly indomitable Serbian juggernaut and the related Vietnam analogies that had helped the West, and particularly the United States, convince itself to stand by as the Serbs committed genocide.[151] Wayne Bert comments that, "the psychological impact of this abrupt reversal of fortune could not help but be dramatic, and this lesson in military initiative undoubtedly helped lift a psychological barrier that had until then discouraged Western action. With the Serbs shorn of their aura of invincibility, and given the ease with which the Croatian army had routed the Bosnian Serbs, the allies could now summon the courage to conduct their own offensive against them."[152]

American momentum suffered a temporary but tragic setback on August 19, when three Americans on Holbrooke's team—the State Department's Robert Frasure, Air Force Colonel Nelson S. Drew from the National Security Council staff, and Dr. Joseph J. Kruzel from the Defense Department—died in a road accident on their way to Sarajevo. The death of the American negotiators inspired Holbrooke to secure the peace to which the three men were committed. Holbrooke's personal motivation would soon be bolstered by power from the air.

When, on August 28, 1995, a Serbian mortar attack killed over thirty-five people in Sarajevo, the Serbs had overreached; their luck was up. The attack came as the United States launched its new effort to end the three-and-a-half-year war and just hours before Holbrooke was to meet in Paris with Bosnian leaders. Facing domestic criticism of their own over Bosnia, the European allies demonstrated a new receptivity to the strike option once again promoted by the Clinton administration. National Security Adviser Anthony Lake renewed American diplomatic efforts to win NATO approval. His efforts succeeded, and NATO responded with vigor. More than sixty U.S. fighter jets joined the raids against Serb positions two days after the mortar attack. NATO air attacks and artillery bombardment from the European Rapid Reaction Force deployed outside Sarajevo pounded the Serbs relentlessly and "put the Bosnian Serbs on the receiving end of overwhelming firepower for the first time."[153] The Western response also meant indirect air support for continued Bosnian and Croatian military movements. This time, not only did the Serbs soon pull back their heavy weapons from Sarajevo, but they lost more and more territory. After over

3,500 allied sorties, the Bosnian Serbs' self-declared parliament in Pale indicated their willingness to negotiate seriously.

Within months, Serb control of territory in Croatia had fallen from 55 percent to less than 23 percent; in Bosnia it dropped from 70 percent to under 50 percent. The actual balance of power on the ground at that point almost exactly mirrored the 51/49 formula proposed in the Contact Group plan in June 1994. With Karadzic's rebel Serb forces on their heels, Milosevic emerged in a much stronger bargaining position. Milosevic delivered, and the parties concluded a cease-fire in mid-September. In November 1995, after three years of fighting and genocide and hundreds of thousands dead, the presidents of Bosnia, Serbia, and Croatia joined Holbrooke at Wright-Patterson Air Force Base in Dayton, Ohio, to settle the Yugoslav conflict.

JUSTICE IN DAYTON AND BEYOND

America's policy toward war and genocide in Bosnia entered the justice phase with the signing of the Dayton Peace Accords. The details of the Dayton process and the resulting accord themselves are subjects of involved analyses.[154] In sum, the agreement reached at Dayton and signed in Paris in December 1995 divided Bosnian territory according to the 51/49 plan. The negotiated framework established a single state called Bosnia-Herzegovina comprised of two entities, the Federation of Bosnia and Herzegovina and the Serb Republic (Republica Srpska). A NATO-led peacekeeping force (Implementing Force, or IFOR) of 60,000 troops, including 20,000 Americans, was deployed to Bosnia to maintain separation between the two previously warring sides. As of this writing, 3,500 American military personnel remain in the region. As far as genocide is concerned, Dayton's greatest significance is that it ended the war and with it the ethnic cleansing. Beyond that, the Dayton Accords include unprecedented provisions for human rights and attempts to deal with accused and indicted war criminals.

Some key elements of the accord include the following:

1. The parties are obligated to cooperate fully with the International War Crimes Tribunal for the former Yugoslavia in its investigations of war crimes and other violations of international humanitarian law and to comply with its orders.
2. Stipulations that individuals indicted for war crimes who do not comply with the tribunal's orders cannot run for or hold elected or appointed office in Bosnia and Herzegovina.
3. The sanctions suspension resolution adopted by the Security Council follow-

ing Dayton includes provisions that will assist in enforcing compliance with these provisions.

4. On the recommendation of the commander of IFOR or the high representative, if parties are found to be "failing significantly" to meet their obligations, sanctions will be reimposed unless the Security Council decides otherwise.
5. In addition, an "outer wall" of sanctions will remain available, if necessary, in the form of denying access by noncompliant parties to international organizations, international financial institutions, and foreign assistance.

The tribunal, established in 1993 to deal with war crimes in the former Yugoslavia and which the Dayton agreement works to support, is the centerpiece of a postwar effort to secure justice for the victims of war crimes and genocide. As part of its unique history, the International War Crimes Tribunal for the former Yugoslavia (ICTY) was established by the UN Security Council *during* the conflict. In fact, the work of the tribunal added one more factor to the already difficult negotiations throughout the war. American and European negotiators found themselves having to negotiate with men accused of war crimes. Nonetheless, it was not at all clear how to achieve agreement on any settlement such as Vance-Owen or Dayton without discussing it and bargaining, at least unofficially, with war criminals such as Radovan Karadicz. Although distasteful, the United States and Europe had to deal with some of those responsible for genocide in the name of ending the war. Thus, in the end, the United States and its European allies sought justice for war crimes, atrocities, and genocidal acts that they remained unwilling to stop.[155]

Under the leadership of Madeleine Albright, the United States led the effort to create the tribunal and subsequently emerged as its most important supporter. To promote the ICTY, the United States has contributed more than $120 million, and countless U.S. government personnel have assisted with its work. Additionally, the Clinton administration supported the work of the tribunal by providing important information about war crimes and atrocities, including some material taken from classified sources. The tribunal began work in the summer of 1994 under the guidance of South Africa's Judge Richard Goldstone. While the Dayton Accords include specific provision supporting the ICTY, the tribunal served a purpose itself over the course of the Dayton negotiations. Richard Holbrooke explains that "during our negotiations the tribunal emerged as a valuable instrument of policy that allowed us, for example, to bar Karadzic and all other indicted war criminals from public office."[156] However, the real impact of the ICTY has come in the aftermath of Dayton.

To further the cause of the Yugoslav trial and other such initiatives and to institutionalize and centralize that effort, President Clinton in May 1997 nominated David J. Scheffer to the new position of ambassador-at-large for war crimes issues. Scheffer, trained in international law, previously served as legal counselor to Madeleine Albright during her stint as U.S. ambassador to the United Nations and also represented her at the National Security Council. Not an insignificant development, the creation of the War Crimes Office at the State Department and Scheffer's appointment demonstrated Clinton and Albright's interest in strengthening the ability of the United States to deal with the complex and delicate issues of justice for international crimes. With ambassador rank, Scheffer has been able to better coordinate efforts between bureaus at the State Department, to urge cooperation between U.S. agencies, and to consult with other governments. In this way, the administration created "an action office to make sure things gets done" relating to war crimes and genocide.[157]

The United States has taken steps to help bring the accused to the ICTY for trial, although there have been stops and starts. The United States initially expressed considerable reluctance to use its peacekeeping contingent (IFOR) as a posse to round up suspects. Military leaders in particular voiced their concerns about getting bogged down in guerrilla warfare—the Somalia experience no doubt gave substance to their opposition. Throughout the postwar period, the Clinton administration favored the use of behind-the-scenes pressure to push the Dayton signatories to comply with the requirement that they transfer alleged war criminals to The Hague.

To accelerate the slow process of apprehension, the United States in late 1996 and early 1997 proposed the creation of a specially trained police force to hunt down war criminals in Bosnia. Such a unit would remove the policing burden from the increasingly reduced peacekeeping force. Then-Chairman of the U.S. Joint Chiefs of Staff General John Shaliskavili said NATO troops were not trained for police-type work. To fill that role, the general said, "I think a way must be found where a police force can be constituted that would take care of those instances where the signatories to the agreement continue to refuse to turn over those war criminals." However, the proposal met stiff resistance from the European allies, especially France and Italy.[158] Opponents feared that "search and capture" missions by any force would result in costly firefights and could provoke reprisals against IFOR units. The plan faded, and NATO maintained its formal policy of arresting suspects only if troops came across them while fulfilling their normal duties.

Over time, U.S. pressure combined with frustration at the snail's pace of arrests to push NATO toward a more proactive stance. Discontent in the United States and Europe was magnified by the fact that the two "big fish" indicted for genocide and crimes against humanity—Radovan Karadzic and Ratko Mladic—continued to move about freely. Karadzic reportedly even passed through NATO-operated checkpoints. The War Crimes Tribunal provided NATO with additional incentive to act: it began issuing sealed, secret indictments. This approach prevented suspects from knowing that they could be at risk of being apprehended.

This mix of frustration and opportunity produced results on July 10, 1997, when NATO troops killed one Bosnian Serb wanted for genocide in a gunfight and arrested a second wanted for the same crime. British troops carried out the operation with American forces providing logistical support. The July operation signaled a new aggressiveness on the part of the United States and NATO. For example, on January 22, 1998, American forces apprehended Serb Goran Jelisic, wanted for genocide and crimes against humanity. Later in 1998, U.S. troops netted a bigger fish when they arrested General Radislav Krstic, the highest-ranking war crimes suspect yet taken to The Hague for prosecution. The tribunal charges Krstic, who served just under Ratko Mladic, with genocide for his actions during the July 1995 "cleansing" of the safe haven at Srebrenica. The indictment states that troops under his direct command massacred thousands of Muslim civilians. Krstic entered a plea of not guilty to the charges brought against him, including genocide, complicity to commit genocide, extermination, murder, and persecution.

Karadzic and Mladic remain at large. A *New York Times* report claims that at one point the United States had actually developed secret plans to capture both men. According to a former State Department official, "There was a big effort to collect intelligence and to make plans," an effort that cost tens of millions of dollars and included training commandos. The administration eventually shelved the plans out of concerns about potentially bloody clashes with the men's bodyguards and French reluctance to allow such a clandestine mission in their zone of occupation.[159]

The United States nonetheless continues to voice its commitment to the cause of justice in Bosnia, including the eventual trial of Karadzic and Mladic. In May 1999, the State Department launched the War Criminal Rewards program for the former Yugoslavia. Under that program, the United States offers a reward of up to $5 million for information leading to the arrest or conviction of persons indicted for serious violations of international humanitarian law by the International Criminal Tribunal for the former Yugoslavia.

Prospects for postgenocide justice in the Balkans took a positive turn when the new Yugoslav regime under the leadership of Vojislav Kostunica (which took power in a popular revolt in October 2000) arrested Slobodan Milosevic. As of this writing, Milosevic is behind bars facing charges of abuse of power and corruption. Specifically, the charges state that Milosevic overstepped his official authority and conspired with top aids to steal about $390 million from Yugoslavia's treasury. The arrest came as an American deadline passed for the Kostunica government to prove that it was cooperating with the tribunal or risk losing at least $50 million of desperately needed economic aid. Despite U.S. insistence that Milosevic stand trial for atrocities committed under his watch, the Yugoslav government has indicated no plans yet to transfer Milosevic to The Hague, where the ICTY has indicted him for his leadership role in war crimes against Kosovo Albanians. He has so far escaped indictment for his role in the Bosnian conflict, in part because of his central role as a guarantor of the Dayton Accords, but tribunal prosecutors say that the charges could be expanded to include genocide. Milosevic and his brothers in crime Karadzic and Mladic have been targets of what has been termed "Operation Saturation," which involved distributing throughout Bosnia and Serbia a "most wanted" poster identifying the three indictees. According to Ambassador Scheffer, "We recognize that our work is not finished, and that much more needs to be accomplished. We share the impatience and frustration arising from the fact that some of the major indictees, including Radovan Karadzic and Ratko Mladic, reaming at large. But their day before the Yugoslav Tribunal will come; there are no deals to cut."[160]

CONCLUSION

In a televised address to the nation, President Bill Clinton announced, "My fellow Americans, today our Armed Forces joined our NATO allies with air strikes against Serbian forces. . . . We act to protect thousands of people. . . . We act to prevent a wider war; to diffuse a powder keg at the heart of Europe that has exploded twice before in this century and with catastrophic results. And we act to stand united with our allies for peace. By acting now we are upholding our values, protecting our interests, and advancing the cause of peace." Less than a month later, the president stressed, "We must not allow, if we have the ability to stop it, ethnic cleansing or genocide anywhere we can stop it—particularly at the edge of Europe." Just a few weeks after that statement, Clinton wrote in a letter to the *Times* of London, "Today in the Balkans, forces from the United States, the United Kingdom, and our NATO allies are standing strong against ethnic cleansing, working to end the atrocities, save lives, and restore hope." Unfortunately for the people of Bosnia, those stirring words came in 1999 in response to Serbian violence against Kosovo.[161]

In Bosnia, it took years of war and genocide and over 200,000 lives lost before the United States finally demonstrated resolve, brought force to bear from the air, and in large part helped end the tragedy and trauma there. The Bosnian Muslim/Croat entente, the end of the war, and the subsequent Dayton Peace Accords did represent a triumph of American diplomacy, but those eighteen weeks of activity were hardly representative of U.S. efforts over the course of the conflict. Resignation, abdication, and hesitation best sum up the U.S. response to European genocide in the 1990s.

Early on, the Bush administration had a unique leadership opportunity to change the course of events in the Balkans and edify the moral call to action contained in the UNGC. The Serbs responded to a strong use of American-led NATO force in August and September 1995. It is not difficult to imagine a similarly effective use of force against the Serbs much earlier in the conflict, maybe even years earlier. An American ultimatum backed up with military power might have forced the Serbs to end the assaults on Dubrovnik and Vukovar and could very likely have altered their calculations about the costs and benefits of a wider war complete with "ethnic cleansing." The result would have been an entirely different course for the crisis in the region.

Instead, having already prosecuted a war in the Persian Gulf in early 1991 and with significant forces still deployed in that region, the administration displayed reluctance to contemplate a new conflict later in 1991 that could become a significant theater of battle.[162] Despite having proclaimed a "new world order," the Bush administration "during late summer and fall of 1991 turned aside suggestions that American warplanes and ships attack Serb gunners shelling Dubrovnik and Vukovar; and Bush in early 1992 turned aside a French suggestion that peacekeepers be sent to Bosnia to prevent war from breaking out."[163] Ambassador Zimmerman concludes in his memoirs, "The refusal of the Bush Administration to commit American power early was our greatest mistake of the entire Yugoslav crisis. It made an unjust outcome inevitable and wasted the opportunity to save over a hundred thousand lives."[164]

In addition to the temporal proximity of the Persian Gulf War, memories and analogies drawn from the Vietnam War never drifted far from mind. Statements by several prominent policymakers throughout the conflict revealed the continued spectral presence of the chastening "lessons" of Vietnam. Unfortunately for the Bosnian Muslims struggling against a genocidal adversary, the powerful urge to avoid another quagmire—or even the potential risk of one—paralyzed the United States. In turn, the Vietnam syndrome let the Serbs carry out their murderous agenda with a free hand.

This reluctance to intervene continued long after the Persian Gulf War. Despite revelations of concentration camps and the ongoing criminal siege of Sarajevo, the Bush administration refused to get involved. Such staunch refusal to intervene against massive genocidal atrocities contrasts sharply with the same administration's willingness to intervene militarily in Panama in large part to remove a dictator who had defied Washington one time too many.[165]

To his credit, President Bush avoided the rhetorical excess of his successor. He matched consistency of policy on Bosnia with consistency in public pronouncements; the Bush team spoke prudently on the issue for the most part. While administration officials did criticize and condemn the Serbs, they nevertheless "never promised that the U.S. cavalry might be on the way." Having willfully declined to stop the atrocities in Bosnia, the Bush administration left that job and the mistake of misleading rhetoric to the incoming Clinton team.

As already discussed in detail, for too long Bill Clinton promised much and delivered nothing for Bosnia. To craft an effective policy posed a large enough challenge for the new administration. President Clinton made it even tougher with his bold speechifying. Clinton thus grappled with a dilemma in part his own creation: "He had promised justice but fulfilling that promise meant that he must commit major diplomatic attention and most likely some military force, make speeches, and spend political capital—and thereby risk, as his political advisors warned him, the domestic reforms he had come to Washington to make."[166] A harsh but accurate judgment comes from former Secretary of State Henry Kissinger, who explained that Clinton

> committed his administration to acting on an aggressive, forceful policy of reversing Serbian seizures of land, of protecting Bosnia as a multi-ethnic society. And, from the beginning, he never adopted the level of force necessary to achieve these large aims. From the beginning, he proposed objectives that were totally incompatible with the means proposed for those objectives. These commitments to higher moral principles unmatched by higher use of force led to gradual emasculation of the people we were supposed to be protecting. . . . We drifted into a pattern of behavior in which we were not willing to stop the war by force. But we were also not willing to accept a peace plan that could stop it by diplomacy. Thus, we inflamed the situation without providing the means for dealing with that inflammation.[167]

When the use of force did come, it was inadequate. David Gompert observes that "the belief of some in 1992–1994 that once hurt, the Serbs would become reasonable overlooked the fact that the Serbs had been given to understand that the selective use of force was not a prelude to, but rather a substitute for, significant intervention. Indeed, the failure until 1995 of the United States and its allies to use air power in a truly punishing way, combined with the advertised fears of U.N. authorities that force would endanger relief personnel and operations, created a classic situation of 'escalation dominance' favoring the (objectively weaker) Serbs."[168]

Foreign policy leadership on an issue with grave moral and life-or-death implications gave ground with little resistance to leadership at home on domestic issues. As James Gow summarizes, the administration found itself "torn between understandable emotional reaction, outrage, and a stand on principle, on the one hand, and facing up to inescapable realities and responsibilities of action, as well as President Clinton's surpassing devotion to domestic policy on the other."[169] Clinton relished leadership at home on issues such as health care, but he ran from it on the Bosnian genocide. For the former Arkansas governor, the choice to lead an intervention against Serb aggression and genocide—by no means an easy choice—was made more difficult by his own predilections and troublesome military background.

However, the choice to act could have been made. Interests could have been redefined, newly formulated, and explained to a concerned American public. The administration preferred to believe in an isolationist American public. However, National Opinion Research Center polling conducted over fifty years has consistently shown that from 61 to 79 percent of those surveyed believe "it will be best for the future of this country if we take an active role in world affairs."[170] Detailed studies on American public attitudes specifically on U.S. involvement in Bosnia conducted in 1994 and 1995 by the Program on International Policy Attitudes (PIPA) found strong public support for more forceful action.

PIPA, a joint program of the Center for the Study of Policy Attitudes and the Center for International and Security Studies at the University of Maryland, found that over half those polled wanted the UN force in Bosnia to get tougher in the face of Serb aggression. Only about 30 percent of those polled favored withdrawal. Support for intervention and the use of force climbed steeply when respondents were asked about ethnic cleansing and genocide. When those polled were asked their opinion if a UN commission determined that Serb actions constituted genocide, 80 percent answered that the United States and the United Nations should intervene to stop the atrocities.[171] The support existed—all it needed was leadership. However, the Clinton administration chose to cede rather than lead.

An unwilling and risk-averse administration continued Washington's new post–Cold War act of deference to Europe. Unfortunately, "America's decision to rely on its European partners to take the lead in Yugoslavia proved to be a grave mistake that compounded the West's failure."[172] The minimal response from Europe and the United States sent a message to Serbia: There will be no Balkan version of Desert Storm or meaningful European intervention, so continue with your actions and pay no heed to mediators or ultimatums.[173]

Both the Bush and the Clinton administration failed the Bosnia leadership test. The fact that the American public would have supported some form of action, that the American people were almost looking for leadership on the issue, only magnifies the shortcomings of Bush and Clinton. The public would have supported action and often felt that "something should be done," but neither administration took advantage of this attitude to craft an effective, proactive policy and actually lead.[174] Rather, they indulged in selective rhetoric, choosing the best phrases depending on pressing needs. When Bill Clinton needed a campaign issue, and then sporadically during his presidential tenure, he spoke of the need to combat naked Serb aggression to stop atrocities. When either administration sought to justify inaction—or, worse, to cover tracks when backing away from tough threats—U.S. spokesmen described Bosnia as a civil war with fault on all sides, a problem too complicated to understand, let alone solve from the outside, and in any case a problem for Europe to solve.

Yet in terms of normative progress, the United States, not Europe, possessed the influence and could command the respect and resources to make it happen. The deployment of adequate American leadership and force would have made a powerful and precedent-setting contribution to ethics and law in the emerging "new world order." With unrivaled military power and a firm claim to world leadership, the United States held in its hand an ethical leadership moment primed for evolution in international affairs: the opportunity to make an effective, forceful stand against not only aggression but also genocide. Basking in the glow of its "unipolar moment," the United States squandered this chance to serve as a norm entrepreneur and implement the prevention side of the UNGC.

In terms of normative advancement, two developmental "tracks" dominate this story. The first and most obvious is the failure of the United States to exert itself fully as an entrepreneur on behalf of the UNGC. In large part because of traditional realist concerns, such as costs of intervention and loss of public support at home, two presidents of different party affiliations and often wildly diverging public policy stances prevented the United States from putting its hegemonic ability and moral authority to work for the UNGC. Without a clear vital national interest at stake (at least not according to a classically realist definition), the United States could argue that Bosnia did not merit attention because it fell short on the interest scale. The "antigenocide" norm remained too weak to compel great-power action.

At the same time, however, a noteworthy body of evidence points to at least minimal progress in the development of the punishment side of the norm. This evolution includes the establishment of a war crimes tribunal complete with indictments for genocide, unique features of the Dayton Accords, and the creation in the United States of the State Department's Office of War Crimes Issues. The American hesitancy to use the word "genocide" itself when referring to Bosnia also hints (ironically) at a norm growing in stature, perhaps despite U.S. policies. Despite the overarching failure to stop genocide in progress, these other advances are not insignificant. Gradually, these acts continue the gradual strengthening of the UNGC and the norms contained therein.

Writer Susan Sontag's comment about Bosnia's fate applied equally to the UNGC itself: "So might instead of right has triumphed. Nothing new in that—see Thucydides, Book V, 'the Melian Dialogue.' "[175] The Sontag/Thucydides proposition, the status of the convention, and the commitment of the Clinton administration would face an unprecedented second challenge in the 1990s. In 1994, a crisis in central Africa would present another opportunity—another ethical leadership moment—for the United States to align pledge with policy by preventing genocide and saving hundreds of thousands of lives.

NOTES

1. See Robert J. Donia and John V. A. Fine Jr., *Bosnia & Hercegovina: A Tradition Betrayed* (New York: Columbia University Press, 1994).

2. Susan L. Woodward, *Balkan Tragedy: Chaos and Dissolution after the Cold War* (Washington: The Brookings Institution, 1995). Woodward emphasizes the economic aspect of Yugoslavia's dissolution and descent into violence in chapters 3 and 4.

3. Richard Holbrooke, *To End a War* (New York: Random House, 1998), 23–24.

4. Warren Zimmerman, "The Last Ambassador: A Memoir of the Collapse of Yugoslavia," *Foreign Affairs* 74, no. 2 (March/April 1995): 4–5.

5. Warren Zimmerman, *Origins of a Catastrophe: Yugoslavia and Its Destroyers* (New York: Times Books, 1996), 11.

6. Roger Cohen, *Hearts Grown Brutal: Sagas of Sarajevo* (New York: Random House, 1998), 431.

7. Cohen, 432.

8. Milosevic and others drew inspiration and material for their nationalist vision from a document known as "The Memorandum" drafted by scholars in the Serbian Academy of Arts and Sciences. Parts of the nationalist tract, which in part decried Serbian subjugation in Tito's Yugoslavia, appeared in the Serb press.

9. Mark Danner, "America and the Bosnia Genocide," *New York Review of Books,* December 4, 1997, Web edition, 37.

10. Zimmerman, *Origins of a Catastrophe,* 120–22.

11. Noel Malcolm, *Bosnia: A Short History* (New York: New York University Press, 1994), 252.

12. Quoted in Danner, "America and the Bosnia Genocide," 37.

13. Final Report of the Commission of Experts Established Pursuant to Security Council Resolution 780 (1992), Document S/1994/674, 43, 71.

14. Ted Galen Carpenter, "Serbian Analogy . . . and Perspective," *Washington Times,* June 12, 1994, B4.

15. Testimony before the U.S. House Armed Services Committee, May 26, 1993.

16. Roy Gutman, *A Witness to Genocide* (New York: Macmillan, 1993), 170; Tom Gjelten, "Blaming the Victim," *New Republic,* December 20, 1993, 14–16.

17. *Wall Street Journal,* February 23, 1993, A1.

18. *New York Times,* March 9, 1995, A1.

19. Thomas Cushman and Stjepan G. Mestrovic, eds., *This Time We Knew: Western Responses to Genocide in Bosnia* (New York: New York University Press, 1996), 15, 33, n. 24.

20. Zimmerman, *Origins of a Catastrophe,* 224.

21. Quoted in Danner, "America and Bosnia Genocide," 33.

22. Roger Cohen, 168–69.

23. For initial reports, see Amnesty International, *Yugoslavia: Torture and Deliberate and Arbitrary Killings in War Zones* (New York: Amnesty International, 1991).

24. Gutman, 46.

25. Gutman, 44–45.

26. "Final Report of the Commission of Experts Established Pursuant to Security Council Resolution 780 (1992)," UN Security Council Document S/674, May 27, 1994, 51–55.

27. Philip Cohen, "The Complicity of Serbian Intellectuals in Genocide in the 1990s," in Cushman and Mestrovic, eds., 53. See also Retzak Hukanovic, "The Evil at Omarska," *New Republic,* February 12, 1996, 24–29.

28. Helsinki Watch, "Omarska Detention Camp," in *War Crimes in Bosnia-Herzegovina, Volume II* (Helsinki: Human Rights Watch/Helsinki Watch, 1993), 108.

29. Gutman, 93.

30. See UN Economic and Social Council, "Rape and Abuse of Women in the Territory of the Former Yugoslavia," Document E/CN.4/1994/5, June 30, 1993; UN Security Council, "Final Report of the Commission of Experts Established Pursuant to Security Council Resolution 780 (1992)," General Document S/1994/674, May 27, 1994; and UN Security Council, "The Situation of Human Rights in the Territory of the Former Yugoslavia," Document A/48/92, S/25341, February 26, 1993.

31. Gutman, "The Rapes of Bosnia," in *A Witness to Genocide,* 68; "Victims Recount Nights of Terror at Makeshift Bordello," in *A Witness to Genocide,* 74: "A Pattern of Rape: A Torrent of Wrenching First Person Testimonies Tells of a New Serb Atrocity: Systematic Sexual Abuse," *Newsweek,* January 11, 1993, 32–36.

32. Beverly Allen, *Rape Warfare: The Hidden Genocide in Bosnia-Herzegovina and Croatia* (Minneapolis: University of Minnesota Press, 1996), 58.

33. Allen, 57.

34. Allen, 60.

35. Philip Cohen, 47. See also Catherine MacKinnon, "Rape, Genocide, and Women's Human Rights," *Harvard Women's Law Journal* 17 (spring 1994): 5–16, and Alexandra Stiglmayer, ed., *Mass Rape: The War against Women in Bosnia-Herzegovina* (Lincoln: University of Nebraska Press, 1994).

36. David Rieff, *Slaughterhouse: Bosnia and the Failure of the West* (New York: Simon and Schuster, 1995), 121.

37. Quoted in Danner, "America and the Bosnia Genocide," 24.

38. Philip Cohen, 47. See also Gutman, "Unholy War: Serbs Target Culture, Heritage of Bosnia's Muslims," in *A Witness to Genocide,* 77; Robert Fisk, "Waging War on History: In Former Yugoslavia, Whole Cultures Are Being Obliterated," *Independent* (London), June 20, 1994, 18.

39. Michael Sells, *The Bridge Betrayed: Religion and Genocide in Bosnia* (Berkeley and Los Angeles: University of California Press, 1996), 1–5.

40. UN Security Council, "Final Report of the Commission of Experts . . . ," 66–69.

41. Tom Gjelten, *Sarajevo Daily* (New York: HarperCollins, 1995), 3.

42. Jan Willem Honig and Norbert Booth, *Srebrenica: Record of a War Crime* (New York: Penguin, 1997), 177. See also David Rohde, *Endgame: The Betrayal and Fall of Srebrenica, Europe's Worst Massacre since World War II* (New York: Farrar, Straus & Giroux, 1997).

43. Under the resolution establishing the safe haven, UN peacekeepers were required to disarm the Muslim population.

44. Rohde, 375.

45. *New York Times,* November 7, 2000, A3.

46. Philip Cohen, 53.

47. UN Security Council, "Final Report of the Commission of Experts . . . ," 51–55; Philip Cohen, 53.

48. Mark Danner, "Clinton, the UN, and the Bosnian Disaster," *New York Review of Books,* December 18, 1997, 69.

49. Wayne Bert, *The Reluctant Superpower: United States' Policy in Bosnia, 1991–1995* (New York: St. Martin's Press, 1997), 136.

50. U.S. Department of State dispatch, July 1, 1991, 468.

51. Ibid., September 30, 1991, 723; October 7, 1991, 748.

52. David Gompert, "The United States and Yugoslavia's Wars," in Richard H. Ullman, ed., *The World and Yugoslavia's Wars* (New York: Council on Foreign Relations, 1996), 129.

53. Zimmerman, *Origins of a Catastrophe,* 158.

54. "The Future of the Balkans: An Interview with David Owen," *Foreign Affairs* 72, no. 2 (spring 1993): 6.

55. Quoted in Joshua Muravchik, *The Imperative of American Leadership* (Washington, D.C.: AEI Press, 1996), 91.

56. "Crisis in Yugoslavia; EC Dashes into Its Own Backyard," *Financial Times,* July 1, 1991.

57. David Gompert, "How to Defeat Serbia," *Foreign Affairs* 73, no. 4 (July/August 1994): 35.

58. Bert, 138.

59. Misha Glenny, *The Fall of Yugoslavia* (New York: Penguin, 1992), 150–51.

60. Quoted in Danner, "America and the Bosnia Genocide," 31; *The Gates of Hell,* Program 4, "The Death of Yugoslavia" (UK Version), Brian Lapping & Associates, for the Discovery Channel, Laura Silber, consultant.

61. Macedonia also sought recognition that the United States was reluctant to grant because of Greek concerns over the historical significance of the name.

62. Danner, "America and the Bosnia Genocide," 30–31, taken from unbroadcast section of ABC News, "While America Watched: The Bosnia Tragedy," March 17, 1994, ABC-51.

63. Paula Franklin Little, "US Policy toward the Demise of Yugoslavia: The Virus of Nationalism," *East European Politics and Societies* 6, no. 3 (fall 1992): 314.

64. Ralph Johnson, testimony before the Senate Committee on Foreign Relations, October 17, 1991, 312.

65. Elizabeth Drew, *On the Edge: The Clinton Presidency* (New York: Simon and Schuster, 1994), 139.

66. Bert, 150.

67. Quoted in Danner, "America and the Bosnia Genocide," 17; See also James A. Baker III, *The Politics of Diplomacy: Revolution, War, and Peace, 1989–1992* (New York: Putnam, 1995), 635–36.

68. ABC News, "While America Watched: The Bosnia Tragedy," Peter Jennings (correspondent), Mark Danner and David Gelber (writers), March 17, 1994, ABC-51, 3.

69. Danner, "America and the Bosnia Genocide," 17.

70. Warren Strobel, *Late-Breaking Foreign Policy: The News Media's Influence on Peace Operations* (Washington, D.C.: United States Institute of Peace), 129; Danner, "America and the Bosnia Genocide, 50.

71. ABC News, "While America Watched," 9.

72. See Richard Johnson, "The Pinstripe Approach to Genocide," in Stjepan G. Mestrovic, ed., *The Conceit of Innocence: Losing the Conscience of the West in the War against Bosnia* (College Station: Texas A&M Press, 1997), 65.

73. Quoted in Danner, "America and the Bosnia Genocide," 44, from unbroadcast section of ABC News, "While America Watched." As a signatory to the UNGC, the United States joins other nations to "confirm that genocide, whether committed in time of peace or in time of war, is a crime under international law which they undertake to prevent and to punish." No mechanism, apart from moral obligation and shaming, exists to compel signatory states to fulfill their obligation.

74. Johnson, 65.

75. Roger Cohen, 217.

76. See note 75.

77. *New York Times,* August 27, 1992, A22; *Los Angeles Times,* August 29, 1992, A4.

78. Johnson, 67.

79. UN General Assembly Resolution A/47/92, December 17, 1992.

80. U.S. Department of State dispatch, September 1992, 1–3, 25.

81. U.S. Department of State dispatch, September 1997, 14.

82. Bert, 152; *New York Times,* August 28, 1992, A6.

83. Gompert, "The United States and Yugoslavia's Wars," 133.

84. Bert, 154–55.

85. Danner, "Clinton, the UN, and the Bosnian Disaster," 66, quoted in "Method to the Madness," *Decision Brief* (Washington, D.C.: Center for Security Policy, October 2, 1992), 3.

86. *New York Times,* September 22, 1992, A1; *New York Times,* October 8, 1992, A35; Bert, 158; Baker, 648–50.

87. U.S. Department of State dispatch, September 1992, 13–16, 25.

88. President Bush, "Remarks at a Meeting of the American Legislative Exchange Council," March 2, 1991, *Weekly Compilation of Presidential Documents* 27, no. 9: 233. President Bush also declared that "the specter of Vietnam has been buried forever in the desert sands of the Arabian peninsula" (ibid., 245).

89. Quoted in Danner, "America and the Bosnia Genocide," 20.

90. Warren Zimmerman, "Yugoslavia: 1988–1996," in Jeremy R. Azrael and Emil A. Payin, eds., *United States and Russian Policymaking with Respect to the Use of Force* (Santa Monica, Calif.: Rand, 1996), 191.

91. Gompert, "The United States and Yugoslavia's Wars," 132.

92. Gompert, "How to Defeat Serbia," 38.

93. Muravchik, 101.

94. *New York Times,* January 10, 1993; Muravchik, 101.

95. Quoted in Roger Cohen, 175.

96. Danner, "America and the Bosnia Genocide," 67, from unbroadcast portion of ABC News, "While America Watched."

97. Quoted in Gutman, *A Witness to Genocide,* xxxviii, xli.

98. According to David Rieff (in *Slaughterhouse*, 27), he raised the issue of Clinton's campaign rhetoric on Bosnia with a Clinton operative who asked him in exasperation, "Why do people nowadays take campaign promises so seriously?"

99. Dick Morris, *Behind the Oval Office: Winning the Presidency in the Nineties* (New York: Random House, 1997), 245.

100. Rieff, 29.

101. Colin Powell, *My American Journey* (New York: Ballantine, 1995), 560–61.

102. James Gow, *Triumph of the Lack of Will: International Diplomacy and the Yugoslav War* (New York: Columbia University Press, 1997), 212.

103. Drew, 150.

104. *Washington Post,* April 23, 1993, A1.

105. See note 104.

106. Rieff, 155.

107. *New York Times,* April 22, 1993, A15.

108. John Newhouse, "No Exit, No Entrance," *The New Yorker,* June 28, 1993, 49; Bert, 274, n. 13; *New York Times,* January 31, 1993, A17.

109. Bert, 184.

110. Marshall Freeman Harris, "Clinton's 'European' Bosnia Policies," in Mestrovic, ed., 242.

111. Gompert, "The United States and Yugoslavia's Wars," 137.

112. Quoted in Danner, "Clinton, the UN, and the Bosnian Disaster," 75.

113. Paul A. Goble, "Dangerous Liaisons: Moscow, the Former Yugoslavia, and the West," in Ullman, ed., 186. See also Ivo H. Daalder, *Getting to Dayton: The Making of America's Bosnia Policy* (Washington, D.C.: Brookings Institution Press, 2000), 17, and Martin Walker, *The President We Deserve: His Rise, Falls, and Comebacks* (New York: Crown Publishers, 1996), 267.

114. Harris, 248–49.

115. Harris, 249.

116. Drew, 159.

117. Drew, 157. See also Robert Kaplan, *Balkan Ghosts: A Journey through History* (New York: St. Martin's Press, 1993).

118. Daalder, 19.

119. Thomas L. Friedman, "Bosnia Reconsidered," *New York Times,* April 8, 1993; Susan Woodward, 307.

120. Muravchik, 103.

121. Quoted in Muravchik.

122. Gompert, "The United States and Yugoslavia's Wars," 138.

123. Drew, 284.

124. Gow, 220.

125. *New York Times,* September 26, 1993, 15.

126. David Owen, *Balkan Odyssey* (New York: Harcourt Brace, 1995), 232.

127. Zimmerman, *Origins of a Catastrophe,* 226–27.

128. Muravchik, 106.

129. Gompers, "The United States and Yugoslavia's Wars," 138.

130. *Washington Post,* February 6, 1994, A26.

131. *New York Times,* February 22, 1994, A1.

132. NATO shot down four Serb aircraft violating the zone.

133. Laura Silber and Allan Little, *Yugoslavia: Death of a Nation* (New York: Penguin Books, 1996), 312–13.

134. *New York Times,* April 8, 1994, A1.

135. Muravchik, 107.

136. Gompert, "The United States and Yugoslavia's Wars," 139.

137. See note 136.

138. *Washington Post,* June 30, 1994, A20.

139. Muravchik, 109; Bert, 216.

140. Quoted in Peter Maass, *Love Thy Neighbor: A Story of War* (New York: Alfred A. Knopf, 1996), 272.

141. Honig and Booth, 115.

142. *New York Times,* October 29, 1995.

143. Rieff, 234.

144. Judge Fouad Riad, "The Prosecutor v. Radovan Karadzic, Ratko Mladic. Review of the Indictment," International Criminal Tribunal for Yugoslavia, IT-95–18-I, November 1995, 16. For other details on Srebrencia, see "United Nations Report of the Secretary General Pursuant to Security Council Resolution 1019 on Violations of International Humanitarian Law in the Areas of Srebrenica, Zepa, Banja Luka, and Sanski Most," Document S/1995/988, November 27, 1995, 1–8.

145. Bob Woodward, *The Choice* (New York: Simon and Schuster, 1996), 260.

146. Woodward, 262.

147. Bert, 223.

148. Holbrooke, 66.

149. Holbrooke, 67.

150. Rieff, 257.

151. Bert, 222.

152. Bert, 223.

153. Gow, 278.

154. Obviously, indispensable on Dayton is Richard Holbrooke, *To End a War.* See also United States Institute of Peace, "Dayton Implementation: The Apprehension and Prosecution of Indicted War Criminal," *Special Report* (Washington, D.C.: United States Institute of Peace, 1997). See also the previously mentioned *Getting to Dayton* by Ivo Daalder.

155. The tribunal was established under Security Council Resolution 827, May 25, 1993.

156. Holbrooke, 190.

157. Author interview with Ambassador David Scheffer, Charlottesville, Virginia, December 18, 1998.

158. On France's hesitation, see Chuck Sudetic, "The Reluctant Gendarme," *Atlantic Monthly,* April 2000, 91–98.

159. *New York Times,* July 26, 1998, A1.

160. David J. Scheffer, ambassador at large for war crimes issues, U.S. State Department, address at Washington College of Law, American University, Washington, D.C., March 31, 1998.

161. President Clinton, "Address to the Nation," Washington, D.C., March 24, 1999; *Buffalo News,* April 4, 1999, H2; *Sunday Times* (London), April 18, 1999 (available at <www.cnn.com/ALLPOLITICS/stories/1999/04/18/clinton.letter/>).

162. See Gompert, "The United States and Yugoslavia's Wars," 143, n. 2.

163. Mark Danner, "Slouching towards Dayton." *New York Review of Books,* April 23, 1998, 60.

164. Zimmerman, *Origins of a Catastrophe,* 216.

165. See Robert W. Tucker and David C. Hendrickson, *The Imperial Temptation: The*

New World Order and America's Purpose (New York: Council on Foreign Relations Press, 1992), 46–47.

166. Danner, "Clinton, the UN, and the Bosnian Disaster," 75.

167. Quoted in Michael Kelly, "Letter from Washington: Surrender and Blame," *The New Yorker,* December 19, 1994, 44–51.

168. Gompert, "The United States and Yugoslavia's Wars," 138.

169. Gow, 220. See also David Hendrickson, "The Recovery of Internationalism," *Foreign Affairs* 73, no. 5 (September/October 1994): 26–43.

170. Cited in *Daily Yomiuri,* August 6, 1994, 5.

171. Steven Kull, "Americans on Bosnia: A Study of US Public Attitudes," Program on International Policy Attitudes, Washington, D.C., May 1995, 1–4. See also Steven Kull and Clay Ramsay, "U.S. Public Attitudes on U.S. Involvement in Bosnia," Program on International Policy Attitudes, Washington, D.C., May 1994; Steven Kull, "What the Public Knows That Washington Doesn't," *Foreign Policy* 101 (winter 1995–96): 102–15.

172. Gompert, "The United States and Yugoslavia's Wars," 127.

173. Bert, 147.

174. See Richard Sobel, "U.S. and European Attitudes toward Intervention in the Former Yugoslavia: Mourir pour la Bosnie?" in Ullman, ed., 145–81.

175. Susan Sontag, "A Lament for Bosnia," *The Nation,* December 25, 1995, 818–20.

Chapter Four

Eyes Wide Shut: The United States and the Rwanda Genocide

On March 11, 1998, the White House press secretary released a statement announcing that President Bill Clinton would add a stop in Rwanda to his previously planned tour of several nations in sub-Saharan Africa. According to the statement, the visit would "provide an opportunity for the President to pay respect to the victims of the 1994 genocide." Three weeks later, on an overcast and drizzly March 25, President Clinton arrived in the Rwandan capital of Kigali for a brief airport visit. The president began his stopover by meeting with several survivors and witnesses of the three-month campaign of genocide by Hutus against Tutsis in the spring of 1994. As people such as Josephine Murebwayire and Venuste Karasira recounted profoundly disturbing tales of unbelievable violence, President Clinton listened intently and then thanked them in a noticeably shaking voice. He then told the small group, "We in the United States and the world community did not do as much as we could have done to try to limit what occurred in Rwanda in 1994."[1]

The president followed up on this emotional meeting with a brief but powerful speech. With a crowd of Rwandan diplomats and officials before him, President Clinton commented on the tragic events of April–June 1994 and the striking silence and passivity of the United States. He declared to those assembled, "We did not act quickly enough after the killing began. We did not immediately call these crimes by their rightful name—genocide." Although short, the president's message was clear and not insignificant—the United States and the rest of the world owed an apology to Rwanda for inaction in the face of a genocide that ended up claiming upward of a million lives.

This chapter examines American foreign policy and the 1994 genocide in Rwanda. It builds on the work of the previous chapter by further studying the Clinton administration and its reaction to a second genocide during its watch, this time in central Africa. The challenge of two genocides within two years was unprecedented and created for the United States difficult but influential political and moral leadership choices for the dawn of the so-called new world order. The Rwanda genocide came fast and furious; it was an "accelerated" genocide compared to the deadly slow burn occurring in Bosnia at the time. The suddenness and swiftness of the killing shocked the world and demanded that the international community take notice.

The brutal events in central Africa once more put the United Nations Convention on the Prevention and Punishment of the Crime of Genocide (UNGC) and the hegemonic influence of the United States to the test; Rwanda dared the outside world to act against a heinous international crime it had pledged to arrest. However, at the outset, the United States preferred not to take notice and instead hedged and obfuscated. The tragedy of Rwanda is particularly dramatic because the opportunity clearly existed for the United States and its partners to intervene effectively, save hundreds of thousand of lives, and invigorate as never before the ethical vision embedded in the text of the UNGC.

Following a quick tour of ethnic tension in Rwanda's history, this chapter briefly documents the path of genocide pursued by the Hutu majority against Rwanda's minority Tutsi population after the crash of President Habyarimana's plane in April 1994. Following premeditated plans and responding to murderous radio broadcasts, Hutu militias, civilians, and military forces sought to exterminate the Tutsis. The focus then turns to the reporting of events in Rwanda and the initial U.S. reaction to the news.

For some time, the United States viewed the conflict predominantly in civil war and peacekeeping terms. It did not take long, however, for the genocidal nature of events in central Africa to become frighteningly clear. As information about Rwanda's nightmare became more available and the facts ever more obvious, the Clinton administration ducked. As with Bosnia, the United States sought to avoid, minimize, and redefine a genocide in progress. This case is significant for what it once again shows both about the power of the word "genocide" and the contortions the "indispensable nation" went through to avoid using it.

This chapter also explores the major intervention debates and options, most of them floated at the United Nations and sunk by the United States. Domestic politics, the legacy of Somalia, and narrowly defined interests produced consistent delay and obstruction by the Clinton administration. Inaction reigned as tens of thousands continued to fall under the Hutu's genocidal assault. This chapter asks specifically if intervention was feasible and explores other avenues for moral action and leadership short of deploying troops.

The story of the United States and Rwanda in the spring of 1994 also advances the discussion of the broader implications of the American response to genocide, namely in terms of normative progress. With unrivaled leadership potential during a genocidal crisis, the United States held in its hands the power to revivify the UNGC and give it a significant role in shaping the emerging world order. Thus, the events and actions discussed here again relate directly to notions of "ethical leadership moments," "norm entrepreneurship," and U.S. contributions to the reification of the genocide prohibition and punishment norm found in the convention. The determination of the United States not to act and even to impede effective action by other parties suggests the continued weakness of the prevention clause in the UNGC. Yet, once again, it appears that the punishment component of the UNGC continues to enjoy slow but steady forward progress, in part thanks to the United States.

BACKGROUND

Contrary to the perceptions of many outside observers, the genocide in Rwanda was not simply the result of ancient hatreds between two ethnic groups. In the aftermath of World War I, the 1919 Versailles Treaty sought to remake the world after a shattering conflict in Europe. As part of the treaty, Belgium received Rwanda as a League of Nations trust territory. As part of their subsequent colonial rule, the Belgians elevated the so-called Tutsis to positions of prominence in the colonial administration. Up to that point, however, the terms "Tutsi" and "Hutu" did not represent strictly defined ethnic groups as they do today. Early on, the Tutsi dominated the central state apparatus. Outside that circle, other members of the Tutsi owned cattle and represented the court in the hinterland. The "Hutu" were predominantly farmers. However, this was not a rigid, unbending caste system. In fact, "Hutu could and did become 'Tutsi' as chiefs were incorporated into the ruling elite, or farmers became wealthy and acquired cattle." Inequalities certainly existed, "but the ethnic boundary was permeable."[2]

This permeability disappeared over time as Belgian colonists and Roman Catholic missionaries viewed Rwandan society through the since discredited lens of "Hamitic" ideology.[3] According to this worldview, any developed or "civilized" institutions in Africa (such as Rwanda's centralized state structure) resulted from invasion by "Hamites," also referred to variously as "African Aryans," "white coloureds," or "black Caucasians," and seemed to represent a missing link between the races. Applied to Rwanda, this fantastic racial typography in large part rewrote the region's history and received bolstering from general physical distinctions emphasized by Western observers who explained that Tutsis were generally "taller, thinner, and more European-looking than Hutus." Belgian doctor J. Sasserath described the Tutsi as a "superior race" who were tall and slim with "straight noses, high foreheads, thin lips. The Hamites seem distant, reserved, polite and refined." Sasserath contrasted this portrait with that of the Hutus, often called Bantu. Sasserath wrote, "The rest of the population is Bantu . . . possessing all the characteristics of the negro: flat noses, thick lips, low foreheads, brachycephalic skulls. They are like children, shy and lazy and usually dirty."[4]

This Hamite myth, overlayed on a developed colonial system, strengthened the minority Tutsi at the expense of the Hutu. Belgian authorities put racial division into practice by requiring each and every Rwandan to carry identification cards classifying them as either Tutsi or Hutu, a practice continued even until the outbreak of violence in 1994.[5] The written recording of ethnic group membership amplified the importance of such distinctions and heightened their rigidity.

Over the years, a previously permeable and mutable society hardened into a nation sharply divided along strictly interpreted racial classifications, complete with concomitant discrepancies in economic and social power. Alain Destexhe sums up succinctly that "in short, if the categories of Hutu and Tutsi were not actually invented by the colonisers, the policies practiced by the Germans and the Belgians only served to exacerbate them. They played an essential role in creating an ethnic split and ensured that the important feeling of belonging to a social group was fuelled by ethnic, indeed racial, hatred."[6]

Eventually, the system would turn upside down, and the Hutu majority would gain the upper hand in Rwandan society. Facing international criticism for their colonial administration and feeling growing "sympathy for the suppressed masses," Belgium began removing Tutsis from positions of power and replacing them with Hutus. Hutu agitation for expanded power culminated in 1959 with riots, massacres, and a revolution. In what many observers consider the first genocide in Rwanda, more than 20,000 Tutsi perished as the Hutu grasped power and sought to eliminate Tutsis along the way. By the time of Rwandan independence in 1962, thousands of Tutsi had gone into exile abroad, while those that remained became increasingly marginalized and disenfranchised and, more often than not, scapegoats in any and every political crisis.

It is worth mentioning that neighboring Burundi, Rwanda's "false twin," also suffered ethnic violence between the minority Tutsi and the majority Hutu. In 1965, political instability and a power struggle led to violence. The Tutsi gained control in a previously mixed regime and attempted to liquidate the Hutu elite following an apparent coup attempt by Hutu politicians and military officers. In 1975, further upheaval led the Tutsi military regime to commit genocidal massacres of 100,000 to 200,000 people, mostly educated Hutus. Ethnic conflict again led to atrocities in 1988, with some 20,000 Hutu killed by Tutsi. Since 1993, an estimated 150,000 Tutsi and Hutu have lost their lives in intercommunal violence in Burundi.[7]

Rwanda entered a fairly long period of relative peace and stability following a successful coup by Hutu leader Juvenal Habyarimana in 1973. By the 1990s, however, the nation faced serious economic problems as coffee prices fell on the world market and poor weather contributed to food shortages. With domestic concerns already growing steadily, the Hutu regime had to deal with military incursions from Uganda by Tutsi in the Rwandan Patriotic Front (RPF), an opposition group composed primarily of Tutsi exiles but also with some moderate Hutus in its membership. External enemies and internal economic disruptions provided fertile conditions for deadly tensions and violence. Massacre was reinvigorated as a political tool. From late 1990 to 1993, militia forces and Hutu militants attacked and killed hundreds of Tutsi in separate incidents.

The growing violence and dangerous instability did not go unnoticed. Under the auspices of the United Nations, both sides met in Arusha, Tanzania, to negotiate the end of the civil war and to create a viable multiethnic democracy in Rwanda. Signed on August 4, 1993, the Arusha Accords set up a system of power sharing and political reform. A transitional government included representatives from the RPF, and the UN Assistance Mission for Rwanda (UNAMIR) was charged with overseeing the implementation of the accords. A group of military observers from the Organization of Africa Unity (OAU) also went to Rwanda to monitor the cease-fire. The initial UNAMIR force was composed of 800 soldiers with a total of 2,500 envisioned for final deployment.

While President Habyarimana did open the government to Tutsi representatives and appointed a moderate, opposition party Hutu, Agathe Uwilingiyimana, as prime minister, he "had no principled commitment to the accords and temporized on their implementation at every step."[8] Instead, Habyarimana was a devotee of the "Hutu power" ideology based on the belief in Hutu superiority, Hutu rule and domination, and the need to deal harshly with the supposedly subversive Tutsi minority. Furthermore, for hard-line, Hutu extremists, the Arusha Accords were a betrayal and Habyarimana their Judas.

The case of genocide in Rwanda stands on the opposite spectrum from Cambodia in terms of knowledge and forewarning. In Cambodia, few if any predicted genocide and massive atrocities, and reliable information trickled out at best. Rwanda, on the other hand, had been the subject of countless reports and warnings leading up to the explosion of violence in May 1994. Hindsight is 20/20, but in this case the signs were there for those who wanted to see and care.

As early as December 1993, UN peacekeepers received an anonymous letter from Hutu army officers warning of a plan for assassinations and massacres. On January 11, 1994, UNAMIR commander General Romeo Dallaire reported urgently to the UN Peacekeeping Office information he had received about weapons stockpiles, government and militia plans to exterminate Tutsis, and plans to kill Belgian soldiers "and thus guarantee Belgian withdrawal from Rwanda."[9] The details came to Dallaire from an informant working with Hutu militias and government officials. Urging action, Dallaire closed the fax in French, writing, "Peux ce que veux. Allons-y" ("Where there's a will, there's a way. Let's go").

The peacekeeping office, headed by Kofi Annan, replied that same day. They instructed Dallaire to take not action but to share the information with the Belgian, French, and American missions and with the Habyarimana government. Dallaire followed his orders; information was shared, and no arms caches were raided. According to Iqbal Riza, chief of staff to Kofi Annan, "We said, 'Not Somalia Again.' "[10]

In February, Belgium sought an extended mandate for the UN forces in Rwanda following Dallaire's prediction of impending violence. Belgian Foreign Minister Willy Claes asked the Security Council for more authority to act, namely to strengthen the Belgian-led force and allow it to seize weapons caches. However, the United States wanted no additional risk for UNAMIR. A declassified cable from Belgium's UN delegation to Brussels reports that the United States vetoed Belgium's request to augment its own forces on the ground.[11]

At the end of January 1994, the Central Intelligence Agency (CIA) concluded a study that "suggested if combat were to begin in Rwanda, that it would include violence against civilians—with a worst-case scenario of the deaths of half a million people." As French scholar Gerard Prunier notes, "In Rwanda, all the pre-conditions for a genocide were present: a well-organized civil service, a small tightly controlled land area, a disciplined and orderly population, reasonably good communications, and a coherent ideology containing the necessary lethal potential."[12] This body of evidence warning of potential ethnic violence on a large scale caused little concern in the United States and the United Nations. In fact, when the Clinton administration came to power and had the Pentagon perform a foreign policy review to identify potential crisis areas, Deputy Assistant Secretary for African Affairs James Woods put Rwanda and Burundi on the list. According to Woods, "I won't go into personalities, but I received guidance from higher authorities: 'Look, if something happens in Rwanda-Burundi, we don't care. Take it off the list. US national interest is not involved and we can't put all these silly humanitarian issues on lists like important problems like the Middle East, North Korea, and so on. Just make it go away.' "[13]

Rwanda, not surprisingly, did not simply go away. Instead, the powder keg received its spark on April 6, 1994. On that date, Rwandan President Juvenal Habyarimana and his Burundian counterpart Cyprien Ntariyamira were killed when their plane crashed in Kigali. Fingers of blame immediately pointed to the Tutsi and the RPF for shooting down the plane. Many observers now attribute the crash of the plane to extremist Hutus in the Rwandan army.

GENOCIDE

Almost immediately after the plane crash, Rwanda's colonial past, ethnic mythology, economic difficulties, political opportunists, and a vociferous campaign of hate fused seismically to produce a staggering genocide—staggering both in number and in savagery. Contrary to the perceptions of many observers then and now, the strife in Rwanda did not result from a "failed state" situation as occurred in Somalia when central government collapsed. Instead, the racist Hutu power leadership of an activist and centralized state apparatus put into motion a premeditated, well-conceived, and deliberate plan to exterminate the Tutsis. The bloodshed in Rwanda constituted as clear a case of genocide as the twentieth century had seen.

In the Rwandan capital, the killing of Tutsi was particularly centralized and preconceived. Presidential guards followed plans to eliminate "priority targets—the politicians, journalists, and civil rights activists—within less than six hours."[14] Lawyers, businessmen, and any potentially "threatening" Tutsi or moderate Hutu intellectuals also faced death. Among these first victims were several members of the transition government, including Prime Minister Agathe Uwilingayamana and Supreme Court President Joseph Kavaruganda. The hideous torture and slaying of the Belgian soldiers guarding the prime minister was part of the orchestrated campaign of genocide. The blueprint called for the Hutu to provoke the Belgians to use force, kill them, and thus create for Rwanda what the death of U.S. Rangers created for Somalia—Western withdrawal.[15]

Before news of Habyarimana's death was even released, government forces established roadblocks to prevent anyone from leaving Kigali. Thousands perished at barricades set up to keep them in Kigali and make them easy targets. The cause of "Hutu power" and its goal of eliminating Rwanda's Tutsi minority was aided and abetted significantly by extremist radio broadcasts. From the start, Hutu-controlled radio combined popular music with hate-filled commentaries and exhortations. As early as January 1994, in response to the Arusha Accords, the extremist Hutu-controlled Radio-Television Libres des Milles Collines (RTLMC) began calling for the extermination of the Tutsi, referred to as "inyenzi" (cockroaches).[16] Following the president's plane crash in April, Rwandan hate radio asserted itself, first blaming Tutsi rebels and UN forces for Habyarimana's death. Then the announcers called for murder "to avenge the death of our president."[17] Within a month, the genocidal voice of RTLMC declared maliciously, "By 5 May, the country must be completely cleansed of Tutsis."[18]

Through its endless stream of malicious propaganda, RTLMC helped recruit and organize the *Interhamwe* militias and frighten Hutu citizens into believing that all Tutsi were enemies to be destroyed. To ensure a successful genocide, radio announcers read lists of names of Tutsi and moderate Hutus to be killed, often including their addresses or last known locations. One broadcast told listeners things such as "You have missed some of the enemies in this or that place. Some are still alive. You must go back and finish them off."[19] One listener referred to RTLMC as "vampire radio" because it openly urged more bloodletting and killing.[20]

Outside Kigali, the implementation of genocide fell to provincial Hutu militia groups, namely the *Interhamwe* (those who attack together) and the *Impuzamugambi* (those who only have one aim). Both groups, with combined memberships reaching some 50,000, canvased the Rwandan countryside under orders from political leadership. Armed with rifles, grenades, and machetes, the militiamen searched for Tutsis and Hutu moderates to exterminate. For much of the genocidal killing spree, the militias received direction from local leaders and civil servants. The town and village authorities "received their orders from Kigali, mobilised the local *gendarmerie* and *interahamwe,* ordered the peasants to join in the manhunts and called for military support if the victims put up too much resistance."[21]

For the most part, resistance was not a problem, and genocidal slayings in Rwanda continued at a pace faster than Nazi Germany's "Final Solution." To track down their victims, the killers and their leaders made use of election rolls, census figures, and national identification cards. They also demonstrated a merciless blood lust, sparing no one anywhere. When news spread of the killings, many Tutsi sought safety in their places of worship, but churches provided no refuge at all. In many instances, "local officials ordered Tutsi to gather in churches, schools, and stadiums. But the end result was no protection but a lure, a trap, and a grave."[22] Across the country, churches were left filled with the butchered bodies of defenseless Tutsis. Churches ended up hosting some of the worst massacres: 2,800 people in Kbungo, 6,000 in Cyahinda, and 4,000 in Kibeho.[23]

The parish at Nyarubuye serves as a shocking example of events repeated across the country. In his account of the genocide in Rwanda, Fergal Keane provides survivor witness accounts of the massacre at Nyarubuye and describes his visit to the church shortly thereafter. Following the guidance of local *bourgmestre* of Rusomo, Sylvestre Gacumbitsi, some 3,000 Tutsis went to the church for safety. In short time, *Interhamwe* militiamen, army troops, and police arrived and killed every Tutsi they could hunt down. The *genocidaires* "killed all day at Nyarubuye. At night they cut the Achilles tendons of survivors and went off to feast behind the church, roasting cattle looted from their victims in big fires and drinking beer. . . . And in the morning, still drunk after whatever sleep they could find beneath the cries of their prey, the killers at Nyarubuye went back and killed again."[24] Horror stories such as the Nyarubuye atrocities come to light only because a handful of people such as Flora Mukampore survived the nightmare. As Keane relates, "When they had killed everyone, or so they thought, Gacumbitsi's gang left. But underneath the mounds of corpses lay survivors including Flora. For a week and a half she hid under the bodies venturing out at night to try to find water, and then returning to her grim hiding place for the day."[25]

In other areas, not only did the parishes afford no protection, but the clergy themselves proved complicit in the genocide. In a prominent case, Adventist Pastor Elizaphan Ntakirutimana allegedly betrayed his Tutsi followers at the Mugonero church complex. Rather than protect his flock, Ntakirutimana used his position of authority to "instruct" Tutsis to seek refuge at the Adventist compound. Later, the pastor and his physician son led a group of attackers to the site where the congregation was slaughtered. In the ensuing months, both father and son "searched for and attacked Tutsi survivors and others, killing or causing seriously bodily or mental harm to them."[26]

These murderous scenes and others like them repeated themselves across the country. Addressing the scope of the tragedy, journalist Fergal Keane exhorts his readers to "remember the figures, never ever forget them; *in one hundred days up to one million people were hacked, shot, strangled, clubbed, and burned to death. Remember, carve this into your consciousness: one million.*"[27] Philip Gourevitch of *The New Yorker* underscores the same point when he writes, "Take the best estimate: eight hundred thousand killed in a hundred days. That's three hundred and thirty-three and a third murders an hour, or five and a half lives terminated every minute."[28]

Death figures, of course, fail to account for the countless people maimed, tortured, and psychologically devastated and the systematic serial rape of Tutsi women. Nor do figures manage to capture fully the absolute horror and brutality of the Rwandan tragedy. Bodies polluted and clogged the Akagera River. Children and babies were slain, often smashed to death against rocks or hurled alive into pits.[29] In some instances, militias offered mercy to women if they would kill their own children. Pregnant women were eviscerated. Victims were commonly mutilated before being killed, with penises and breasts often chopped off.[30] To avoid such agony, people with money offered to pay their assassins to get the job done quickly with a bullet rather than suffer death by machete.[31]

The point here (as in earlier chapters) is not to sensationalize the topic at hand. Such details are an integral part of understanding the full story of genocide in Rwanda and then placing it into an appropriate political context. As Gerard Prunier notes, "The gruesome physical and psychological reality of the genocide has to be present to the mind when the political situation is being assessed. Whether one consider the possibilities of a coalition government in post-genocide Rwanda or the depth of foreign responsibilities, one should never forget how great were the horrors which the survivors experienced."[32]

As fighting raged in Kigali between the Rwandan Armed Forces (FAR) and the Tutsi-led RPF, which had launched a massive attack to protect its personnel in the capital, stop the killing, and overthrow the Hutu regime, the wholesale slaughter of Tutsi civilians continued apace. At the same time, the United States and the rest of the world community balked. Responding to the murder of its soldiers, Belgium quickly removed its remaining 420 troops from the UNAMIR contingent, thus depriving General Dallaire's force of its best-trained members. UNAMIR was soon further reduced by the departure of troops from Bangladesh and Ghana. Belgium's decision sent a distinct message to American policymakers. As one high-ranking State Department official explained, "You can't overstate the impact on our policy process of the Belgians leaving."[33] Human rights lobbyist Holly Burkhalter repeats a similar discussion with a American diplomat who explained that "people were saying, 'How can we get in, if it's so bad the Belgians had to leave.' "[34]

REPORTING RWANDA

As unimaginable genocidal atrocities got under way in Rwanda, the outside world initially struggled to make sense of what was happening. The word "genocide" itself was slow to appear in both press coverage and in statements from governments such as the United States, although genocide clearly best captured the main thrust of events in Rwanda. The print media dominated coverage—Rwanda's killers made a determined and successful effort to keep television cameras out while they set on completing their ghoulish task. As a result, for some time, the Western media portrayed the violence as a civil war (in part correct) between the FAR and the Tutsi-led RPF while missing completely the genocidal component of the Hutu power plan. Instead, coverage described a civil war emerging from ancient tribal (as opposed to "ethnic") forces. Early reports mentioned the death of the two central African presidents but then generally focused on the evacuation of foreign nationals in Rwanda "caught in tribal fighting." Articles with titles such as "Western Troops Arrive in Rwanda to Aid Foreigners" were the lead stories for any Rwanda coverage.[35]

As the death toll climbed, coverage remained limited to simplistic accounts and explanations of the violence. Major newspapers often reduced the differences between the groups to the old physical stereotypes and overgeneralizations explored earlier in this chapter. The actual story lay hidden behind passages such as "the Tutsis—the tall, Nilotic people also known as the Watusi—make up 14 percent of Rwanda's population, while the Hutus—a short stocky people—make up 85 percent"[36] or "for centuries the Tutsi, a tall Hamitic people who originated in Ethiopia, ruled as lords over far more numerous and shorter Bantu

Hutus."[37] As Burkhalter critically notes, "The media did a hideous job covering the early days of the genocide, talking about fat people and thin people."[38]

Beyond these limited and limiting attempts at analysis, the media tended to describe Rwanda's violence as war and not as genocidal massacres of civilians. To be sure, civil war between the Hutu government forces and the Tutsi RPF remained an important component of the story. However, as the record clearly shows, from the start the vast majority of killings were not casualties of any war but victims of a systematic campaign of extermination. The closure of Rwanda's borders by government troops only exacerbated the problem of accurate reporting. Stories such as "Anarchy Rules Rwanda's Capital" and "Drunken Soldiers Roam City" continued to misportray the violence as chaotic and military in nature, not planned, and predominantly civilian.

By mid-April, news reports estimated that some 20,000 Rwandans had been killed in fighting, while close to 100,000 people had fled Kigali. In his April 17 column, *Seattle Times* writer Jerry Large drew attention to the fact that his own paper seemed more concerned with Rwanda's endangered gorilla population than with the tens of thousands of people being killed and driven from their homes. Large conceded that the gorilla piece was important since "there are only 600 mountain gorillas left in the world thanks to us big-brained humans." However, he remained troubled that the story about 300 animals in Rwanda sat at the top of the paper, while "the story underneath talked about 100,000 humans fleeing the nation's capital."[39]

The newsworthiness of gorillas versus humans demonstrated in one edition of the *Seattle Times* does not represent fully either coverage across the nation's media outlets or the value they placed on the lives of those in Rwanda. Instead, it highlights the difficulty the media had in gauging the nature of "yet another" crisis in Africa. Still, at a deeper level, the primacy of stories about evacuating westerners or protecting gorillas does suggest that, for some, these groups were in some way considered more important—at least more newsworthy—than the tens and hundreds of thousands of people perishing around them.

EARLY U.S. REACTION

Just as the media proved itself slow to understand the catastrophe in Rwanda, the United States was slow to address the horror in any meaningful way. In the immediate aftermath of the deaths of the presidents of Rwanda and Burundi, President Clinton issued a statement expressing his shock and sadness at hearing the news. Clinton said, "Their deaths are a tragic blow to the long-suffering Rwandan and Burundian people." Within a week or so of the plane crash, the

United States did act, but only to remove its citizens from harm's way. French, Belgian, and U.S. troops were sent into Rwanda to evacuate expatriates.

On advice from its ambassador to Rwanda, David P. Rawson, the United States evacuated its citizens via overland convoy to Burundi, while France and Belgium removed their larger contingents by plane. Meanwhile, President Clinton sent some 300 Marines stationed off the Somali coast to Burundi to protect the Americans once they arrived and to act as backup "in case things get ugly," as one official explained.[40] The evacuation of Americans complete, the United States clearly took a step back from the situation in Rwanda, not to assess it but to avoid it. With no action forthcoming, Karl Inderfurth, a member of the U.S. delegation at the United Nations commented, "We pray that the killing will stop."[41]

By relying on prayer instead of action, the United States abdicated world leadership, relegated its values to the realm of rhetoric, and lost a critical opportunity to change the course of events in Rwanda.

The firmest subsequent action taken by the United States for the next few months was an evacuation of most of the remaining UN force in Rwanda. At UN Security Council discussions about UNAMIR following the outbreak of violence, the United States consistently argued that the remaining 2,000 troops could no longer carry out their mandate as established at Arusha and could not be adequately protected from expanding hostilities. As Michael Barnett, then at the U.S. mission to the United Nations, summarizes, "The general attitude was that 'We now have to close down the operation.' "[42] The United States, therefore, called for the complete removal of the force. At the urging of UN Ambassador Madeleine Albright, the administration indicated a willingness to settle for something less than total removal of the force. In an April 21 vote, the United States won the day for the most part as the Security Council voted a sharp reduction in the peacekeeping mission. In a unanimous decision, the Security Council reduced UNAMIR to a contingent of just 250. Thus weakened, particularly by the loss of its well-trained and equipped Belgian members, the UN force could hardly uphold its initial mandate, never mind protect civilians or intervene to stop massacres and fighting. The remaining "symbolic" force was to monitor events, help with humanitarian assistance, and continue to press for a cease-fire.[43] The resolution also sent an important and fairly unmistakable message to Rwanda's leaders: Kill as you please, we don't really care, and in fact we'll watch.

No support existed on the fifteen-member Security Council for a second option proposed by the secretary-general: to strengthen the UN force so that it could intervene and halt some of the killing.[44] That proposal urged "the immediate and massive reinforcement of UNAMIR and a change in its mandate so that it would be equipped and authorized to coerce the opposing forces into a cease-fire, and to attempt to restore law and order and put an end to the killings."[45] The independent inquiry by the United Nations into the organization's actions during the genocide concluded that the UNAMIR reduction was "a decision which the Inquiry finds difficult to justify. The Security Council bears a responsibility for its lack of political will to do more to stop the killing."[46]

SOMALIA SYNDROME

The United States sounded a particularly strident voice of caution over the issue of an expanded UN presence in Rwanda. As events unfolded in Rwanda, American policymakers faced the specter of the Somalia disaster as they deliberated possible options. In December 1992, American forces entered Somalia as part of a UN mission to feed starving people in a nation wracked by internal chaos. With CNN broadcasting images of the soldiers coming ashore to rescue the at-risk population, this gesture of international goodwill seemed destined for success.

Over the next year, the mission expanded from humanitarian relief to include elements of "nation building," helping Somalia establish some sort of workable, democratic polity. As a result of this so-called mission creep, American forces found themselves at odds with local Mogadishu warlords. This conflict culminated on October 3, 1993, with a firefight between American Rangers, members of the Army's elite Delta Force, and forces loyal to Mohammed Aideed. After hours of intense fighting, eighteen Americans lay dead and seventy-three wounded.[47]

Any of loss life is difficult enough, but Somalia earned its lasting legacy when triumphant Somalis dragged the body of a perished American helicopter pilot through the streets of Mogadishu. Covered in the news complete with video footage, the episode seared powerful images into the memories of Americans—policymakers, politicians, the public, and military personnel alike. Somalia became "a sobering and formative experience for U.S. policy, one that sent shockwaves through the Pentagon and White House."[48] The equation for intervention in Africa then appeared to have a maximum of risk with limited returns at best.

In the military establishment, an angry belief that the Clinton administration had failed to provide requested equipment and irritation at its subsequent hasty withdrawal from Somalia following the Battle of Mogadishu contributed to a reluctance to commit American forces to another UN mission, especially one in Africa.[49] At the same time, the dictates of domestic politics suggested few if any influential constituencies for American involvement in Africa following the Somalia debacle. To put it simply, the president feared losing more votes and opinion poll percentage points than he would gain over any African intervention.

Despite the Somalia episode, it is important to note that policymakers did not share a monolithic view about the appropriate and necessary response to the Rwanda crisis. In fact, according to administration officials, the State Department's Africa Bureau, headed by George Moose, urged an expanded and more vigorous UNAMIR presence. Deputy Assistant Secretary Prudence Bushnell and Central Africa Office Director Arlene Render "argued fiercely at interagency meetings within the executive branch for a stronger mandate and a troop increase for UNAMIR as well as for a number of diplomatic measures to isolate and stigmatize the rump regime."[50] Madeleine Albright reportedly opposed a bystander role for the United States.[51] However, proponents of stronger action faced an uphill battle within the administration, particularly with the Pentagon.

The Pentagon based much of its position on a Somalia analogy, arguing that an all-too-fine line existed between sending in UN forces and eventually having to follow up with American soldiers. Pentagon officials were quite wary of having to bail out a floundering UNAMIR and, therefore, opposed multilateral involvement at any level.[52] This was an understandable concern but one born of selective memory—the costly Battle of Mogadishu had been an American not a UN operation. One official said the Pentagon was so determined to avoid entanglement in a "messy country without significant US interests at stake, that they purposely undercut the Africa bureau."[53] Underhanded organizational politics aside, proponents of intervention in any form were outranked in Clinton administration discussions. A lower-level official such as Bushnell had a difficult argument made even more challenging by having to go head to head with more senior officials from the Pentagon, including Undersecretary of Defense John Deutch.

According to lobbyist Holly Burkhalter, "As one administration official in the intelligence community described it, the Africa bureau's Moose, Bushnell, and Pender were completely outgunned. . . . When you have George Moose debating John Deutch, guess who wins?"[54] Compounding this "outgunning" was an apparent lack of interest or support from higher-ups in the State Department. Peter Tarnoff, the undersecretary of state for political affairs and the overseer of the Africa Bureau and other regional departments, "apparently had no interest in Rwanda," while Tim Wirth, undersecretary of state for global affairs, "seemingly played no role at all in the question of US policy during the genocide, even though his brief included human rights."[55] Meanwhile, at the National Security Council (NSC), senior officials there demonstrated their disinclination toward any sort of action.[56] Throughout the administration, policymakers saw Rwanda "through the prism of Somalia." As a result, they thought in terms of a failed state and incorrectly reasoned that "any intervention would have to be large-scale and costly and would probably produce no measurable improvement anyway."[57]

From even the limited details available about administration thinking about Rwanda during the early phase of the crisis, it appears that the United States operated under a significantly flawed understanding and interpretation of events. In large part, the Clinton administration first mistakenly identified and therefore discussed the Rwanda issue as a peacekeeping matter, as a more or less "traditional" conflict between two armed forces. Therefore, any proposed action to alleviate the situation in Rwanda fell under the rubric of "peacekeeping" and was far more likely to fall victim to flawed analogies from the Somalia experience. It also made more likely—and perhaps more understandable and defensible—extreme caution and trepidation at the thought of interposing any foreign force between the warring parties no matter what the reported loss of life.

Civil war in a traditional sense was practically a sideshow in Rwanda—the main act and the cause of the massive casualties and acts of inhumanity was genocide, pure and simple. It is important to note that intervention in any form may not have been more likely or come more quickly had the administration more quickly and more accurately gauged events in Rwanda to be genocide. Framing the issue properly as a case of massive violations of human rights with thousands of civilian casualties might have led to a different administration orientation. Then again, the United States proved willing and overly eager simply to avoid calling genocide "genocide" when the evidence was clear and present.

PDD-25

This "peacekeeping frame of mind" and its peculiar outgrowth from the Somalia syndrome became manifest with the public release on May 5, 1994 (in the midst of the genocide in Rwanda), of Presidential Decision Directive 25 (PDD-25). PDD-25 marked a determined effort to redefine the conditions and contexts for U.S. participation in UN peacekeeping operations. Bill Clinton came into office trumpeting support and enthusiasm for multinational operations on issues ranging from nonproliferation to international crime. Candidate Clinton even spoke openly of the establishment of a UN rapid reaction force to intervene on humanitarian grounds.[58]

However, as is often the case, where one stands depends on where one sits, and candidates and presidents occupy very different chairs. Clinton's proclaimed vision of assertive multilateralism dissipated; caution and "prudence" filled the gap. Speaking to the United Nations on September 7, 1993, President Clinton said the United Nations must learn "when to say no." He urged the United Nations to ask "hard questions" about potential interventions, including "Is there a real threat to international peace? Does the proposed mission have clear objectives? Can an end point be identified? How much will the mission cost?"[59] These "hard questions" are certainly reasonable, but as one critic suggested, "With such criteria requiring answers in advance, the United States would never have entered World War II had it not been attacked first."[60]

With newfound "prudence" and the haunting "precedent" of Somalia in the background, the Clinton administration formulated an official reassessment of U.S. support for UN peacekeeping initiatives. Termed "the first comprehensive U.S. policy on multilateral peace operations suited to the post-Cold War era," PDD-25 represented a response to hard questions about when, where, and how to intervene.[61] The document defined the American national interest in terms of limited involvement and low cost. Furthermore, it declared that American involvement in such UN missions would occur only if it had a "direct bearing on U.S. national interests." The nebulous and subjective term "national interest" is always open and subject to interpretation. However, within the context of PDD 25, "direct bearing on U.S. national interests" suggested a fairly limited rather than expansive reading and one that would more than likely exclude a place such as Rwanda.

In the press briefing designed to introduce the directive, National Security Adviser Tony Lake stated that "the central conclusion of the study is that properly conceived and well-executed, peacekeeping can be a very important tool of American foreign policy." Shortly thereafter, though, Lake added a qualification pregnant with echoes from Somalia: He noted that while the United States can sometimes help other countries in times of need, "we can never build their nations for them."[62] Lake did not specifically mention whether the United States could help protect unarmed civilians from genocidal butchers.

Specifically, the policy review addressed six major issues: (1) making disciplined and coherent choices about which peace operations to support, (2) reducing U.S. costs for UN peace operations, (3) clearly defining policy on command and control of U.S. forces, (4) reforming and improving the ability of the United Nations to manage peace operations, (5) reforming and improving the ability of the United States to manage peace operations, and (6) improving cooperation between the executive, the Congress, and the American public on peace operations.[63] Among a variety of factors, PDD-25 stresses that the United States will participate in a UN peace mission when the mission (1) responds to a threat to or breach of international peace and security, (2) advances U.S. interests (with unique and general risks weighed appropriately), (3) includes acceptable command and control arrangements, and (4) includes clearly defined objectives with realistic criteria for ending the operation (i.e., an exit strategy). At the policy unveiling, National Security Adviser Lake discussed each of these six imperatives and highlighted the notion that "peacekeeping is a part of our national security policy, but it is not the centerpiece. The primary purpose of our military force is to fight and win wars."

The public announcement of PDD-25 and comments like those made by a senior foreign policy official such as Tony Lake did not bode well for any American support for a strengthened UN response to the crisis in Rwanda and certainly not for any intervention by American forces. To repeat, the thrust of PDD-25 and its release during Rwanda's convulsions suggest that some policymakers mistakenly viewed any mission to central Africa as a more or less "traditional peacekeeping" expedition to maintain a cessation of hostilities between two fighting parties. For the most cynical interpreter, the directive essentially placed any significant initiatives to help Rwanda outside the bounds of reality since none could realistically succeed or even be implemented without American support.

To a very real extent, a more cynical view was not unjustified. PDD-25 meant a potential vicious circle or catch-22 for future deployment of UN forces: "The United States would refuse any new deployment of UN Blue Helmets unless all the necessary conditions (logistical, financial, troop deployments, etc.) were fulfilled—yet they could never be fulfilled *without* the active support of the superpower."[64] Commenting on PDD-25 and its application to Rwanda, Richard Dowden of Britain's *Independent* newspaper called it the result of a "poker mentality: Problem: Somalia. Response: Intervention. Result: Failure. Conclusion: No More Intervention."[65] From Congress, Representative David Obey (D-Wis.) explained the policy as a fulfillment of the American public's desire for "zero degree of involvement and zero degree of risk and zero degree of pain and confusion."[66] The PDD-25 mind-set significantly influenced administration thinking and policy even prior to its public announcement.

UNAMIR REVISITED

As the calendar moved into late April and early May, Rwanda's death toll continued its rapid ascent into the hundreds of thousands as killings spread like a contagion into the countryside. At the same time, Rwanda's internal crisis was becoming a serious regional problem. The UN High Commissioner for Refugees (UNHCR) reported that some 250,000 Rwandan refugees were pouring across the border into neighboring Tanzania, "the largest and fastest such exodus hitherto witnessed by the world body."[67] Similarly, the International Committee of the Red Cross and Red Crescent Societies was monitoring the movement of refugees at the time and called it "a major humanitarian disaster," and they expected "the number to swell to over 500,000."[68]

In response, UN Secretary-General Boutros Boutros-Ghali urged the Security

Council again to take up the Rwanda situation and this time provide UNAMIR with a bolstered version of its mandate, previously diminished on April 21. In an April 29 letter to the Security Council, the secretary-general wrote that "it has become clear that that mandate does not give UNAMIR the power to take effective action to halt the continuing massacres." In calling for forceful action, Boutros-Ghali fully realized that "such action would require a commitment of human and material resources on a scale which member states so far proved reluctant to contemplate."[69] To avoid typical UN delay, Boutros-Ghali "urged member states to make bilateral arrangements in order to quickly match troops with the equipment and transport that would be needed by UNAMIR II."[70] Despite the imposing obstacle of demonstrated reluctance, the secretary-general envisioned sending 5,500 troops to Kigali. From there, they would spread out and create several protected zones or safe havens.

Here, PDD-25 served as a booster shot for American reluctance. Responding to the proposal in the language of the new directive, Madeleine Albright told the Security Council, "Sending a UN force into the maelstrom of Rwanda without a sound plan of operations would be folly." [71] To be fair, the United States was not alone in proceeding with such care. Even though other African nations expressed dismay at the impotent UNAMIR, they were slow to pledge their own troops and eventually would do so only if someone else paid to equip them.[72] The United States could finance such an operation but instead still hesitated, much to the dismay of Boutros-Ghali. Although he did not mention the United States and its "Somalia syndrome" by name, the secretary-general clearly had American policymakers in mind when he said, "We must accept that in certain operations we will not be successful. And the fact that you are not successful in a certain operation must not be an obstacle to additional operations all over the world."[73]

The United States instead countered with a plan to establish protected zones across Rwanda's borders in neighboring countries ("outside-in" vs. Boutros-Ghali's "inside out"), an approach it considered safer and more realistic. One could reasonably argue that the American proposal had merit. Kigali remained an unstable area with a relatively high level of potential risk to outside forces. At the same time, however, relief officials stressed that the majority of at-risk Rwandans remained at the center of the country and not outside its borders.[74] Consultation continued and focused mainly on amendments presented by the United States. According to the United Nations itself, American proposals included "an explicit reference to the need for the parties' consent, the postponement of later phases of deployment pending further decisions in the Council, and requirement that the Secretary-General return to the Council with a refined concept of operations, including among other elements the consent of the parties and available resources."[75] As discussion and debate continued over these qualifications and requirements, the dying continued in Rwanda at an obscenely accelerated pace.

As a second alternative to direct Western intervention, the United States floated the idea of organizing and paying for an all-African force to stop the bloodshed in Rwanda. As a result, the Security Council followed up on Boutros-Ghali's appeal for more forceful action by asking him to consult with the Organization of African Unity (OAU) to explore such an alternative means of ending the crisis.[76] The United States recognized the likelihood of having to provide any African force—probably drawn from Rwanda's weak neighbors—with equipment, supplies, and logistical support to make them effective. Such an African intervention had a contemporary precedent—a Nigerian-led peacekeeping force had been deployed in Liberia to help end that country's civil war. Furthermore, Chapter 8 of the UN Charter calls on regional organizations such as the OAU to try to resolve disputes in their areas before turning to the Security Council.

However, the UN undersecretary-general in charge of peacekeeping at the time, Kofi Annan of Ghana, questioned the efficacy of such an all-African force. Speaking before the Senate Foreign Relations Subcommittee on Africa, Annan said, "Given the limitations of the OAU, if we want urgent and immediate action, I'm not sure that is the organization to turn to. The only African country that could . . . contain the situation and help bring about law and order would be South Africa, but it's too soon to turn to them."[77] According to its own study, the OAU and a large majority of African heads of state engaged in a silence described as "a shocking moral failure."[78] Indeed, the OAU offered minimal initiative at best during the slaughter. Only Senegal sent new forces to the region once the killing started (as part of France's "Operation Turquoise"). In reality, any realistic attempt at military intervention required American leadership. Unfortunately for Rwanda's besieged civilians, that leadership proved elusive.

Finally, on May 17, 1994—almost three weeks after Boutros-Ghali's request—the Security Council approved a 5,500-troop deployment for UNAMIR with a broader mandate. Under Resolution 918, UNAMIR was authorized "a) to contribute to the security and protection of displaced persons, refugees, and civilians at risk in Rwanda, including through the establishment and maintenance, where feasible, of secure humanitarian areas; b) to provide security and support for the distribution of relief supplies and humanitarian relief operations."[79] The Security Council also voted to impose an arms embargo on Rwanda.

Yet PDD-25 still exercised influence. Although it accepted the plans according to Resolution 918, the United States successfully insisted that at first only 150 unarmed observers travel to Rwanda to assess the situation, followed by a force of 800 to secure the airport in Kigali. The future deployment of the remainder of the 5,500 troops "would depend on a further report regarding the cooperation of the parties, the duration of the mandate, and the availability of troops."[80] The United States made final adjustments to its position during Security Council deliberations as Ambassador Albright consulted with Washington via cell phone, while at the United Nations, American representative Karl Inderfurth emphasized that "the true key to the problems in Rwanda is in the hands of the Rwandese people."[81] Albright later testified before Congress that the U.S. insistence on more careful and detailed mission plans was the first implementation of PDD-25.[82]

The May 17 Security Council vote to strengthen UNAMIR was an important step in reviving any hope of ameliorating the ongoing genocidal catastrophe in central Africa. However, Resolution 918 still required implementation, which in turn required a certain amount of additional political will and initiative from member states. Once again, this side of the equation proved troublesome; the United States demonstrated a distinct lack of focus or compelling interest in making a difference. As noted previously, troops from some nine African countries were "theoretically" ready for an intervention in Rwanda, but they required funding and equipment from wealthier countries. In this area, as throughout the crisis, delay dominated the process. A central example is the case of the United States and the armored personnel carriers (APCs), a tale that sadly has come to epitomize American failure to act to help Rwanda.

Shortly after the decision to establish UNAMIR II, Ghana offered several hundred troops to start the deployment. To support this force of Ghanaians authorized for deployment to Kigali, the United Nations requested fifty APCs from the United States. A week later, the United States agreed to provide the APCs and transport them to Uganda. Soon thereafter, however, the United States and the United Nations debated and discussed whether the vehicles would be purchased or leased and for how much. These negotiations lasted for weeks, during which the United States also expressed irritation that officials from Ghana were padding their requests to obtain more equipment than they needed (upward of 200 artillery pieces for fewer than 1,000 men). Meanwhile, the APCs had yet to be moved from their base in Germany to Entebbe because "Pentagon regulations stipulate that no step to carry out a contract can be taken until a lease is signed, and the White House never pressed to waive the restrictions."[83]

Furthermore, the United States was even unwilling to provide in-service vehicles. The APCs available for rent were taken among army stocks of mothballed transporters. Simply getting them out of storage and achieving agreement between the United Nations and the U.S. State Department took three weeks.[84] By the time the vehicles did arrive in mid-July, they were still unpainted and without radios or machine guns.[85] Such delays and concerns over payment while thousands were massacred daily hardly gave the impression of a United States devoted to making a difference in Rwanda. As one Pentagon official explained, "U.N. procurements procedures are incredibly slow. In the Rwanda case, we could have done it the normal—that is the slow—way, or somebody could have said, let's get that equipment over there fast, and then cut the red tape to get it done. We didn't do that."[86] People died en masse while the United States delayed. James Woods, deputy assistant secretary of defense from 1986 to 1994, adds, "It became almost a joke as to the length of time and the, you know, ever-emerging details of things that had to be decided in order to get the bloody APCs on their way. And they got all bogged down into issues of the exact terms of a lease, what color, who would paint them where, what kind of stenciling would go on and all of the other little details."[87] The APCs finally crossed into Rwanda on July 30 and were ready for use the first week of August—when the genocide was over.

AVOIDING THE "G" WORD: ACT II

At the time of the secretary-general's late April request, it had become apparent to observers and analysts the world over that genocide was taking place in Rwanda, not simply a bloody civil war. By this time, refugees who had witnessed the appalling slaughter in Rwanda helped confirm the genocide that many already suspected. Refugee after refugee interviewed in camps across the region described a systematic campaign of killing, coordinated between political leaders, the military, and paramilitary groups. Many also pointed to the frightening incitement power of the Hutu-controlled radio stations.[88] On April 28, just a day before the renewed call for a bolstered UNAMIR, Oxfam announced that "the systematic killing of the Tutsi minority in Rwanda clearly amounted to genocide."[89] In a letter to British Prime Minister John Major, the director of the U.K.-based aid group said that events in Rwanda represented "genocide on a truly horrific scale, with a level of killing the world has not seen since Cambodia in the 1970s."[90] Oxfam and other groups urged the United Nations to send adequate troops back into Rwanda to protect civilians from the genocidal slaughter that had raged unmitigated for almost a month.

Alison Des Forges, a noted Rwanda expert and a consultant for Human Rights Watch, lent her distinguished voice to the charge of genocide. On May 4, 1994, Des Forges testified to the House Subcommittee on Africa that the Hutu government was behind a planned program of genocide. Des Forges explained to the subcommittee that the April death of President Juvenal Habyarimana was being used as an excuse to wipe out the minority Tutsi population. She also made specific reference to Radio-Television Libres des Milles Collines, which, she explained, "operating with the tacit support of the Rwandan government, is asking for the annihilation of the Tutsis" with announcements such as "The grave is half full. Who can help fill it by Monday?"[91] Des Forges also spoke critically of U.S. support for withdrawing the UN peacekeepers from Kigali, a move that she said "made it easier for the violence to occur and spread."[92] On the same day, Boutros-Ghali appeared on ABC's *Nightline* and referred to Rwanda's disaster as "genocide."

Des Forges followed up her congressional testimony with an editorial a week later in the *New York Times* titled "Genocide: It's a Fact in Rwanda." She charged governments with hesitating "to call the horror by its name, for to do so would oblige them to act: signatories to the Convention for the Prevention of Genocide, including the United States, are legally bound to 'prevent and punish' it."[93] She urged the United States and others to act even in some minimal way, from firm public denunciations to denial of international aid to the regime, no matter what they chose to call or not to call the genocide.

While President Clinton used the word almost a dozen times during his 1998 apology in Kigali, for most of the crisis the United States willfully chose not to call events in Rwanda "genocide." Throughout the early stages of Rwanda's upheaval, American policymakers more understandably referred to it as "civil war," "ethnic conflict," and other such related terms. At the time, information was less abundant and less reliable, leading to the mischaracterization of the situation mentioned earlier. However, in little time the picture of genocide in Rwanda became ever more clear and eventually irrefutable. According to a Frontline report, "a secret intelligence report by the State Department had called the killings genocide as early as the end of April."[94] However, the United States held firm to its reluctance to use the "G" word. By early June, the secretary-general of the United Nations and even the French government (with historically close ties to the Hutu regime) were describing the violence in Rwanda as genocide.

Rather than follow that lead, the Clinton administration instructed its spokesmen not to describe the situation in Rwanda as genocide. At one of the daily conferences on Rwanda between officials in Washington, the potential domestic political impact emerged as a concern. Tony Marley, a State Department military adviser, relates that "one official even asked a question as to what possible outcome there might be on the congressional elections later that year were the administration to acknowledge that this was genocide taking place in Rwanda and be seen to do nothing about it. The concern obviously was whether it would result in a loss of votes for the party in the November elections."[95]

The Eminent Personalities report on Rwanda produced by the OAU also points to American domestic political circumstances as an important factor in U.S. inaction. Republicans voiced hostility to any UN mission, and the 1994 "Contract with America" midterm election loomed on the political horizon.

According to the OAU report, "With negligible American interests to consider, Clinton was left with the choice between pandering to local political advantage or trying to save an untold number of lives in Rwanda."[96]

The effort to avoid applying the label "genocide" to Rwanda had as much to do with appearances and public perceptions at home as with potential legal obligation. While Article I of the UNGC does call on signatories "to undertake to prevent" the crime, it is unlikely that internal State Department analyses suggested any risk of being "judged" in violation of that provision. This lack of legal concern arises in large part from U.S. reservations to the convention. Specifically, the United States opposed the terms of Article IX of the UNGC, which states,

> Disputes between the Contracting Parties relating to the interpretation, application, or fulfillment of the present Convention, including those relating to the responsibility of a State for genocide or for any of the other acts enumerated in Article III, shall be submitted to the International Court of Justice at the request of any of the parties to the dispute.

Behind forceful pressure from Senator Jesse Helms, the United States ratified the convention with a reservation to Article IX, which reads,

> That with reference to Article IX of the Convention, before any dispute to which the United States is a party may be submitted to the jurisdiction of the International Court of Justice under this article, the specific consent of the United States is required in each case.[97]

In this way, the United States excluded itself from the jurisdiction of the International Court of Justice concerning implementation of the convention. Still, the administration recognized the power of the word "genocide" whether legally binding or not—and rightly so. Work by the Program on International Policy Attitudes found in July 1994 that 80 percent of respondents favored intervention if a UN commission concluded that genocide was occurring in Rwanda.[98] The Clinton administration, however, expressed no interest in demonstrating leadership on the issue and tapping this base of latent public support.[99]

For a president and an administration most keenly interested in domestic policy, the Rwanda issue (like Bosnia) was perceived more as a threat to the legislative agenda and approval ratings at home. Since American officials heard no widespread outcry from the American people, they generally avoided creating one and remained content not to hear much opposition to their nonresponse. At a meeting on Rwanda, President Clinton reportedly asked his staff if the Congressional Black Caucus had agitated at all on the issue, and he was reportedly told they had not. When a representative from Human Rights Watch asked

National Security Adviser Anthony Lake how to make progress in influencing U.S. policy, Lake answered, "Make more noise."[100]

The noise certainly was not forthcoming from the administration since it preferred not to see genocide in Rwanda on the public radar. The State Department and the NSC told their officials to limit their phrasing to the statement that "acts of genocide may have occurred." Said a senior administration official, "Genocide is a word that carries an enormous amount of responsibility." The official went on to explain that if the United States described the slaughter in those terms, "it would be natural—and unwelcome—for voters to expect that the response would include dispatching troops."[101] Ambassador to Rwanda David Rawson made a similar point, arguing that "as a responsible government, you don't just go around hollering 'genocide.' You say that acts of genocide may have occurred and they need to be investigated."[102]

The difficult and disingenuous nature of this "semantic squirm"[103] became apparent at a State Department press briefing on June 10, 1994. Two months after the start of genocide in Rwanda, the United States still refused to come right out and call it by its name. Department spokeswoman Christine Shelly told the assembled reporters that "based on the evidence we have seen from observations on the ground, we have every reason to believe that acts of genocide have occurred in Rwanda." She carefully added that in terms of the applicability of international law (i.e., the UNGC), "clearly not all of the killings that have taken place in Rwanda are killings to which you might apply that label." Already in a difficult position as a mouthpiece for this convoluted and purposely twisted position, she was then asked, "How many acts of genocide does it take to make genocide?" "That's just not a question that I'm in a position to answer," she replied, adding, "There are formulations that we are using that we are trying to be consistent in our use of."

In a follow-up question, a member of the press pushed the issue, saying, "So you say genocide happens when certain acts happen, and you say that those acts have happened in Rwanda. So why can't you say that genocide has happened?" To this, Shelly answered, "Because, Alan, there is a reason for the selection of words that we have made, and I have—perhaps I have—I'm not a lawyer. I don't approach this from the international legal and scholarly point of view. We try, best as we can, to accurately reflect a description in particularly addressing that issue. It's—the issue is out there. People have obviously been talking about it."

A less semantically painful but more revealing answer came when she stressed that "there are obligations which arise in connection with the use of the term." Those obligations are clearly spelled out in the UNGC (as discussed earlier, the United States became party to the convention in 1989). However, as its record on Rwanda in the two months leading up to that painful press conference plainly revealed, the United States defined its national interest as avoiding its signed commitment. Commenting on the press conference exchange, Philip Gourevitch writes, "She [Shelly] meant that if it was a genocide, the Convention of 1948 required the contracting parties to act. Washington didn't want to act. So Washington pretended that it wasn't a genocide. Still, assuming that the above exchange took about two minutes, an average of eleven Tutsis were exterminated in Rwanda while it transpired."[104]

The White House faced criticism from several fronts for its word games and diplomatic evasions. Following a visit to refugee camps in Tanzania, Representative Tony P. Hall (D-Ohio) said, "I believe it is genocide and we need to stop sitting on the sidelines." Commenting on the position of the Clinton administration, Hall stated, "They keep avoiding calling it genocide because they know that as a ratifier [of the UNGC] we are required by international law to find the parties responsible and go after them. We need to go after the people who are guilty. We know who they are." Similarly, in a June 10, 1994, letter to President Clinton, Human Rights Watch President Kenneth Roth explained that since the killing began "only 4 days ago, Human Rights Watch/Africa has gathered evidence that perhaps as many as 500,000 helpless civilians, mostly of the Tutsi minority, have been slaughtered. How can this be anything but genocide?"[105]

A week before Shelly's challenging press conference, former Bush administration secretary of state for African affairs, Herman Cohen, wrote an op-ed in the *Washington Post* highly critical of the administration's position. Cohen charged that the United States was entirely wrong to continue viewing and labeling Rwanda "as a traditional peacekeeping problem when it is really a 'call 911' problem." He denounced the administration for its "current wimpish approach to the genocide in Rwanda" and said, "If anything is going to destroy the credibility of the international community in the area of conflict resolution, the American policy is going to do it." Cohen concluded that "another Holocaust may have just slipped by, hardly noticed."[106]

Meanwhile, Secretary of State Warren Christopher, traveling in Turkey, suggested some progress when he said to reporters, "If there's any particular magic in calling it a genocide, I have no hesitancy in saying that."[107] However, Christopher's magical invocation did not reveal any actual change in policy. In a manipulative legal interpretation not entirely unexpected from the Clinton administration, they argued that the UNGC did not, in fact, obligate signatories to prevent and punish the crime. Rather, "the White House determined that the convention merely 'enables' such preventive action."[108]

PROSPECTS FOR INTERVENTION/ PREVENTION

No mission, no matter how noble the cause and the intentions, should proceed without first determining that the proposed action has a high chance of succeeding and improving the situation at hand. The case of the Rwanda genocide and American foreign policy is no different. Fairness and thoroughness dictate that one at least briefly examine the simple but crucial question, Could a reasonable intervention have made a difference? The short answer is a definitive yes. A UN force backstopped by—indeed, shaped by—U.S. leadership and its unrivaled military capability could have saved thousands of lives. Could they have "prevented" the genocide? No, if prevention means keeping it from happening in the first place. That level of prevention could have occurred only with a reinforced UNAMIR with a vigorous mandate and a major economic assistance package already in place well before the events of the spring of 1994.

Instead, the "prevention" at issue here involves minimizing the carnage to the greatest extent possible once the genocide had already begun. While critics such as Alan Kuperman rightly discount a maximum intervention of say 15,000 Americans, they too quickly discount the value of other options.[109] Rwanda revisionists display the same lack of vision and creative leadership shown by American policymakers at the time. All fail to recognize—or recognized but failed to implement—a combination of several minimum interventions that taken together could have had a close to maximum effect.

Canadian Major General Romeo Dallaire, the former commander of the UNAMIR force, has argued forcefully and consistently that the United Nations could have halted the 1994 genocide had it been willing to commit more troops with authority to take decisive, preventive action. Dallaire first made his views public in five and a half hours of testimony at the UN International Criminal Tribunal for Rwanda in February 1998. He was testifying at the trial of Jean-Paul Akayesu, a mayor accused and later convicted of facilitating genocide in central Rwanda.[110] Dallaire explained how he urged the United Nations to send him more troops and broaden his mandate, even before the crash of Habyarimana's plane, but the recommendations went nowhere. Asked directly during the trial if he could have stopped the progression of the genocide, Dallaire answered, "Yes, absolutely. We had a time frame of two weeks [the first two weeks of the crisis] easily where we could have made the task of killing much more difficult for these people."[111]

Dallaire suggested that one obvious tactic would have involved preventing Hutus from establishing their network of roadblocks and barricades that kept Tutsis from fleeing and aided in rounding them up for massacres. Instead, according to the general, his force was too small, ill equipped, and inadequately trained and without legal mandate to intervene.[112] Dallaire said that an effective force could and should have been assembled and deployed in April 1994, but the United Nations lacked the political will to do so. Defense attorney Nicolas Tiangaye said, "It seems to me you regret that, Major General." Dallaire replied, "You cannot even imagine."[113]

At an earlier date, General Dallaire also stated, "I came to the United Nations from commanding a mechanized brigade group of 5,000 soldiers. If I had had that brigade group in Rwanda, there would have been hundreds of thousands of lives spared."[114] With the major general's provocative comment in mind, the Carnegie Commission on Preventing Deadly Conflict, the Institute of the Study Diplomacy at Georgetown University, and the U.S. Army convened a panel of senior military leaders to investigate whether such a force in Rwanda could have had any significant impact on the situation there.

The report produced by that distinguished panel includes rather detailed military analysis with elaborate strategic and tactical details about the theoretical force. However, most important, the conference participants concluded that "the hypothetical force described by General Dallaire—at least 5,000 strong, depending on the method of employment, and armed with the equipment and capabilities to employ and sustain a brigade in combat—could have made a significant difference in Rwanda in 1994."[115]

The report includes a number of reasonable qualifications and requirements for any intervention force. For example, the panel stressed that commanders in the field would require adequate latitude to increase or decrease the use of force as they deemed necessary, with emphasis on the freedom "to respond instantly to or prevent violent acts."[116] Still, the panel stated its overall finding quite clearly: "The rapid introduction of robust combat forces, authorized to seize at one time critical points throughout the country, would have changed the political calculations of the participants. The opportunity existed to prevent the killing, to interpose a force between the conventional combatants and re-establish the DMZ, and to put the negotiations back on track."[117]

Elaborating on political and military realities, the panel recognized that the creation of any such capable force "requires the participation of a modern, sophisticated national military force—in this case, U.S. participation would have been essential—to marshal the resources, provide critical functions, and achieve mission goals."[118] Written most plainly, it seems likely that 5,000 troops, with American military support, could have saved tens and even hundreds of thousands of people from genocidal slaughter in Rwanda.

Such a military intervention did not necessarily mean 5,000 Americans. Had it been willing to exercise dynamic and creative "ethical leadership" at this critical moment, the United States could have assembled a powerful multinational force to effectively—even easily—deal with undisciplined hordes of machete-wielding thugs.

Had the Western forces that had been sent in to evacuate expatriates joined the UNAMIR contingent, a strong likelihood existed that they could have halted the genocide's progress in Kigali, with arresting ripple effects from the capital to the countryside. Reflecting on this lost opportunity, the commander of Belgian forces in Rwanda wrote,

> The responsible attitude would have been to join the efforts of the Belgian, French, and Italian troops . . . with those of UNAMIR and to have restored order in the country. There were enough troops to do it, or at least to have tried. When people rightly point the finger at certain persons presumed responsible for the genocide, I wonder after all if there is not another category of those responsible because of their failure to act.[119]

UNAMIR Deputy Commander Brigadier Henry Anyidoho agrees, stating, "Had they been deployed, we had enough troops. . . . There was a moment. We just missed it. It was a fleeting opportunity, and we just missed it. Because there was no political will."[120]

While genocide swept through Rwanda, 18,000 UN troops were in Somalia, including over 2,000 American Marines off the coast as part of the USS *Peleliu* Amphibious Ready Group. When it finally decided to act (mixed motives notwithstanding), France deployed 2,500 troops to carve out a safe zone in southwestern Rwanda. India maintains a highly trained cadre of soldiers essentially "on call" for the UN Security Council. The pieces of the puzzle lay strewn about—well-equipped and highly trained forces from the United States, France, Britain, and Italy, potentially buttressed by soldiers from South Africa, India, and Nigeria, would have been more than capable of establishing even minimal safe havens. All such a strategy required was a leadership vision demanding that those pieces be assembled to save a maximum number of lives.

THE PMC OPTION

If unwilling to risk American or allied lives to save hundreds of thousands of Rwandan civilians, the United States had at its disposal a nontraditional, certainly controversial, but likely effective option: employing private military companies (PMCs), which essentially are the post–Cold War incarnation of mercenaries. With the end of the U.S.-Soviet standoff has come fairly significant military downsizing around the world, creating a talent pool of highly trained and skilled military professionals. However, unlike many of their "dogs of war" ancestors, several contemporary PMCs, such as Executive Outcomes (no longer operating) and Sandline International, are formally incorporated businesses, complete with charters and codes of conduct that claim to align with international law and human rights norms. Of course, they nonetheless exist to make money; like any business, their motive is profit. In a world of globalization, capitalization, and violence, individual mercenaries and PMCs have found a niche.

Best known among PMCs was Executive Outcomes (EO), a company formed in 1989 and composed mainly of former members of the South African Defense Force. Executive Outcomes enjoyed high-profile successes providing training and conducting military operations for the Angolan government and then in helping Sierra Leone beat back Foday Sankoh's rebellious Revolutionary United Front in 1995.[121]

Unwilling to risk its own forces—the world's best-trained and -equipped soldiers—to halt the slaughter in Rwanda, the United States and its allies could have pushed the UN Security Council to contract with a PMC such as EO to move into Kigali and surrounding areas with a mandate to establish safe havens for hunted Tutsi and Hutu. According to a former EO official, the company considered such a role (but was never asked) and could have successfully defended the lives of countless Rwandans. In an unpublished report, Chris Grove, former the chief of staff of EO, details a plan of action and the costs of such a mission.

According to the analysis, EO could have had armed troops on the ground in fourteen days and could have fully deployed over 1,500 personnel, complete with air and communications support, within six weeks. Grove writes, "Executive Outcomes, a Private Military Company, could at the time, if approached by the UN or the OAU, supply personnel, equipment and heavy transport planes (regarded as a key to success in African peace operations) to rapidly deploy a reaction force to the Rwandan region, to deal with the crisis as it developed (similar to EO's assistance in Sierra Leone to counter the RUF about one year later)."[122] The report estimates the cost for a six-month operation at $150 million (compared to $100 million spent each month by the United Nations on failed peacekeeping in Sierra Leone). The employment of mercenaries, sanctioned by the United Nations and the United States, from a PMC for a humanitarian mission in Rwanda would have generated a firestorm of criticism. The PMC issue brings with it a host of questions about motives, accountability, and ethics. However, another question merits serious debate: How much moral squeamishness about mercenaries can the United States and the world community allow themselves in the face of genocide? Writing about the PMC solution to the second Sierra Leone crisis in the spring of 2000, novelist Frederick Forsyth (of *Dogs of War* fame) editorialized in the United Kingdom, "If we are not prepared to watch mass butchery and do nothing, and we are not prepared to commit our own armed forces, not just to evacuate our British nationals, but with a clear mandate to defeat the thugs, destroy them, capture the psycho who lead them and hand him over to the elected government, why not use mercenaries?"[123]

The PMC option for Rwanda would have been far from ideal. More broadly, it probably represents a short-term fix until the international community can decide and commit to some sort of UN rapid reaction force or until the political leadership in the United States and elsewhere overcomes their policy of combatant immunity. In the meantime, however, we face the evidence that a well-known, professional military group was willing and able to operate under UN mandate to prevent the death of tens of thousands of Rwandans. An American administration that was determined not to risk American lives in the heart of Africa but aware that something must be done to live up to the pledge of "never again" could have seized on the PMC alternative as an imperfect solution to a horrific situation.[124]

The Rwanda "revisionism" suggesting that little could have been done in time to make a difference simply falls short. A number of scenarios existed for saving lives at every stage of the crisis. Granted, once started, the genocide could not be prevented, but it could have been stopped or seriously curtailed. Intervention at some level by military forces, be they state or nonstate, could have minimized—even dramatically reduced—the final death toll. Not being able to save all 800,000 victims is hardly reason to stand by and save none.

NONMILITARY INTERVENTION

The United States did have options open to it, short of military intervention, to influence, at least minimally, events in Rwanda and to express its outrage at the Hutu regime. Primary among these was dealing with Rwandan hate radio. According to genocide scholar Frank Chalk, the U.S. Foreign Broadcast Service and Britain's BBC monitored hate radio transmissions in Rwanda.[125] Given the prominent role played by the murderous radio broadcasts of stations such as Radio-Television Libre des Milles Collines, disabling those stations would have helped minimize incitement and propaganda and hinder communication between radical Hutus. Aware of the powerful impact these broadcasts were having, General Dallaire, a few international human rights groups, and several U.S. senators called for them to be jammed, but nothing was done.[126] The RPF even sent a letter calling on the Security Council to jam or destroy RTLMC.[127] The U.S. aircraft Volent Solo, used to disrupt Iraqi communication during the Persian Gulf War, could have put an end to the extremist radio incitement in Rwanda. Instead, the Clinton administration, citing legal problems, never seriously investigated the radio option. Pentagon lawyers even argued that jamming state radio in Rwanda would be contrary to the U.S. constitutional protection of press and speech rights.[128] Volent Solo stayed grounded at a Pennsylvania airbase.[129]

While hate radio spewed its genocidal venom, the regime behind it maintained its representation at the United Nations and in the United States. Rwanda continued to hold its rotating seat on the Security Council throughout the genocide, even as the Security Council discussed and voted on issues concerning the slaughter. The Rwandan representative certainly reported back to the government the attitude of the United Nations and important member states such as the United States. No member state "contested the right of representatives of a genocidal regime to sit at the table of a council supposedly devoted to the maintenance of peace."[130] Says Michael Barnett, "Nobody said, 'Stop it.' Nobody said, 'Your presence here disgusts me.' Nobody said, 'Why don't you just get out of the room?' There was never a real moment in which they dressed him [the Rwandan representative] down because if you did, you would be breaking the rules."[131] In Washington, the Clinton administration withdrew recognition from the genocidal regime and shut down its embassy only after the RPF had asserted its control in Kigali.

OPERATION SUPPORT HOPE

In a strange, perverse, or ironic twist of fate, when decisive American action finally came in response to events in Rwanda, its primary beneficiaries were the Hutus. With few people left to kill, the genocide began to wind down, and a new human disaster—this time "made for television"—emerged as an endless caravan of human beings fled their torn-apart homeland. Civil war blazed in Rwanda. Tutsi forces of the RPF had struck with success at government forces. As the RPF advanced across the country and stood poised to take firm hold of Kigali, the "Hutu power" architects of the genocide made a desperate final attempt to salvage some sort of control and deny final victory to the Tutsi forces. Again turning to their hate radio broadcast machine, the Hutu leadership painted a horrifying picture of the advancing RPF and what their rule would be like for Hutu civilians. The broadcasts urged people to flee the country to save themselves as individuals and the Hutu as a group. In an interview, Hutu leader Jean-Bosio bragged, "Even if the RPF has won a military victory, it will not have the power. It has only the bullets, we have the population."[132] The messages proved quite effective, precipitating the exodus of almost the entire nation.

July and August saw two million Rwandans, the vast majority of them Hutu (most Tutsi were dead), flee their country. A report on the refugee flow by the UNHCR estimated almost 300,000 in northern Burundi, over half a million in Tanzania, and close to one million refugees in Zaire. In a three-day period, an estimated one million Rwandan Hutus poured across the border to the Zairean town of Goma—a rate close to 500 people a minute. The United Nations and cooperating relief agencies were quickly overwhelmed by the mass of humanity. Monstrous conditions—including lack of food, water, shelter, and medicine—only worsened as unsanitary living spaces led to an epidemic of cholera running rampant throughout the Goma camp, which sat at the base of a volcano on the shores of Lake Kivu. Doctors Without Borders documented the "hell on earth" at Goma, where some 50,000 died in two weeks.[133]

For some observers, the suffering had an aspect of poetic justice or divine retribution for the Hutus in the camps, many of whom (but certainly not all) had participated in some capacity in the genocide just weeks prior. Philip Gourevitch relates the story of a reporter familiar with the Hutu conspiracy against the Tutsis arriving to cover the camps who said he looked up at the volcano at Goma and prayed, "God, if that thing erupts right now and buries the killers, I will believe that You are just and I will go to church again every day of my life."[134]

The Hutu *genocidaires* did not meet a volcanic end. Instead, in a situation strikingly reminiscent of Cambodia and the Khmer Rouge, the Hutu power leadership quickly assumed positions of power and influence in the camps. With hundreds of thousands of people to deal with, workers with the United Nations and nongovernmental organizations (NGOs) could not organize and manage aid distribution on their own. They had to rely considerably on local personnel—on Hutu leaders and *bourgmestres,* many of them criminals involved in and responsible for the genocide. Given Rwanda's history and tradition of obedience to authority, many refugees organized themselves village by village, region by region, under the guidance of their local leaders.[135] Prunier explains that the Hutu leadership "kept almost total control of their subjects. Whoever disagreed with them was quickly murdered, a quick way to stop returns to Rwanda after the first few weeks. They monopolised the distribution of humanitarian aid and inflated the numbers of people actually registered to get more than what was needed. In the distributions, they gave first priority to themselves, and then to the ex-FAR or *Interahamwe.*"[136] In addition, Hutu leaders would sell extra rations and use the funds collected to finance planned military operations.[137]

Donors and relief providers faced an unpalatable situation and a difficult problem: how to aid those in need without providing *genocidaires* with the means of reviving their murderous program. The dilemma had no easy solution if any at all; one could not visually distinguish the guilty from the innocent. The UNHCR workers learned that their mission had earned a telling nickname: "*Hauts Criminels Reassasies*" (Well-Fed High Criminals).[138] Even more troubling was the news that armed guerrilla groups nourished at the camps were waging attacks into Rwanda just weeks after their arrival as "refugees."[139] A then-confidential UN report struck a tone of despair at the situation: "Former soldiers and militiamen have total control of the camps. . . . They have decided to stop by force in necessary any return of the refugees to Rwanda. . . . It now looks as if these elements are preparing an armed invasion of Rwanda and that they are both stockpiling and selling food aid distributed by cariative organizations in order to prepare for this invasion."[140]

As analysts such as Alain Destexhe and Gerard Prunier have noted, the humanitarian horror at Goma and the other camps had the effect of glossing over and even diminishing the genocide that had just occurred. The media could not cover the genocide in action but could capture the terrible suffering at the camps on film and broadcast it around the world. Even the print media responded with notably dramatic stories with titles such as "Descent into Hell" and "Land of the Dead and Dying."[141] Destexhe, writing at the time, commented,

> Yesterday the genocide of the Tutsi by the Hutu militias, today the genocide of the Hutu refugees by cholera? This comparison, which one can see widely used in the press, puts on the same plane things which have nothing to do with each other. Through this confusion the original, singular, and exemplary nature of the genocide is denied and the guilt of the perpetrators becomes diluted in the general misery.[142]

The "genocide" by cholera did dominate the news and muted the June 28 UN report on the actual genocide against the Tutsis. The investigations conducted by special reporter Rene Degni-Segui confirmed a preplanned, systematic, and coordinated program of genocide. Degni-Segui called for criminal charges against those responsible to be handled by an international tribunal.[143] Gerard Prunier echoes much of the Destexhe analysis, noting that following the UN report, "the pressure to create a tribunal was partly weakened by the shock of the refugee ordeal in Goma, according to an unspoken argument which could be roughly summed up as 'What these people need is food and medicines, not a tribunal.' "[144] The death of a "mere" 50,000 in front of cameras displaced the loss of upward of a million Tutsis who perished at the hands of their countrymen, out of sight of the Western media.

Still, the refugees at Goma and elsewhere, Hutu or not, *genocidaires* or not, did desperately need assistance. Caring for international criminals was the price exacted for saving the lives of innocent children. Since the UNHCR and beleaguered NGOs simply could not handle the size and scale of the camps and the death in them, they appealed to the international community for help. Although it had impeded UN action in Rwanda at almost every turn, cast Rwanda and the genocide of the Tutsis outside the bounds of its national interests, obscured the UNGC, and refused to label as genocide an obvious and large-scale commission of that crime, the United States moved with surprising alacrity to buttress the humanitarian effort to save the refugees. Seemingly oblivious to the genocide that preceded and caused the refugee crisis, President Clinton called Goma "the worst humanitarian crisis in a generation."[145] In stark contrast to American inaction, lack of interest, and delay during the three months of genocide in Rwanda, the Clinton administration quickly pledged $100 million and was the first to offer military support for the delivery of "600 tonnes of food and 500 tonnes of medical equipment the UN had estimated was required daily for sustaining the displaced population."[146]

Carefully describing the effort as a disaster relief operation and not a peacekeeping mission, President Clinton announced Operation Support Hope, a vigorous American response to the needs of the massive displaced population. Within a month, the operation counted over 2,000 American troops working in Rwanda, Kenya, Uganda, and eastern Zaire. To combat the cholera epidemic, American forces flew a nonstop flight from California to Goma, complete with three in-flight refuelings, to transport a water purification plant capable of processing 24,000 gallons an hour. The transport also brought two California fire engines to help pump water from Lake Kivu.[147] Said one U.S. Army major of the effort, "You've only got to go out and look, and your heart says this is the right place to be and the right thing to do."[148]

Shortly after the Clinton administration recognized the new RPF government on July 31, Secretary of Defense William Perry traveled to Entebbe and Kigali to review and improve the relief operation and to meet with President Pasteur Bizimungu and Vice President Paul Kagame of Rwanda. During his trip, the secretary pledged that American noncombat forces would remain with Operation Support Hope "as long as needed to do our mission even if that meant a year or longer."[149] Traveling with Perry, Congressman Donald Payne (D-N.J.) said, "We will, as the leading power in the world, be asked in many instances to take the lead in such humanitarian efforts."[150] During his stopover in Kigali, Perry said, "This is a very important mission to the future of where we go as a nation. There are two schools of thought in the U.S. Congress, one that perhaps we should be more isolationist and not involve ourselves in operations of this nature and those of us who feel as leader of the free world we should be involved."[151]

The significant relief efforts undertaken by the United States under Operation Support Hope undoubtedly made a difference and saved the lives of thousands of Rwandan refugees. The effort merits praise. At the same time, the decisive and effective response to the humanitarian disaster puts in marked relief the similarly determined noneffort to save lives during the genocide itself. In a comment crying out for context, President Clinton stated that "from the beginning of this tragedy, the United States has been in the forefront of the international community's response."[152] Of course, he was referring to act II of the tragedy; the United States had shunned the stage during the act I genocide.

Although a driving factor behind PDD-25 was cost cutting, the United States ended up spending at least fifty times the amount of money it balked at months earlier. As one analyst sharply noted, "The U.S. has been niggardly about peacekeeping but no one seems to worry about spending many many more times the amount of money now to save lives."[153] It is almost surreal and difficult to square how, on the one hand, the United States haggled for weeks over rental payments for old APCs while genocide ran its course and how, on the other hand, just a few months later the wallet opened to the tune of well over $300 million for relief. According to American estimates, the world community has spent almost $5 billion on humanitarian, economic, and military programs for Rwanda, with the United States alone spending $1.23 billion.[154] In the end, one prefers to resist the notion, however slight, that Rwandans perished by the hundreds of thousands in part because the United States sought to save money.

THE UNITED STATES AND POSTGENOCIDE JUSTICE IN RWANDA

American largesse toward postgenocide Rwanda did not end with Operation Support Hope. Along with its dedication to humanitarian assistance for Rwanda's refugees, the Clinton administration spoke out strongly in favor of seeing those guilty of genocide brought to justice. In fact, U.S. agitation for a tribunal began as early as July, when it was still hindering efforts to stop the crimes it was interested in seeing prosecuted.[155] To this end, the United States backed the November 8, 1994, UN Security Council Resolution 955, which outlined a plan "to establish an international tribunal for the sole purpose of prosecuting persons responsible for genocide and other serious violations of international humanitarian law committed in the territory of Rwanda and Rwandan citizens responsible for genocide and other such violations committed in the territory of neighboring states, between 1 January 1994 and 31 December 1994."[156]

Ambassador Albright applauded the resolution, which she said marked "the culmination of months of very hard and persistent work by our respective governments, the Secretariat, the Commission of Experts, and this Council to create a new ad hoc tribunal for the investigation and prosecution of genocide, crimes against humanity, and war crimes in Rwanda."[157] Albright expressed U.S. willingness to assist with the tribunal and with the rebuilding of Rwanda's judicial system. She closed her statement expressing the administration's "hope that the step we have taken here can promote both justice and national reconciliation, lest the Rwandan people be unable to escape the memory of madness and barbarism they have just been through."[158] As of the end of 2000, the United States had committed over $80 million to the Rwanda tribunal. The United States has also provided desperately needed computers and other office equipment, and dozens of Americans have served in the office of the prosecutor, some of them on leaves of absence from the Department of Justice.[159]

The tribunal in Tanzania suffered from the start, battling primitive facilities, unhelpful nepotism, and intermittent power and telephone service.[160] Concerned about the problems plaguing the International Criminal Tribunal for Rwanda (ICTR) and inhibiting its effectiveness, the United States applied pressure on the United Nations to formally audit the administration of the court and demand changes. The United Nations did act and stimulated slow but certain change. After finding in February 1997 that "not a single administrative area functioned effectively," a UN inspector-general released a report a year later finding "significant progress in the work of the prosecutors and an overhauled management."[161]

With improvements made and judges and prosecutors at work, the tribunal made progress, culminating in the fall of 1998. On September 2, 1998, the ICTR handed down the first international conviction ever for genocide, finding former Rwanda mayor Jean-Paul Akayesu guilty of organizing genocidal massacres in the Rwandan village of Taba. Judges from Senegal, South Africa, and Sweden ruled that Akayesu used his authority to incite and supervise mass killings of more than 2,000 people and the rape of dozens of Tutsi women in April 1994. Akayesu was also found guilty of inciting villagers to commit genocide in an inflammatory speech on April 19, 1994, in which he called on Hutu followers to exterminate Tutsi civilians.[162] Prior to Akayesu's conviction, no one had ever been punished by an international court for the crime of genocide.

The next day, the tribunal followed up on this historic conviction with an equally momentous sentencing. On September 4, 1998, former Rwandan Prime Minister Jean Kambanda was condemned to life imprisonment for his role in the genocide. Kambanda pled guilty in May to six counts of genocide and crimes against humanity. The court rejected defense arguments for leniency in sentencing because of his cooperation—he provided over ninety hours of testimony incriminating others involved in planning and implementing the genocide. Chief Judge Laity Kama of Senegal wrote, "Genocide is the crime of crimes" and explained that "Jean Kambanda abused his authority and the trust of the population. Nor has he expressed contrition, regret, or sympathy for the victims in Rwanda, even when given the opportunity." The court found that Kambanda witnessed systematic killings, knew that massacres were taking place, and failed to use his powers to stop those below him from organizing and executing a program of genocide.[163]

The United States certainly deserves some credit for these milestone events in international law. As the primary donor, the United States provided the financial and in-kind support without which the tribunal could not function. American insistence on reform of the tribunal helped the court finally function properly and eventually make history with its convictions and sentencing. The State Department's Office of War Crimes Issues continues to monitor judicial developments and provides assistance and expertise to the tribunal to help it bring justice in as many cases as possible. In 2001, the State Department launched a Rewards for Justice Program in support of the ICTR. Like its counterpart for the Yugoslav tribunal, the program offers rewards of up to $5 million for information leading to the transfer to or conviction by the ICTR of any individual indicted by the tribunal for his or her actions regarding the Rwandan genocide.

The post-Rwandan genocide response by the United States has not been limited to the Arusha tribunal. One component of that newfound commitment to Rwanda and the entire central African region is the Great Lakes Justice Initiative (GLJI). Unveiled in Addis Ababa in December 1997 by Secretary of State Madeleine Albright during a meeting of the OAU, the project is designed based on the belief that in the Great Lakes region—Rwanda, Burundi, and the Democratic Republic of Congo—cycles of violence and instability have led to a situation in which "a majority of the population lives outside of the rule of law where corruption and violence are perpetuated with impunity."[164] To combat that negative climate and head off future explosions of violence across national and ethnic boundaries, the GLJI adopts a combined regional, international, and multiagency approach to help the public and private sectors develop justice systems that are "impartial, credible, and effective in combating the culture of impunity and violence that has ravaged Central Africa."[165] The initiative addresses judicial issues at a variety of levels, including efforts to reform courts, prosecutors, police, and prisons and to assist professional associations, universities, and other areas of civil society to formulate improved laws and institutions. The GLJI also pays attention to the role of the military, its system of justice, and adherence to international human rights standards.[166] In Rwanda particularly, the initiative targets the government's colossal caseload as it attempts to prosecute thousands of people detained under its own genocide law. On a broader, more regional level, the program supports independent human rights monitors, conflict resolution mechanisms, and educational efforts. In support of the GLJI, the United States has committed over $30 million to date.

American support for genocide prevention efforts in central Africa now also extends into the military sphere. The United States helped draft and now sponsors in part the Africa Crisis Response Initiative (ACRI) as a means of enhancing the capacity of African nations to prevent and contain disasters on the continent. The ACRI functions as a training partnership among African and non-African militaries with the ultimate goal of creating an effective, mobile African force available to the United Nations for peacekeeping and conflict resolution missions. With American funding and military personnel, battalions of African soldiers receive training appropriate to deployment on regional missions for the United Nations. The ACRI is an international effort that "corresponds to the desire within the region to find African solutions to African problems."[167] The project simultaneously enjoys the full support of the American Joint Chiefs, who view it as an excellent way to avoid sending in American forces in the case of a future genocide in the region.[168] After the initial training sessions, ACRI plans to hold follow-up sessions every six months over the course of two and a half years. The training targets all levels of soldiers, staff, and commanders. With an overarching "train the trainer" model, ACRI includes classroom instruction, field training, and computer-based simulations. As of early 2001, ACRI had provided training and equipment to over 5,000 troops with training missions held for Malawi, Benin, Senegal, and Ghana. Obviously, ACRI is not designed to handle the major conflict that has plagued central Africa—namely, the Democratic Republic of Congo (formerly Zaire)—since 1997.

All together, these American efforts and contributions to prevent another "Rwanda" from occurring fall under what is termed the International Coalition Against Genocide, a systematic attempt at avoiding the resurgence of genocide in central Africa. The coalition's aims include "fostering international coordination in support of regional efforts to enforce anti-genocide measure; providing a forum for high level deliberations on long-term efforts to prevent genocide in the future; and ensuring international support for the findings of the OAU Eminent Personalities Study of the Rwanda Genocide and the Surrounding Events."[169] The International Coalition Against Genocide also plans to revive the UN Arms Flow Commission and to accelerate programs to bring criminals against humanity to justice.[170]

CONCLUSION

When the horrific genocide of 1994 began to decimate Rwanda, a pivotal opportunity arose to strengthen the norm embodied in the UNGC. As a superpower and a convention signatory, the United States faced an unparalleled ethical leadership moment to invigorate its human rights rhetoric with action and through that action save hundreds of thousands of lives. Instead, the United States emerged not as a world leader committed to an important norm of human rights and international law but as an unexpected stumbling block to effective action to stop a genocide that the American president later called "the most intensive slaughter in this blood filled century we are about to leave."[171] America's shortcomings during the carnage in Rwanda were so prominent and so influential for the prospects of *any* international action that official reports from the United Nations, the OAU, Human Rights Watch, and the Belgian and French legislatures roundly criticized the Clinton administration, singling out the United States for its obstinate refusal to act or to help others do so in an effective and timely manner.[172] The United States has had no formal inquiry into its action during the Rwandan genocide.

The evidence that emerges from the U.S. response to genocide in Rwanda suggests a still weak norm of genocide prevention. The preventive side of the norm lacked the "bite" and internalization to force the administration's hand. Realist-related concerns, such as a lack of traditional strategic interest in Rwanda and domestic political self-interest in the United States, bolstered by a misapplied analogy drawn from the Somalia experience, undermined a fertile moment for ethical leadership on the world stage. Strangely, however, as genocide ran its course, the normative framework of the UNGC did cause the United States to "not act" in a certain way. The convention and the term "genocide" had at least enough standing and clout to compel the Clinton administration to consciously avoid using the term for fear of the pressure and criticism it might entail given their determined policy of passivity. The semantic game played by the Clinton administration suggests that the UNGC has in fact armed the word "genocide" with normative and policy implications that the United States does not ignore even if it ultimately chooses not to intervene.

Despite the inaction of the United States, it did eventually express public contrition and pursued important policies with noteworthy norm-building potential. In fact, the strong public apologies by the president and the secretary of state are important milestones in the development of a norm to prevent and punish genocide. To be sure, some critics see Clinton's statement at the Kigali airport as empty and self-serving. Michael Barnett is particularly sharp in his judgment, calling the president's speech "meaningless" and "hollow."[173] Clinton did dissemble somewhat. His statement that "all over the world there were people like me sitting in offices day after day after day who did not fully appreciate the depth and the speed with which you were being engulfed by this unimaginable terror" does not hold up. The administration had the information before them but chose not to see or at least to turn away from what they saw.

Still, cynicism should not permit us to ignore the importance of an apology by the American president. It could not bring back the hundreds of thousands of victims. However, with its expression of remorse, the administration recognized not only that they did not do what they could have but also that they did not do what they *should have*. United States action in Rwanda's postgenocide period has not been limited to saying, "We're sorry." Instead, the Rwanda case once again reveals the pattern of nonintervention during genocide with subsequent humanitarian assistance to address its aftermath and efforts at accountability and justice. The sizable airlift to provide aid to the refugee camps, international judicial work such as the Arusha tribunal and the GLJI, and politicomilitary projects such as the ACRI help Rwanda recover from its trauma.

These posttragedy efforts support the goals of the UNGC in a substantive way and mark the slow march of normative evolution.

This delayed norm entrepreneurship by the United States holds out some hope and represents legitimate ethical progress. As secretary of state, Madeleine Albright spoke in such terms when she declared in a speech on American policy toward Rwanda that "there is an opportunity to move ahead on the basis of international norms."[174] However, this movement fails to erase the missed opportunity of April–June 1994, an opportunity consciously avoided with eyes wide shut. From the start of the genocide in Rwanda, the United States had before it a menu of policy options running the full range of the intervention spectrum. From a policy buffet of political, military, and diplomatic initiatives, the United States chose *none,* and it could have been different. Katelijne Hermans, a Belgian journalist evacuated from Kigali during the crisis, succinctly captured the opportunity lost when she said, "It could have been different. But somebody has to decide it will be different, and nobody took the decision."[175] As Philip Gourevitch acutely concludes, the Clinton administration policy on genocide in Rwanda was not a failure, "it was actually a success of a policy not to intervene. The decision was not to act. And at that we succeeded greatly."[176]

NOTES

1. *New York Times,* March 26, 1998, A1.

2. Rakiya Omaar and Alex de Waal, "U.S. Complicity by Silence: Genocide in Rwanda," *Covert Action Quarterly* (available at http://caq.com/CAQ52Rwanda.html), 4.

3. Hamism derived from the biblical story of Ham, Noah's son. According to the Book of Genesis, Ham and his descendents were cursed because he had seen his father unclothed. The curse was black-colored skin.

4. J. Sasserath, *Le Ruanda-Urundi, etrange royaume feodal* (Brussels, 1948), quoted in Alain Destexhe, *Rwanda and Genocide in the Twentieth Century* (New York: New York University Press, 1995), 39.

5. In most cases, ownership of ten or more cattle earned one "Tutsi" status, while fewer than ten meant one was "Hutu." A third group also exists in Rwanda: the Twa people. A forest-dwelling pygmy minority, they represent only 1 percent of the population and have never been central to the politics or economics of the region.

6. Destexhe, 41.

7. See Stephen R. Weissman, "Preventing Genocide in Burundi," *Peaceworks,* no. 22 (Washington, D.C.: United States Institute of Peace, July 1998); Rene Lemarchand, *Burundi: Ethnic Conflict and Genocide* (Washington, D.C.: Woodrow Wilson Center, 1996); Stanley Meisler, "Holocaust in Burundi, 1972," in Willem A. Veenhoven, ed., *Case Studies on Human Rights and Fundamental Freedoms: A World Survey,* vol. 5 (The Hague: Martinus Nijhoff, 1976).

8. Holly Burkhalter, "The Question of a Genocide: The Clinton Administration and Rwanda," *World Policy Journal* 11, no. 4 (winter 1994/95): 44.

9. Fax from General Romeo Dallaire to UN Department of Peacekeeping Operations, January 11, 1994.

10. Frontline, "The Triumph of Evil," no. 1710, January 26, 1999, interview with Iqbal Riza, 5.

11. Nat Hentoff, "The Holocaust without Guilt," *The Village Voice,* March 16, 1999, 28; Alan J. Kuperman, "The Rwanda Failure," *Washington Post,* December 29, 1998, A15.

12. Gerard Prunier, *The Rwanda Crisis: History of a Genocide* (New York: Columbia University Press, 1995), 238.

13. Frontline, interview with James Woods.

14. Prunier, 243.

15. United Nations, "Report of the Independent Inquiry into the Actions of the United Nations during the 1994 Genocide in Rwanda" (available at <www.un.org/News/ossg/rwandareport.htm>),December 15, 1999, 6.

16. RTLMC, popularly known as "Radio Milles Collines," was set up in 1993 by two men closely connected to President Habyarimana. One was Alphonse Ntimavunda, his brother-in-law. The second was Felicien Kabusa, his son-in-law.

17. Prunier, 224.

18. Destexhe, 32. For more on the impact of Rwanda's malicious broadcasts, see Frank Chalk, "Hate Radio in Rwanda," in Howard Adelman and Astri Suhrke, eds., *The Path of a Genocide* (London: Transaction Publishers, 1999), and Linda Melvern, *A People Betrayed: The Role of the West in Rwanda's Genocide* (London: Zed Books, 2000), 70–73.

19. Prunier, 224.

20. Prunier, 189.

21. Prunier, 244.

22. "Rwanda's Carnage," *Christianity Today,* February 6, 1995, 52.

23. Destexhe, 31.

24. Philip Gourevitch, *We Wish to Inform You That Tomorrow We Will be Killed with Our Families: Stories from Rwanda* (New York: Farrar, Strauss & Giroux, 1998), 18.

25. Fergal Keane, *Season of Blood: A Rwandan Journey* (New York: Viking/Penguin, 1995), 90.

26. Gourevitch, 36. The elder Ntakirutimana was extradited from the United States to stand trial in Rwanda.

27. Keane, 29.

28. Gourevitch, 133.

29. African Rights, *Rwanda: Death, Despair, and Defiance* (London: African Rights, 1995), 342–44.

30. Prunier, 256.

31. See note 30.

32. Prunier, 257.

33. Author interview with State Department Official (confidential), December 1998.

34. Holly Burkhalter, "A Preventable Horror?," *Africa Report,* November–December 1994, 18.

35. *New York Times,* April 10, 1994, A1.

36. See note 35.

37. *Los Angeles Times,* April 14, 1994, A12.

38. Holly Burkhalter, "The United Nations Genocide Convention at 50" (address at Institute of Genocide Studies conference, New York, December 1998).

39. *Seattle Times,* April 17, 1994, B11.

40. *New York Times,* April 10, 1994, A6.

41. UN General Assembly, April 14, 1994, Document A/48/PV.93, 4.

42. Frontline, 11.

43. UN Security Council Resolution 912, Document S/RES/912, April 21, 1994. Despite the vote, the actual force number did not fall below 470.

44. *Washington Post,* April 22, 1994, A1.

45. UN Special Report of the Secretary-General on UNAMIR, Document S/1994/470, April 20, 1994, 3.

46. United Nations, "Report of the Independent Inquiry into the Actions of the United Nations during the 1994 Genocide in Rwanda" (available at <www.un.org/news/ossg/rwandareport.htm>), 29.

47. A total of thirty Americans died over the course of the Somalia mission. For a riveting account of the Battle of Mogadishu and an excellent epilogue on the political dynamics in the background, see Mark Bowden, *Black Hawk Down: A Story of Modern War* (New York: Penguin USA, 2000).

48. *Los Angeles Times,* September 10, 1094, A1.

49. Author interview with Pentagon official (confidential), December 1998.

50. Burkhalter, "The Question of Genocide," 47.

51. *Washington Post,* July 10, 2000, A4.

52. Author interview with Pentagon official (confidential), December 1998.

53. Author interview with Pentagon official (confidential), December 1998. See also Omaar and de Waal.

54. Burkhalter, "The Question of Genocide," 48.

55. Burkhalter, "The Question of Genocide," 47.

56. Omaar and de Waal, 9–11; author interview with Alison Des Forges, January 1999.

57. Alison Des Forges, *Leave None to Tell the Story: Genocide in Rwanda* (New York: Human Rights Watch, 1999), 624.

58. Burkhalter, "The Question of Genocide," 48.

59. *Washington Post,* September 28, 1993, A1.

60. Milton Leitenberg, "Rwanda 1994: International Incompetence Produces Genocide," *Peacekeeping & International Relations* 23, no. 6 (November/December 1994): 10.

61. White House press briefing by National Security Adviser Tony Lake and Director for Strategic Plans and Policy General Wesley Clark, May 5, 1994.

62. See note 61.

63. Presidential Decision Directive 25, Bureau of International Organizations, U.S. Department of State, Washington, D.C.

64. Destexhe, 50.

65. *The Independent* (London), May 18, 1994.

66. Reuters, May 5, 1994.

67. *SIPRI Yearbook, 1995: Armamants, Disarmament, and International Security* (Stockholm: Stockholm International Peace Research Institute), 106.

68. *New York Times,* April 30, 1994, 1.

69. United Nations, Letter of the Secretary-General to the Security Council, Document S/1994/518, April 29, 1994, 2.

70. *The United Nations and Rwanda* (New York: United Nations Department of Public Information, 1993–1996), 47.

71. In response to a July 2000 report on the Rwanda crisis and the international response, Albright has stated, "I screamed about the instructions that I got on this. I felt they were wrong and I made that point, but I was an ambassador under instructions" (*Washington Post,* July 10, 2000, A4). In his memoirs, Boutros-Ghali notes that he sensed that Albright disagreed with the policy: "I felt sure, without clear authorization from the White House." However, no one resigned in protest.

72. Ethiopia, Ghana, Senegal, Zambia, Zimbabwe, Mali, Malawi, Congo, and Nigeria were among those who expressed an interest in contributing troops.

73. *Los Angeles Times,* September 10, 1094, A1.

74. Burkhalter, "The Question of Genocide," 50.

75. UN Independent Inquiry Report, 19.

76. In the same breath as its discussion with the OAU, the Security Council assigned blame to the Hutu government for the worst of the massacres while not explicitly exonerating the rebels. In careful diplomatic language, the Security Council did not accuse anyone of genocide but reminded the parties that attempts to destroy an ethic group constitute a crime under international law.

77. *Los Angeles Times,* May 3, 1994, A11. At the time, the government of South Africa was undergoing reorganization following all-race elections.

78. Organization of African Unity, "International Panel of Eminent Personalities (IPEP) to Investigate the 1994 Genocide in Rwanda and Surrounding Events," Section 15.87, July 7, 2000.

79. UN Security Council Resolution 918, Document S/RES/918, May 17, 1994, in *The United Nations and Rwanda,* 282–84. The expanded mandate did not include Chapter VII authority.

80. *SIPRI,* 107.

81. Meeting of the Security Council, Document S/PV.3377, May 16, 1994, 6.

82. *The Independent* (London), April 18, 1994; *International Herald Tribune,* April 18, 1994.

83. *New York Times,* June 9, 1994, 10.

84. Prunier, 275.

85. S. Metz, *Disaster and Intervention in Sub-Saharan Africa: Learning from Rwanda* (Carlisle, Pa.: Strategic Studies Institute, U.S. Army War College, 1994), 7.

86. Burkhalter, "The Question of Genocide," 51.

87. Frontline, 23.

88. *Washington Post,* May 8, 1994, A1.

89. *The Times* (London), April 29, 1994.

90. *Toronto Star,* May 4, 1994, A18.

91. *Buffalo News,* May 5, 1994, 18.

92. See note 91.

93. *New York Times,* May 11, 1994, A23.

94. Frontline, 19.

95. Frontline, 19–20.

96. Organization of African Unity, Section 12.50; *Star-Tribune* (Minneapolis/St. Paul), July 14, 2000, A18. See also Richard Haas, "The Squandered Presidency," *Foreign Affairs* 79, no. 3 (May/June 2000), 136–40.

97. For further elaboration on this point, see Lawrence LeBlanc, *The United States and the Genocide Convention* (Durham, N.C.: Duke University Press, 1991), chap. 9.

98. Steven Kull, "What the Public Knows That Washington Doesn't," *Foreign Policy* 101 (winter 1995–1996): 113–14.

99. For a discussion of public attitudes toward intervention and other foreign policy issues, see Steven Kull and Clay Ramsay, "Challenging U.S. Policymakers' Image of an Isolationist Public," *International Studies Perspectives* 1 (2000): 1.

100. Des Forges, *Leave None to Tell the Story,* 624–25.

101. *New York Times,* June 10, 1994, A8.

102. See note 101.

103. Gourevitch, 157.

104. Ibid., 153.

105. Letter, Kenneth Roth to President Clinton, June 19, 1994 (available at <www.hrw.org>).

106. *Washington Post,* June 3, 1994, A28.

107. Gourevitch, 153.

108. See note 107.

109. Alan J. Kuperman, "Rwanda in Retrospect," *Foreign Affairs* 79, no. 1 (January/February 2000): 94–114.

110. To allow Dallaire's testimony, UN Secretary-General Kofi Annan waived part of his diplomatic immunity, but he was still barred from discussing specifics about his communications with his superiors in New York.

111. *Washington Post,* February 26, 1998, A17.

112. See note 111.

113. Since his return from Rwanda, General Dallaire has taken early retirement from the Canadian armed forces in large part due to posttraumatic stress syndrome.

114. Colonel Scott R. Feil, "Could 5,000 Peacekeepers Have Saved 500,000 Rwandans? Early Intervention Reconsidered," ISD Report, vol. 3, no. 2 (April 1997) (Washington, D.C.: Institute for the Study of Diplomacy, Georgetown University).

115. Scott R. Feil, "Preventing Genocide: How the Early Use of Force Might Have Succeeded in Rwanda" (report to the Carnegie Commission on Preventing Deadly Conflict, April 1998; available at <www.ccpdc.org/pubs/rwanda/rwanda.htm>), 37.

116. See note 115.

117. See note 115.

118. Feil, 9.

119. Colonel Luc Marchal, "Rapport Relatif aux Ops d'Evacuation des Expatries au Rwanda," August 5, 1994, 15; Alison Des Forges, "Rwanda: Genocide and the Continuing Cycle of Violence," testimony before the Subcommittee on International Operations and Human Rights, May 5, 1998 (available at <www.house.gov/internationalrelations/hr/wshr5598.htm>).

120. Frontline, 15.

121. See David Isenberg, "Soldiers of Fortune Ltd.: A Profile of Today's Private Sector Corporate Mercenary Firms," Center for Defense Information Monograph, November 1997. See also Herbert M. Howe, "Private Security Forces and African Stability: The Case of Executive Outcomes," *Journal of Modern African Studies* 36, no. 2 (1998): 307–31.

122. Chris Grove, "A Possible Role of Executive Outcomes during the Rwanda Genocide of 1994," unpublished manuscript, July 2000.

123. Frederick Forsyth, "Send in the Dogs of War," *Daily Mail,* May 5, 2000, 10. See

also Frederick Forsyth, "Dogs of War: Send in the Mercenaries," *Wall Street Journal Europe,* May 17, 2000, 10.

124. According to William Shawcross, Kofi Annan investigated the hiring of a private security service to patrol refugee camps in Zaire after the genocide. See William Shawcross, *Deliver Us from Evil* (New York: Simon and Schuster, 2000), 122–23.

125. Chalk, 97.

126. Jamie F. Metzl, "Information Intervention," *Foreign Affairs* 76, no. 6 (November/December 1997): 15–21.

127. UN Independent Inquiry, 21.

128. Frontline, 21.

129. Holly Burkhalter, "US Might Have Avoided Rwanda Tragedy," *Christian Science Monitor,* August 9, 1994, 19.

130. Des Forges, "Rwanda: Genocide and the Continuing Cycle of Violence," 6–7.

131. Frontline, 16–17.

132. African Rights, 657.

133. Destexhe, 56.

134. Gourevitch, 166–67.

135. Destexhe, 57.

136. Prunier, 314.

137. *Agence-France Presse,* November 1, 1994; *New York Times,* November 3, 1994, A5.

138. Prunier, 315.

139. Gourevitch, 167.

140. *Africa News,* November 28, 1994, 1; Prunier, 316.

141. *U.S. News & World Report,* August 1, 1994, 42–46; *The Economist,* July 30, 1994, 36.

142. Quoted in Prunier, 303.

143. United Nations, Report on the Situation of Human Rights in Rwanda, UN Document E/CN.4/1995/7, June 28, 1994.

144. Prunier, 303.

145. *CBS Evening News,* July 22, 1994.

146. *SIRSI,* 109.

147. *St. Louis Post-Dispatch,* July 24, 1994, A3.

148. *Chicago Tribune,* August 1, 1994, 1.

149. *Los Angeles Times,* August 1, 1994, A1.

150. *Los Angeles Times,* August 2, 1994, A4.

151. *Washington Post,* July 31, 1994, A16.

152. *New York Times,* July 23, 1994, A5.

153. Holly Burkhalter, quoted in *The Independent* (London), August 4, 1994, 14.

154. Helen Fein, "The Three P's of Genocide Prevention," in Neal Riemer, ed., *Protection against Genocide* (Westport, Conn.: Praeger, 2000), 44.

155. Author interview with Ambassador David Scheffer, December 1998.

156. U.S. Department of State dispatch, November 21, 1994, vol. 5, no. 47, 781. The government of Rwanda voted against the tribunal because it did not include the death penalty for the guilty.

157. See note 156.

158. U.S. Department of State dispatch, November 21, 1994, 780.

159. First Lady Hillary Rodham Clinton, "Statement at the International Criminal Tribunal for Rwanda," Arusha, Tanzania, March 24, 1997; David J. Scheffer, "Human Rights and War Crimes Issues" (address at Dartmouth College on United Nations Day, 1997); and David J. Scheffer, "Remarks at Conference on War Crimes Tribunals: The Record and the Prospects," Washington, D.C., March 31, 1998.

160. See "On 1994 Blood Bath in Rwanda, Tribunal Hews to a Glacial Pace," *New York Times,* November 21, 1997, A1. Rwanda's own judicial system struggled mightily as well. Its facilities, designed to hold 19,000, were jammed with some 65,000 prisoners. See "Wave of Arrests Jam Rwanda's Ailing Prisons," *Washington Post,* January 29, 1996, A12.

161. *New York Times,* November 21, 1997, A1.

162. *New York Times,* September 2, 1998, A1.

163. *Washington Post,* September 5, 1998, A1.

164. U.S. Agency for International Development, Congressional Presentation, Great Lakes Initiative, 1999.

165. Susan E. Rice, assistant secretary for African affairs, Statement before the Subcommittee on Africa, House Foreign Relations Committee, March 17, 1998.

166. John Shattuck, assistant secretary for democracy, human rights, and labor, statement before House Committee on Appropriations, Subcommittee on Foreign Operations, April 1, 1998.

167. Secretary of State Madeleine Albright, "Address on U.S. Policy toward Africa," George Mason University, Fairfax, Virginia, March 19, 1998.

168. Author interview with Colonel Richard Roan, U.S. Marine Corps, December 4, 1998.

169. Entebbe Summit for Peace and Prosperity, "Joint Declaration of Principles," March 25, 1998. Signatories include the United States, Kenya, Rwanda, Tanzania, the Democratic Republic of Congo, Ethiopia, Uganda, and the Organization for African Unity representative.

170. U.S. Department of State, David J. Scheffer, ambassador-at-large for war crimes issues, address at conference on "Genocide and Crimes against Humanity: Early Warning and Prevention," Holocaust Museum, Washington, D.C., December 10, 1998.

171. *New York Times,* March 26, 1998, A1.

172. French National Assembly, "Rapport D'Information Sur Les Operations Militaires Menees par la France, d'autres Pays et l'ONU au Rwanda entre 1990 et 1994," December 154, 1998; Belgian Senate, "Parliamentary Commission of Inquiry regarding the Events in Rwanda" (report in the name of commission of inquiry by Mr. Mahoux and Mr. Verhofstadt, session of 1997–1998, December 6, 1997). The Belgian report charged that "the permanent members of the Security Council, in particular the United States, had excessive weight in a decision where the success of the mission was often subordinated to the selfish and often contradictory interests of the council's members."

173. Frontline, 24.

174. Albright, "Address on US Policy toward Africa."

175. Frontline, 16.

176. Frontline, 25.

Conclusion

"Thus Can We Make It"

In a closing scene of the 1986 film *The Mission,* the Roman Catholic cardinal sent to South America to resolve a territorial dispute between Portugal and Spain receives word from a Spanish diplomat that a beautiful, remote Jesuit mission serving the Guarani Indians on the land in question had been destroyed following the cardinal's order to forcibly close it. Despite his steely political instincts, Cardinal Altamirano is stunned by the brutality and the loss of life of men, women, and children that results. He confronts his secular counterpart:

> *The Cardinal:* You have the affrontery to tell me this slaughter was necessary?
> *Señor Hontar:* You had no alternative, your Eminence. We must work in the world. The world is thus.
> *The Cardinal:* No, Señor Hontar. Thus have we made the world. Thus have I made it.

This exchange captures in dramatic form the essence of American foreign policy and the prevention and punishment of genocide since World War II. We cannot simply shrug our shoulders and explain away American inaction with the broad statement "The world is thus." None of the outcomes discussed in this book were inevitable or predetermined. The realist perspective suggests *likely* decisions in these cases, but each administration facing the issue of genocide, whether in Cambodia, Bosnia, or Rwanda, was not fated but chose to act in a certain way—generally in ways that allowed genocidal atrocities to continue unchecked.

The first American call to action in the fight to prevent another holocaust came from President Truman in 1949, when he remarked that "America has long been a symbol of freedom and democratic progress to peoples less favored than we have been" and that "we must maintain their belief in us by our policies and our acts." Since then, the United States has struggled and stumbled to maintain a credible commitment to suppress genocide despite several prime opportunities. The conflicts explored here—Cambodia, Bosnia, and Rwanda—held relatively little material interest for the United States, but they significantly challenged notions of international society, related norms of human rights and genocide prohibition, and America's position as champion of human rights. The

United States faced crises crying out for leadership, pivotal moments for ethical change on behalf of human rights in a world of sovereign states. This book has illustrated how the United States has failed on many levels to capitalize on those opportunities both to save tens of thousands of lives and to advance the cause of the United Nations Convention on the Prevention and Punishment of the Crime of Genocide. The failure to act or even at times to speak out against perpetrators of genocide was not inevitable or necessary but the product of choices. As a result of those choices, the pledge "never again" has had a hollow ring, and unfulfilled potential sums up the American record on preventing genocide.

The 1999 North Atlantic Treaty Organization (NATO) intervention against Yugoslavia adds a new but incomplete twist to this story. Following failed negotiations in Rambouillet, France, Slobodan Milosevic resorted to his usual violence and launched a brutal offensive against the civilian population to squash a guerrilla campaign by ethnic Albanians for independence. The United States and the world's most powerful alliance faced a familiar question: Would they stand by and watch an entire ethnic community expelled or "cleansed" in NATO's own backyard? In other words, would the United States abdicate leadership as yet another potential genocide unfolded?

The answer was no, or at least a qualified no. NATO launched a massive series of air strikes to stop the bloodshed, to compel Serb withdrawal, and to allow peacekeepers to enter the region. After over 30,000 sorties with no American or allied casualties, Serb forces left the region, and a NATO-led security force entered, ending the violence and creating conditions for the return of hundreds of thousands of refugees.

Whether Serb action in Kosovo was genocide remains unanswered. British officials alleged genocide at the time, the U.S. State Department hinted at it, Milosevic's successor President Vojislav Kostunica has acknowledged genocidal crimes in the province, and investigations by the International Criminal Tribunal for the Former Yugoslavia continue as of this writing. Aspects of Milosevic's crimes in Kosovo certainly fit much of the definition found in the UNGC, including killing members of an ethnic group and deliberately inflicting on the group conditions of life calculated to bring about its destruction in whole or in part. Moreover, as Helen Fein has pointed out, perpetrators of mass killing and genocide tend to be repeat offenders. Given Milosevic's bloody history, it should come as no surprise if Serb actions in Kosovo are ultimately determined to be genocide under international criminal law. Kosovo nonetheless provides a compelling epilogue to the tale of the United States and genocide since World War II—yet another example full of inconsistency and dualism.

On the one hand, the United States and NATO hurdled UN inertia (Russia and China opposed action) and acted forcefully against a perceived genocidal aggression. On the other hand, President Clinton publicly dismissed the use of ground forces and required that military aircraft fly no lower than 15,000 feet to avoid being shot down, despite the negative impact on targeting precision. Meanwhile, the House of Representatives voted 249–180 to refuse funding for ground forces in Kosovo without explicit congressional approval. Clearly, the commitment to halting a potential genocide in Europe had limits, and American intentions were not wholly altruistic. For many, NATO's credibility and very survival were at stake; but humanitarian intervention does not require entirely pure intentions to be justified. More important in the case of Kosovo, limited leadership and constrained political will blunted the sort of decisive and effective ethical action against genocidal aggression that the use of ground forces would have achieved. In the aftermath of the successful air war against Yugoslavia, President Clinton proclaimed a new guiding star for humanitarian intervention in an interview with CNN's Wolf Blitzer:

> While there may be a great deal of ethnic and religious conflict in the world . . . whether within or beyond the borders of a country, if the world community has the power to stop it, we ought to stop genocide and ethnic cleansing.

Rhetorically powerful and clearly aligned with the UNGC, this "Clinton Doctrine" resonates with America's sense of mission and was at least half-heartedly implemented in Kosovo. It remains to be seen if the Clinton Doctrine survives its author and moves beyond intervention only in areas of strategic significance and only through the use of air power.

Kosovo aside, the U.S. record on the prevention and punishment of genocide contrasts sharply with its Wilsonian and Jeffersonian sense of self. As historian H. W. Brands puts it, "From the beginning of American history to the present . . . this sense of obligation to suffering humankind has been a persistent theme in American thought, speech, and writing about the world."[1] This belief in American exceptionalism and the nation's traditional view of its unique mission and legacy of human rights rose to the surface following World War II and spurred the United States to lead the international community in making strong normative statements in favor of protecting human rights and preventing future cases of genocide in the emerging "new world order" of the post–World War II period. The Universal Declaration of Human Rights and the UNGC were among the first documents meant to usher in this new international society. American representatives at the fledgling United Nations assumed leadership roles in the emerging human rights movement and contributed significantly to the final shape of the Genocide Convention.

However, as shown throughout this book, the American follow-up to the drafting of the UNGC did not inspire confidence. For decades, the cosmopolitan goals expressed in the convention remained confined to the pages on which they were written. In the 1950s, with the systemic shock of the Holocaust within recent memory, the United States assigned greater importance to other interests and priorities that for decades prevented it from taking even the symbolic step of simple ratification. A potent mix of anti-Sovietism, isolationism, and constitutionalism—flavored with a dash of anti-Semitism and segregationist sentiment—worked against ratification of the treaty in 1950 and sent the UNGC spiraling into an abyss of inattention and trenchant opposition. The Senate's failure to ratify the treaty provided a sadly fitting prelude to the U.S. response to genocide for the rest of the century.

From the UNGC debate in the Senate onward, domestic politics have influenced America's response to genocidal atrocities abroad. The Vietnam experience has cast an often impenetrable shadow over foreign policy debates at home, especially about the use of military force. In the mid-1970s, this new "syndrome" removed from the realm of political reality *any* military action in Southeast Asia to combat genocide or otherwise. No president could have sold the public or Congress on the use of force to address glaring humanitarian concerns in Cambodia even if he wanted to do it. Therefore, it was not worth discussing, no matter how feasible operationally. On the issue of the Cambodian seat at the United Nations, an issue and policy opportunity far removed from military action, the United States still balked. The Carter administration had no interest in a domestic political squabble over any support, however technical or symbolic, for a Vietnam-installed regime in Phnom Penh, even at the expense of rewarding the Khmer Rouge.

Fear of political consequences at home should American forces suffer casualties during a humanitarian intervention emerged decades later when genocide plagued the 1990s. Since the end of the Cold War, American policymakers have often hurriedly assumed that the public does not have the stomach for American casualties, leading to an unofficial doctrine of "combatant immunity." Thus, the Bush administration punted Bosnia to its successors. In the midst of genocidal atrocities in the Balkans, the Clinton administration hesitated to put American military personnel in harm's way for a humanitarian mission that seemed to lack an obvious and classic national security interest. Intervention had been a serious issue only as a useful election-year tool with which to bash an opponent, not a serious policy option. The desire to avoid unwanted controversy or pressure at home even dissuaded the very use of the term "genocide," even while the bodies piled up from frenzied genocidal slaughters in Europe and Africa.

However, American policymakers needlessly averted the nation's eyes from the heinous crimes being committed. The assumption that support for humanitarian interventions would disappear as soon as American casualties mounted was blindly accepted as an article of faith. For example, in his memoirs, presidential aide George Stephanopoulos writes about the attitude that he and President Clinton shared in the aftermath of the Somalia experience: "Americans are basically isolationists. Right now the average American doesn't see our interests threatened to the point where we should sacrifice one American life."[2]

Detailed survey efforts dispute this belief. ABC and CNN/*USA Today* polls taken after the deadly battle in Mogadishu found, respectively, only 37 and 43 percent of the public in favor of American withdrawal. Most respondents believed that the United States was doing the right thing in Somalia.[3] What was missing was not public support but a sustained leadership effort to explain why the United States was in Somalia and what it was accomplishing after the famine relief effort. Indeed, a significant percentage of the American public embraces the notion of the United States as "the city on a hill" and believes that humanitarian actions are often in the nation's interest.

In a 1994 poll conducted by the Program on International Policy Attitudes (PIPA) at the Center for International and Security Studies at the University of Maryland, 63 percent of respondents said that the United States and the United Nations should "always" or "in most cases" intervene "with whatever force is necessary to stop acts of genocide." Only 6 percent said "never." A full 80 percent favored intervention if the United Nations determined that genocide was occurring in Bosnia or Rwanda.[4] Even when asked to consider a hypothetical humanitarian intervention with several thousand American casualties, 60 percent believed that the United States would have done the right thing by stopping the greater genocidal carnage.[5] Polling by the Pew Research Center for the People and the Press has shown a similar sense of moral obligation to act on the part of the American public when genocide is taking place.[6]

Surveys cannot fully capture or predict how citizens would react to actual events and televised images. Nonetheless, the PIPA and Pew findings highlight that the American public recognizes a moral imperative to intervene to suppress genocide when possible. In other words, the language of the Clinton Doctrine resonates with most Americans—they will not pay any price, but they will pay *some* price in the name of genocide prevention. With leadership, a president could tap this latent American internationalism and belief that a world order free of genocide serves American interests and at times requires the use of force. Even the Cold War required the dramatic rhetoric of the Truman administration to rally Americans behind an unprecedented international cause and commitment. Public support for humanitarian intervention to stop genocide or to military action to arrest war criminals seems likely if coupled with sustained leadership from above.

Military-political analyst Edward Luttwak makes a similar point. Luttwak explains that one should not expect Americans to take to the streets over issues such as Bosnia and Rwanda but that the White House can and should lead on such issues and summon dormant support for intervention to prevent genocide. For Luttwak, "The ethical confusion of our times does greatly expand the potential scope of the moral leadership that the President of the United States could exercise, for example by persuading the American public that Bosnian Muslims should be actively protected, just as if they were spotted owls or bottle-nosed dolphins."[7] As of yet, leadership on the issue of preventing and punishing the crime of genocide has largely been nonexistent, and it remains to be seen if the Clinton Doctrine lives beyond its spokesperson and rises above the level of mere spin and rhetorical nicety.

We should not forget that the history of the UNGC ratification in the United States demonstrates that domestic politics can advance progress in policy. Domestic forces stalled the convention, but other groups working within the system kept the issue alive and made possible its eventual approval, in part by tapping into electoral motives. Domestic politics can be harnessed in favor of a human rights cause because Americans care about and respond to massive atrocities. As Jonathan Rauch argues, "Not even a leader of Churchillian rhetoric and resolve could persuade Americans not to care at all when Serbs massacre thousands of Muslims in Srebrenica, when genocidaires murder hundreds of thousands in Rwanda . . . the public does not have the stomach to turn its back altogether."[8] The rapid growth of the community of nongovernmental organizations dedicated to human rights and the increasing effectiveness of groups such as Human Rights Watch or Amnesty International means that human rights concerns, genocide related or not, will always be on or near the American foreign policy agenda. While one cannot reasonably expect American leaders to ignore the political "domestic consumption" aspect of any foreign policy decision, it hardly seems unreasonable to expect leadership (short of Churchillian will do) at defining moments of crisis and humanitarian disaster.

The struggle of the United States to respond assertively against the crime of genocide has other roots as well. As the cases developed here suggest, international politics and geopolitical contexts have circumscribed American action. Cold War factors played a significant role. Anti-Sovietism colored much of the debate over the UNGC. By the time genocide exploded in Cambodia, Southeast Asia had become a hotbed of East-West proxy war. The dictates of grand strategy for the geopolitical chessboard dropped Cambodia down the ladder of importance and led the United States at least indirectly to support the Khmer Rouge in the name of broader regional gains.

The end of the Cold War left the United States "in a position of preponderance unsurpassed since the Roman empire."[9] Nonetheless, the ghosts of international politics past exerted a powerful spectral influence on policy in the genocidal 1990s. The lingering presence of the Vietnam and Somalia syndromes spooked policymakers as they deliberated responses to Bosnia and Rwanda. The resounding success of the Persian Gulf War failed to exorcise those demons or dampen overdrawn analogies. Quagmire images and phobias time and again found voice in discussions about an American role in stopping the genocidal war in Balkans. Similarly, the death of U.S. Rangers in Somalia stung American decision makers and churned their gut-level apprehensions about public support for another adventure, however just the cause, on the Dark Continent.

The actual relevance of either Vietnam or Somalia to Bosnia and Rwanda or the true materiality of the "lessons learned" mattered little. In both cases, the foreign policy analogy proved stronger than the norm of genocide prevention. Other world politics issues, including a willingness to let the new European Union handle the Bosnia debacle, the delicate management of relations with Russia, and discomfort over the competency and effectiveness of any UN military operation, have all at times stymied American foreign policy at different ethical leadership moments.

A tempered belief in ethical progress urges that we consider windows of opportunity for "moral entrepreneurship," or what have been referred to throughout this book as "ethical leadership moments"—periods ripe for significant normative advance. The cardinal's perceptive confession in *The Mission* echoes Alexander Wendt's statement that "anarchy is what states make of it" and the proposition that therefore it is irresponsible for statesmen to knowingly pursue policies that boost "destructive old orders."[10] The cases presented in this book illustrate that at several significant leadership moments for the prevention and punishment of genocide, the United States balked and lost opportunities to chart a new course for the world. Richard Breitman's assessment of the Roosevelt administration's response to the Holocaust rings true for the U.S. record on genocide since then: "The record generally shows that . . . the US government did not try to do what might have worked."[11] In doing so, the United States and the rest of the international community turned away from opportunities to challenge the destructive status quo and strengthened the dominant or traditional political world where *genocidaires* need not fear outside intervention to stop their barbarity. To paraphrase the cardinal, by their decisions not to act, thus have they made it.

Despite the potent and paralyzing combination of domestic political concerns and geopolitical imperatives that have distracted the United States and stunted its policies on genocide, the United States has made progress; not all opportunities have been missed. This work has documented several instances in which the United States has seized on ethical leadership moments in relation to genocide with noteworthy results. America's potential displayed itself early in the postwar era when the country took the lead on the UNGC. The United States was the prime mover in shaping the treaty; American representatives worked to establish the very high moral standards that the United States has struggled to meet.

Those standards or expectations have been most closely approximated on the punishment side. American efforts have often led the way in seeking justice for victims of genocide and punishing perpetrators. The United States drove the creation of the International Criminal Tribunal for the Former Yugoslavia and has worked behind the scenes to bring Khmer Rouge leaders to trial. American force and diplomacy (and funding for military training performed by a private military company) helped bring the war in Bosnia to a close and produced the Dayton Peace Accords. The U.S.-led NATO peacekeeping force in Bosnia has arrested indicted war criminals as high up the chain of command as a Serb general. The pursuit of justice in Rwanda has also benefited from American financial support and the expertise of U.S. legal personnel. At an institutional level, the Clinton administration founded the State Department's Office of War Crimes Issues (the Bush administration appears willing to maintain this office) and later worked to coordinate information exchange between federal agencies as part of a "genocide early warning center." At the end of the year 2000, President Clinton authorized the United States to sign the treaty creating a permanent international criminal court (ICC). However, Senator Jesse Helms, arch foe of the UNGC, said he would "declare war" on the ICC and make a priority of its defeat in the Senate.

The norm of genocide prevention and punishment has mattered to the United States. The norm need not compel military action to demonstrate relevance and influence. The limited power of the UNGC has failed to produce intervention but has led the United States to use (or avoid) certain rhetoric and work for justice.[12] As one legal observer notes, the birth of the UNGC created in the international legal lexicon "one of the most powerful words to have been coined in this century."[13] The contorted use of language by the United States to avoid the use of the "G" word and President Clinton's Kigali airport apology for not quickly calling the Rwandan atrocities "genocide" each suggest in their own strange way that the ideas enshrined in the UNGC matter and have power and resonance. During his Kigali speech, Clinton spoke the "rightful name" of Rwanda's tragedy eleven times and pledged that "never again must we be shy in the face of the evidence." Of course, the sad fact is that the world has heard these words before. This mixed record on the prevention and punishment of genocide results in both a critical assessment and also moderate optimism for the future.

The most cynical critics unfairly deride American efforts to hold perpetrators of genocide accountable as window dressing or dismiss it as too little too late. These initiatives do tend to take shape after genocide has already claimed its victims, and they are no substitute for intervention to stop genocide. However, the steps taken so far represent milestone achievements for international law and society and hint at the still untapped potential for U.S. action. In short, the

United States can promote ethical evolution when it adopts the mantle of moral entrepreneur and chooses to lead. The American ability to transform sections of the UNGC from aspiration to action demonstrates progress and offers some hope for the future of the treaty, but it also underscores the profound moments of lost opportunity in the struggle against genocide. The United States has contributed to normative progress on behalf of the UNGC, but without consistent and insistent leadership, it has been "slow boring through hard wood."[14]

An issue as compelling and emotional as foreign policy and genocide that deals with catastrophic suffering and loss of life threatens to push proponents of a more vigorous U.S. response into an almost reflexive hypercriticism: One hastily assumes that something could have and should have been done. This book has tempered the impulse to brazenly chastise the United States for its history of inaction with an awareness of the political realities and contexts in which relevant foreign policy decisions were made. This project has also not been a narrowly academic treatise committed to a simpleminded moralism, divorced from political reality. Nor has it squeezed cases into one theory or another or vice versa. This work is laden with the recognition that American foreign policy is not made in a vacuum. Decisions on any issue ranging from humanitarian intervention to global warming treaties and from ballistic missile control to banana imports take place in a decidedly political universe. Both domestic politics and geopolitical considerations shape foreign policy, including high-stakes decisions about preventing genocide. The case studies here, informed by an understanding of the struggle between foreign policy realism and international ethics, have revealed this politically aware approach throughout. However, to recognize and discuss influential obstructionist factors such as geopolitics and domestic political concerns does not require that we excuse or absolve the United States for its failures or that we blindly accept policymakers' rationales for inaction as inevitable or even adequately reasonable.

Realist morality properly directs us to consider means, ends, and consequences. Choices to act with moral intention come with a price and risk unintended consequences: Witness the NATO operation on behalf of ethnic Albanians in the Serb province of Kosovo in 1999 that, while ultimately successful, led Serb forces to accelerate their "ethnic cleansing" before finally stopping it. However, realism also threatens to impose an attitude and stance of resignation in the face of preventable horror. Furthermore, in its emphasis on the human lust for power and self aggrandizement, realism loses sight of the nobler human desire to do what is right and just. David Welch stresses this point and argues that theories of international relations need "to rediscover the human soul."[15]

More progressive views of world politics, such as the theory-heavy constructivist school of thought, start this turn back toward the soul with the proclamation that "ideas matter," including ideas about ethical action and justice. As Lea Brilmayer comments, "Between the polar opposites of Machiavelli and Gandhi fall the large majority of persons making international decisions."[16] Therefore, a progressive perspective and a belief in the power and responsibility of leadership expects more. In each case presented here, opportunity for ethical leadership and intervention at a variety of levels always existed, but when prominent genocides have raged in the post–World War II era, the United States has often neglected those options.

Any realistic and fair-minded discussion about the prevention and punishment of genocide must also take into account the important costs associated with nonintervention. Aside from the staggering loss of life, genocide carries other significant prices to pay: Genocidal violence leads to massive population dislocations. Cambodia, Bosnia, Rwanda, and Kosovo demonstrate starkly the massive refugee flows caused by genocide. The exodus of hundreds of thousands of people inevitably impacts the afflicted country's neighbors. The humanitarian effort to deal with a tidal wave of refugees swallows millions of dollars from both host nations and outside donors such as the United States: Witness Rwanda, where the money spent on humanitarian aid to refugee camps quickly rivaled the likely cost of intervention to prevent genocide in the first place.[17] The mass movement of dislocated peoples also threatens to upset regional stability. Clinton administration Ambassador-at-Large for War Crimes Issues David Scheffer concurs, writing,

> The international community must do everything it can to respond quickly enough to confront genocidal actions. The consequences of genocide are not only the horrific killings themselves, but the massive refugee flows, economic collapse, and political divisions which tear asunder the societies that fall victim to genocide. The international community pays a far higher price coping with the aftermath of genocide than if it were prepared to defeat genocide in its earliest stages.[18]

Unveiling his "Doctrine of International Community," British Prime Minister Tony Blair made a similar point with a blend of realism and idealism. In his April 22, 1999, speech to the Economic Club of Chicago, Blair said that "acts of genocide can never be a purely internal matter." For Blair, action to end such threats is where "values and interests merge" because genocide, civil wars, and refugee crises all influence negatively on national and international stability and security.[19]

Reaching across the realist-progressivist chasm, Stanley Hoffmann also stresses that "the distinction between interests and values is largely fallacious." For Hoffmann, "Moral passivity" in the face of horrors like genocide, however distant, threatens to lead to "a creeping escalation of disorder and beastliness that will, sooner or later, reach the shores of the complacent, the rich, and the indifferent."[20] The fight against genocide is a parallel fight against instability that, should it expand unchecked, could jeopardize the stability of areas more central to American national security.

Nonintervention also sends messages to other would-be *genocidaires* that they can pursue their atrocious agendas with impunity. Roger Winter, head of the State Department's Office of Refugee Resettlement during the Carter and Reagan administrations and head of the nonprofit U.S. Committee for Refugees, expressed his fear that at the end of the twentieth century "we actually have a greater possibility of genocide and ethnic cleansing than we did five or six years ago because all these despots feel they can get away with it."[21] Such a message, however unintentional, sets a terrible precedent and ignores the moral interdependence of nations that mirrors growing economic interdependence.

Critics argue that any such interventions should be avoided since the urge to do something whenever the cause of human rights is raised, noble as it may be, is a woolly-headed, even pernicious approach to foreign policy that leads to overextension and drains resources better dedicated to "true" national interests. While compelling on the surface, this argument is specious. Few argue that the United States must act whenever or wherever human rights are being trampled. This book does not embrace such a universalist position; it does not offer a moral recipe that applies equally to each and every situation. Action in Bosnia or Rwanda hardly compels similar action in Sudan or East Timor. To argue that it does is reductionist and simplistic. As Immanuel Kant reminds us, "ought" implies "can." Leadership in foreign policy requires room for exceptions and subtlety. When the United States and its allies *can* act with a high likelihood of ending a disaster of such magnitude as genocide, then and only then does the "should" rise in prominence.

Foreign policy is made in a world of norms where sovereignty still reigns. However, the 1999 air strikes against Yugoslavia, the tribunals to try individuals for genocide and crimes against humanity in Yugoslavia and Rwanda, Spain's efforts to extradite former Chilean dictator Augusto Pinochet from Britain to stand trial for torture, and the creation of the ICC all point to a growing number of potential normative regicides and rivals challenging the authority of state sovereignty. Efforts by the United States and the United Nations to encourage the support of human rights help establish "a particular vision of how member states should organize their domestic relations," and such organization does not include genocidal policies.[22]

UN Secretary-General Kofi Annan made a telling statement on April 7, 1999, when he noted that the evolution of international norms means that nations intent on committing genocide can no longer hide behind the UN Charter and the privileged status it traditionally extended to national sovereignty.[23] The UNGC and other treaties like it contain "the underpinnings of a radical new reality for the conduct of international relations."[24] Action on behalf of the UNGC, however incremental the steps, contributes to the emergence of new standards of conduct and redefines state interests. As Hedley Bull presciently noted in 1977, "Carried to its logical extreme, the doctrine of human rights and duties under international law is subversive of the whole principle that mankind should be organised as a society of sovereign states."[25]

The atrocities that closed out the bloody twentieth century showed that the former UN undersecretary-general and "father of peacekeeping" Brian Urquhart did not have it quite right when he remarked in 1988 that "we seem at last to have reached a mild and sunny plateau in international relations."[26] If the past 100 years serve as an indicator, the scourge of genocide will continue to haunt the world of the twenty-first century. How the United States chooses to respond to the next genocide will bear heavily on the question that has perpetually challenged the nation and its foreign policy: Who are we?[27] As Richard Holbrooke writes,

> There will be other Bosnias in our lives—areas where early outside intervention can be decisive, and American leadership will be required. The world's richest nation, one that presumes to great moral authority, cannot simply make worthy appeals to conscience and call on others to carry the burden. The world will look to Washington for more than rhetoric the next time we face a challenge to peace.[28]

Likewise, the world will look to the United States the next time it faces genocide. When that horrible circumstance arises, the United States will once again have an opportunity to assert its leadership, save countless lives, and forge an enduring international ethic born of the Genocide Convention.

Hope for such a progressive policy outcome is not based on naive assumptions and dreams about how the world could be. Rather, it is a realistic hope and vision of an ethically progressive policy tempered by a realist eye toward context and best alternatives and guided by an informed visionary leadership. The "hard wood" remains, but the United States has demonstrated its ability to bore through it slowly, even while missing opportunities for dramatic progress. Because of this, the story of the United States and the prevention and punishment of the genocide since World War II leaves room for cautionary optimism. As Harvard University's Cornel West and Roberto Unger stress, "It is easy to be a realist when you accept everything. It is easy to be a visionary when you confront nothing. To accept little and confront much, and to do so on the basis of an informed vision of piecemeal but cumulative change, is the way and the solution."[29]

Small steps matter in the struggle to make "never again" a reality. Taken together, they hopefully will push the United States to embrace fully its power and responsibility and seize on present and future ethical leadership moments.

To do so invigorates America's mission, aligns rhetoric with reality, and strikes a blow for justice against the inhumane.

NOTES

1. H. W. Brands, *What America Owes the World: The Struggle for the Soul of Foreign Policy* (Cambridge: Cambridge University Press, 1998), vii.

2. George Stephanopoulos, *All Too Human: A Political Education* (Boston: Little, Brown, 1999), 234.

3. Steven Kull, "What the Public Knows That Washington Doesn't," *Foreign Policy* 101 (winter 1995–1996): 112.

4. Kull, 113.

5. Kull, 112. For an interesting discussion of public attitudes on humanitarian intervention, see National Public Radio, "Kosovo Roundtable," *Weekend All Things Considered,* April 11, 1999.

6. Pew Research Center for the People and the Press (available at <www.people-press.org/nato99rpt.htm>).

7. Edward Luttwak, "If Bosnians Were Dolphin . . . ," *Commentary* 96, no. 4 (October 1993): 28.

8. Jonathan Rauch, "Two Cheers for the Clinton Doctrine (OK, Maybe Just One)," *National Journal,* May 26, 2000, 1665.

9. Stephen M. Walt, "Musclebound: The Limits of U.S. Power," *Bulletin of the Atomic Scientists,* March 1, 1999, 44.

10. Alexander Wendt, "Constructing International Politics, *International Security* 20 (summer 1995): 80.

11. Richard Breitman, *Official Secrets: What the Nazis Planned, What the British and Americans Knew* (New York: Hill and Wang, 1999).

12. On norms and prescriptive accounts of actors and identities in the state system, see Paul Kower and Jeffrey Legro, "Norms, Identities, and Their Limits," in Peter Katzenstein, ed., *The Culture of National Security* (New York: Columbia University Press, 1996), 453.

13. Dino Kritsiotis, "The Power of International Law as Language," 34 *California Western Law Review* 34, no. 397 (spring 1998): 1.

14. Dorothy Jones, *Code of Peace: Ethics and Security in the World of the Warlord* States (Chicago: University of Chicago Press, 1991).

15. David Welch, *Justice and the Genesis of War* (Cambridge: Cambridge University Press, 1993), 3.

16. Lea Brilmayer, "Realism Revisited: The Moral Priority of Means and Ends in Anarchy," in Lea Brilmayer and Ian Shapiro, eds., *Global Justice* (New York: New York University Press, 1999), 193.

17. The Clinton administration was reluctant to pay $5 million in transportation costs for UNAMIR in 1994. The subsequent U.S. humanitarian effort to address the postgenocide refugee crisis in central Africa cost more than $300 million; see *Financial World,* October 11, 1994, 22.

18. Ambassador David J. Scheffer, "U.S. Policy on International Criminal Tribunals"

(address at Washington College of Law, American University, Washington, D.C., March 31, 1998).

19. Prime Minister Tony Blair, speech to the Economic Club of Chicago, Chicago Hilton and Towers, April 22, 1999.

20. Stanley Hoffmann, "In Defense of Mother Theresa: Morality in Foreign Policy," *Foreign Affairs* 75, no. 2 (March/April 1996): 172, 175.

21. *Seattle Post-Intelligencer,* March 18, 1999, A7.

22. Michael Barnett, "The United Nations and Global Security: The Norm Is Mightier Than the Sword," *Ethics & International Affairs* 9 (1995): 49.

23. *New York Times,* April 18, 1999, 4.

24. Kritsiotis, 3.

25. Hedley Bull, *The Anarchical Society: A Study of Order in World Politics* (New York: Columbia University Press, 1977), 146.

26. Quoted in David Rieff, "The Lessons of Bosnia," *World Policy Journal* 12, no. 1 (winter 1995): 82.

27. See Ernest May, "Who Are We?," *Foreign Affairs* 73, no. 2 (March/April 1994): 135.

28. Richard Holbrooke, *To End a War* (New York: Random House, 198), 369.

29. Cornel West and Roberto Unger, "Progressive Politics and What Lies Ahead," *The Nation,* November 23, 1998, 12.

Appendix

The Genocide Convention

CONVENTION ON THE PREVENTION AND PUNISHMENT OF THE CRIME OF GENOCIDE. ADOPTED BY THE U.N. GENERAL ASSEMBLY (9 DECEMBER 1948)

Article I. The Contracting Parties confirm that genocide, whether committed in time of peace or in time of war, is a crime under international law which they undertake to prevent and punish.

Article II. In the present Convention, genocide means any of the following acts committed with intent to destroy, in whole or in part, a national, ethnical, racial or religious group, as such: a) Killing members of the group; b) Causing serious bodily or mental harm to members of the group; c) Deliberately inflicting on the group conditions of life calculated to bring about its physical destruction in whole or in part; d) Imposing measures intended to prevent births within the group; e) Forcibly transferring children of the group to another group.

Article III. The following acts shall be punished: a) Genocide; b) Conspiracy to commit genocide; c) Direct and public incitement to commit genocide; d) Attempt to commit genocide; e) Complicity in genocide.

Article IV. Persons committing genocide or any of the other acts enumerated in Article III shall be punished, whether they are constitutionally responsible rulers, public officials or private individuals.

Article V. The Contracting Parties undertake to enact, in accordance with their respective Constitutions, the necessary legislation to give affect to the provision of the present Convention and, in particular, to provide effective penalties for persons guilty of genocide or of any of the other acts enumerated in Article III.

Article VI. Persons charged with genocide or any of the other acts enumerated in Article III shall be tried by a competent tribunal of the State in the territory of which the act was committed, or by such international penal tribunal as may have jurisdiction with respect to those Contracting Parties which shall have accepted its jurisdiction.

Article VII. Genocide and the other acts enumerated in Article III shall not be considered as political crimes for the purpose of extradition. The Contracting Parties pledge themselves in such cases to grant extradition in accordance with their laws and treaties in force.

Article VIII. Any Contracting Party may call upon the competent organs of the United Nations to take such action under the Charter of the United Nations as they consider appropriate for the prevention and suppression of acts of genocide or any of the other acts enumerated in Article III.

Article IX. Disputes between the Contracting Parties relating to the interpretation, application or fulfillment of the present Convention, including those relating to the responsibility of a State for genocide or for any of the other acts enumerated in Article III, shall be submitted to the International Court of Justice at the request of any of the parties to the dispute.

Index

About the Author

Peter Ronayne is a senior faculty member at the Federal Executive Institute in Charlottesville, Virginia. He is also an adjunct professor at the University of Virginia.